D0146856

African American Student's Guide to College Success

African American Student's Guide to College Success

F. Erik Brooks and Glenn L. Starks

An Imprint of ABC-CLIO, LLC
Santa Barbara, California • Denver, Colorado

Library of Congress Cataloging-in-Publication Data

Brooks, F. Erik.
African American student's guide to college success / F. Erik Brooks and Glenn L. Starks.
pages cm
Includes bibliographical references and index.
ISBN 978–1–4408–2929–1 (cloth : alk. paper) — ISBN 978–1–4408–2930–7 (ebook)
1. African American college students—Life skills guides. 2. College students—United States—Life skills guides. 3. College student orientation—United States. 4. African American college students—Biography. I. Starks, Glenn L., 1966– II. Title.
LC2781.7.B75 2015
378.1′982996073—dc23 2015022033

ISBN: 978–1–4408–2929–1
EISBN: 978–1–4408–2930–7

19 18 17 16 15 1 2 3 4 5

This book is also available on the World Wide Web as an eBook.
Visit www.abc-clio.com for details.

Greenwood
An Imprint of ABC-CLIO, LLC

ABC-CLIO, LLC
130 Cremona Drive, P.O. Box 1911
Santa Barbara, California 93116-1911

This book is printed on acid-free paper ∞

Manufactured in the United States of America

Contents

Introduction

For most of the 19th and 20th centuries, African Americans were denied the right to pursue higher education. In the United States, graduating from college has traditionally been the means of obtaining a better way of life. African Americans have not always been afforded the opportunity to attend college. Because of the history of slavery and the practice of racial discrimination in the United States, African Americans have looked to higher education as a way of being competitive for jobs, earning higher wages, and providing for their families. Young people in all socioeconomic groups aspire to seek a college degree. African Americans and first-generation college students are underrepresented on many college campuses. When many attend college, they find it frustrating because of the lack of guidance and the lack of knowledge of the ins and outs of higher education and college life. This book has been designed to help these students find success in college. As African Americans and former first-generation college students, we hope this book can serve as a guide to answer all of the questions that we had when we enrolled at our undergraduate colleges. The prevailing question facing those deliberating if they should attend college is "Why should anyone attend college?" To start with, college allows students to meet people from varies races, ethnic groups, and cultures. It allows them to explore new opportunities, interests, and experiences. Most importantly, many college graduates earn more money than those with only a high school diploma. Most good jobs require a college education, not only a high school diploma. Public and private industries want to hire people who are able to think and solve complex problems. Pursuing a college degree exposes students to this complex problem solving. People with associate degrees earn more than those with high school diplomas, and people with bachelor's degrees earn more than both. A great return on an investment comes from earning associate and/or bachelor's degrees, whereas wages for most high school graduates remain stagnate. The Bureau of Labor Statistics (2014) revealed that those with at least a bachelor's degree earn a median weekly income of $1,066. This is compared to $652 for those with only a high school diploma and only $471 for those without a high school diploma. As one's level of education increases, so does their income. Those with a master's degree earn $1,300, those with a doctorate $1,624, and those with a professional degree $1,735. The same trend applies to unemployment, which ranges from 12.4 percent for those without a high school diploma, to 4.5 percent for those with a bachelor's degree, to 2.1 percent for those with a professional degree.

The authors of this book are both first-generation college students who have earned doctoral degrees. We, along with other colleagues, have discussed our experiences and discovered that there are things we wished that we had known before enrolling into college that may have enriched our undergraduate experience at our prospective undergraduate institutions. This book is an attempt to encapsulate some of these conversations to assist African American high school and college students in gaining a better understanding of the factors they should consider when deciding what university they will attend.

Attending college is a major step in transitioning from childhood to adulthood. Some students are excited by the opportunities that await them during their university experience, while others are apprehensive and fearful about this new and exciting adventure. This book also aims to give students a glimpse of what they may experience when they arrive on a university campus. Choosing a college or university is perhaps one of the most important choices one can make in their lifetime. The decision to go to college is a life-changing event in itself, as it can determine not only a person's income for the rest of their life but also other major life decisions. Having a college degree can determine who one will marry, where they will live, one's level of healthiness (because of the ability to obtain good health insurance and live a happy life), and one's ability to adequately take care of their children.

For African Americans, obtaining a college degree is more than simply a choice: it is a necessity. Blacks in the United States suffer disparities in almost every socioeconomic condition. They have the highest percentages of any racial and ethnic group in poverty, unemployment, health disparities, prison, depressed housing conditions, racial discrimination, homes raised by a single parent, and rates of crime. Education is the key to reversing these overall trends. It is not only the cornerstone of living the American Dream but also the key to successfully competing in a global environment.

With so much at stake, for many students, selecting a college can be very stressful. Even with parents, teachers, and counselors assisting them, students understand that the ultimate choice belongs to them to select a school and major they feel comfortable with, will successfully complete, and find success with afterward. For many black students, there may be limited support from parents and school officials. Their parents may not have gone to college, and teachers and counselors may have too many students to provide one-on-one advice. There is also the tendency to focus on a handful of specifically identified students. However, no student should be discouraged.

Many students (particularly black students) do not attend college because of perceived challenges in navigating the higher educational system. The challenge students find include understanding how to navigate the process of applying to colleges and universities, where to find money to pay for their educations, and what skills are needed to successfully complete their programs. The purpose of this book is to provide both a resource and a road map for African American students in preparing, entering, and succeeding in college. It provides information and resources for succeeding not only at the undergraduate level but also in graduate school at the master's and doctorate levels. This book is specifically written to benefit African American students who may face unique challenges getting into college, with the aim of helping them understand some key issues to ensure they succeed. The success stories provided in this book will, for example, provide personal experiences by those who overcame these challenges.

This book is divided into four primary sections to assist African American students. It discusses major steps that must be completed just to get into college. For example, students must focus on their high school grade point averages as early as possible. They should also consider which extracurricular activities will most benefit them getting into colleges. They must achieve minimum scores on standardized tests such as the Scholastic Aptitude Test (SAT). The second section discusses choosing the right college. There are a myriad of choices for students based on their academic interest, grade point averages, scholarship potential, family financial resources, and desire to remain close to or far from home. This includes private and public schools, nonprofit and for-profit institutions, and on-site and online schools. All these schools offer degree programs that are tailored to the needs of different students. For example, many online courses tailor to adult learners rather than college freshmen just graduating high school who desire a full-time on-site degree program. This book also discusses challenges in completing degree programs. Students often face the greatest challenge with independence. They no longer have parents monitoring their whereabouts, teachers who monitor their activities between classes, or anyone making sure they get their homework done. There are also the many social distractions including parties, social clubs, and the negative influence of some students not interested in their academics. Even for those students who are not distracted, they may lack time management skills and become overwhelmed by the level of coursework. All of these challenges require time management skills and study rituals to succeed.

Lastly, the book provides successful stories of African Americans who have completed degrees at the undergraduate and graduate levels. These individuals offer their personal perspectives on the challenges they faced because of their race in choosing the right schools, dealing with peers, and handling personal responsibilities, as well as the strategies they employed to overcome those challenges. Readers will find their stories inspirational as well as useful in dealing with current and future concerns.

PART I

Transitioning from High School to College

STEP ONE

Preparing for College

Transitioning from high school to college can be a time of excitement but also a time of anxiety. Becoming a college student is quite different from being a high school student. In high school, students' academic lives are controlled by teachers. There is not much flexibility in your choice of courses in high school; however, in college there is a wide array of choices of courses, and the student ultimately controls his or her own academic life. Students typically have more freedom than they experienced in high school. Living on their own for the first time allows college students to gain independence and take charge of the many choices that they are presented with. As a college student, you are now responsible for your own decisions. In the past, your parents and teachers may have made decisions for you, but now it is up to you. In making decisions now, you may still get input from your parents, teachers, and mentors, but you will have to own any decisions that you make while you are in college. Parents are no longer there to ensure responsible action or ethical decision making. Students are responsible for waking up and attending classes on time. There is not an immediate guardian to tell students where they can and cannot go or who they can and cannot see. There is a lot of freedom, and with this freedom, there is a lot of unstructured time that can feel overwhelming and less predictable. The freedom to manage and take responsibility for your life and decisions and living with the consequences of your decisions is a learning process. This freedom can be very frightening, but it can be very satisfying. In a university setting, some students are lured into thinking that they have more time than they really have. Many students find it difficult having so much unstructured time, and they do not have the discipline to balance unstructured time and study activities. This transition from high school to college depends on good time management. New students must balance college work and socializing, club participation and other activities, and finances. All first-time college students, not only African American students, face these challenges.

Instead of having all of one's classes in one building as in high school, college buildings are homes to academic disciplines. One building may hold similar disciplines such as social sciences, mathematics and sciences, and humanities. Students may have courses scheduled in one building on the campus, and their next class may be on the other side of the campus. It is the students' responsibility to attend and to be punctual to all classes. A typical day in college is less structured than in high school. The expectations in college are greater; more reading and studying is required outside of class. Because a college day is less structured, to some students, it feels like they have too much free time outside of the classroom. For other students, this unstructured day makes them feel as if they have no free time to do anything but college work.

Transition can also lead to separation anxiety. If your friends do not choose to attend the same college as you, you may experience separation, loneliness, and sadness separating from parents, high school friends, and routines. This sadness may lead to underage drinking and drug use. Universities usually have strict policies against underage drinking on campus. Underage drinking can lead to a judicial hearing and may result in penalties such as fines or even expulsion from the university. While transitioning from high school to college, students may experience some changes in their personal relationships. Your best friend or your entire set of friends may choose to go to other colleges or may not choose to attend college at all. Your experiences at college may distance you from your old friends. You may discover new romantic relationships and the end of old relationships. Students may feel a loss of connectedness and separation from their old neighborhoods and communities and may need to call, text, and e-mail their family or friends a few times a week until they get adjusted to their new environment. Some may use other forms of social media such as Facebook, Twitter, or Instagram to stay connected with their family and friends.

Preparing for college consists of several steps, each of which will be discussed in this section. The following is a checklist of items:

- Request applications from schools you are interested in attending
- Request high school transcripts to be sent
- Take the appropriate standardized tests
- Obtain letters of recommendations
- Write your college essay
- Obtain financial aid forms and related information
- Attend interviews at college campuses
- Submit applications and financial aid forms
- Receive letters of admission
- Receive financial aid award letters

- Send required college deposits
- Notify the college you will attend
- Review and accept financial aid offer(s)

Planning for college should ideally begin as soon as a student starts school. Many parents find this daunting given their child is so young. However, college preparedness involves planning for financial and academic requirements. U.S. students lag behind those in most industrialized countries because nations such as Japan and Sweden begin teaching their children math, sciences, and reading at very young ages, and their school year typically last longer. In the United States, African American students lag behind their peers due to economic and social disparities such as poverty, lack of parental support, and living in economically depressed areas with poor school systems. These challenges can be overcome, even by parents who lack a good deal of money. Parents should start reading to their children at very young ages, enroll them in good preschool and kindergarten programs, and take advantage of such programs as Head Start and summer programs offered by schools, churches, and community centers. Some school systems offer voucher programs whereby parents have a choice of schools for their children even if they do not have the personal financial means to afford it.

In the United States there are several types of colleges and universities. There are community colleges, public colleges, and private colleges. There are large and small colleges, and there are predominately white institutions and historically black institutions. The type of college and university that students choose should be a good fit academically, socially, and financially. Some colleges and universities have open enrollment, while others can have closed enrollment. Open enrollment means that all students are accepted at the institution. An open enrollment policy means that the institution is open to students with a high school diploma, those with a General Education Diploma (GED), and even students who do not have any of the preceding. Those who do not operate under a wholly open policy will have minimal selective criteria and some course requirements to enroll. Closed enrollment means schools are selective and admit students based on a set of criteria. The criteria may include standardized exam scores, high school grade point average, and extracurricular activities. Highly selective universities operate under a closed admission policy, and their criteria can be stringent.

COLLEGES AND ACADEMIC DEPARTMENTS

Many times students hear "college" and "university" used interchangeably. As a student, this can be very confusing especially if you are unfamiliar with the basic organization of a university. Universities are usually divided into colleges. Colleges are usually grouped with similar or nearly similar departments and offer various courses and fields of study. However, this may not always be the case. Each of these colleges has its own requirements for graduation, and the person who leads each college is called a dean. These colleges are also sometimes referred to as schools, so students may hear various terms like the College of Liberal Arts and Social Sciences, College of Social Work, College of Education, or the School of Divinity, School of Graduate Studies, and School of Communication. Departments are units within a specific college or school. A department consists of a group of professors usually in the same or similar field who offer a group of classes within the school or college. This grouping allows students to get specific education or training (major) in a given academic discipline or subject area. Students may take classes with professors from several different colleges, especially if there is a general education course required for their degree.

An academic discipline is a field of study. It is a topic of knowledge that is taught and researched at the college or university level. Within a discipline, students may choose a major. A major is a specific subset of a subject area that students specialize in their studies. Almost half of the courses in which students enroll in college will be in their major. Some people choose to major in two disciplines or fields. These people are called double majors and typically hold two undergraduate degrees when they graduate. A minor is like a major, but usually there are fewer courses to obtain a minor. An academic minor is a student's declared secondary field of study or specialization during their undergraduate studies. Students may also hear the term *multidisciplinary* used on a college campus. This simply means that courses or projects are constructed by people from different disciplines. A multidisciplinary person is someone who studies within two or more academic disciplines. When courses are multidisciplinary, they may be counted for credit in multiple categories for graduation in the curriculum of courses needed for graduation.

ATTENDING PREDOMINATELY WHITE INSTITUTIONS OR HISTORICALLY BLACK COLLEGES AND UNIVERSITIES

In making a final decision about what university to attend, some African American students are faced with the decision of whether to attend a historically black college and university (HBCU) or a predominately white institution (PWI). Each African American student is unique, and to attend either type of college is an individual decision. There is no right or wrong answer when facing this question, but the beauty of this dilemma is that African American students have a choice and this has not always been the case in the United States. HBCUs have been crucial in the development of black professionals and the black middle class. Since their inception, these institutions have educated people who were restricted legally, politically, and socially from being educated. HBCUs were established to train teachers and preachers along with other community professionals, and they have produced the likes of Booker T. Washington (Hampton University), W. E. B. Du Bois (Fisk University), Martin Luther King Jr.

(Morehouse College), John Hope Franklin (Fisk University), Thurgood Marshall (Lincoln University and Howard University), James Weldon Johnson (Clark Atlanta), Zora Neale Hurston (Howard University), Nikki Giovanni (Fisk University), and Oprah Winfrey (Tennessee State University). In determining and selecting the best option between HBCUs and PWIs, students should consider their personal needs and the reputation of the prospective universities. Bottom line, selecting the best college depends on a student's personality, skills, attitude, future goals, and how a degree from a particular university fits into the student's long-range goals.

African American students receiving a degree from a highly elite PWI are usually perceived as better, and these students can use the degree from these universities as passageways to graduate and professional programs. Most predominately white colleges have been typically funded better than historically black institutions due to systemic, racial patterns of discriminatory practices in state funding. Because of larger endowments and budgets, PWIs may have more renowned faculty members and may offer more lucrative scholarships than HBCUs. By no means does it mean that all HBCUs are not competitive as compared to white institutions. When visiting PWI campuses, students might also find larger libraries, professional-looking sports stadiums, gyms, laboratory facilities, movie theaters, and other amenities that may not be offered at some historically black institutions.

African American students may have to be prepared to experience more racially charged encounters at PWIs than they would at an HBCU. Because there may be a small number of other African American students and professors, students may experience more incidents of overt and subtle racism and racial incidents on predominately white campuses. These incidents can range from being attacked on campus to having their ideas belittled and discounted. These slights can come in the form of scathing attacks in the university newspapers or having their accomplishments demeaned by some faculty and staff members. At PWIs, African American students may also not have the opportunity to meet individuals who are the same race as them and share some common experiences. As a result, some African American students may experience isolation or loneliness at PWIs. African American students may also be reluctant to ask counselors or academic advisors for help when struggling academically or adjusting to college for fear of being perceived as inadequate and not suited for college. In combating isolation, African American students must create social outlets on their own campus to commune with other African American students. If there is an HBCU near the PWI that African American students are attending, students should attempt to connect with students at the nearby HBCU and take part in its social activities. If there is not a nearby HBCU, they should create spaces to cultivate black culture and social activities.

While some attempt to paint an inferior picture of HBCUs this is not the case. HBCUs have both tangible and intangible elements that make them a gem in many students' college experiences. HBCUs provide African American students with better leadership opportunities to grow and reach self-actualization. African American students often find these opportunities are available without the added stress of attempting to navigate the sometimes unwelcoming environment of white colleges. HBCUs generally cost less than PWIs; however, with the reduction of state and federal funding, many HBCUs are increasing their costs. African American students attempting to major in African or African American Studies may be shocked to find that very few HBCUs offer these as majors; the majority of these majors are offered at PWIs. At PWIs, these department spaces usually become safe havens for African American students.

At HBCUs, the student population is very homogeneous, and there may be very few opportunities to interact with racially diverse groups. Students also may find very little racial intolerance; however, intolerance may be rooted in other factors such as sexuality, socioeconomics, or gender. For some students, HBCUs may offer a nurturing atmosphere where African American students find more same-race role models. African American students should examine both options before making a final decision of attending a PWI or an HBCU.

University Accreditation

Some undergraduate students do not look to see if a college is accredited, but this stamp of approval and validation confirms that a university is meeting a set standard of criteria. Accreditation is important in the life of a college student because a student cannot receive federal financial aid for an unaccredited university. If a university is not accredited, potential employers may question the quality of students' learning and the merit of their degree. The federal government may not provide any financial assistance to students attending these schools. Accreditation is a voluntary process of self-regulation and peer review adopted by universities. Accreditation is an endorsement of the services and quality of the education that students will receive at a university. Universities voluntarily enter into associations to evaluate each other in accord with an institution's stated goals. In determining a university's accreditation, a committee of specialists review and evaluate each university using the following criteria:

Overall mission: The mission is the overall goal and purpose of a particular university. The mission also offers benchmarks for the university to pursue. The mission captures the essence of what the university is attempting to do.

Objectives and goals: These are specific organizational values that allow a university to focus on particular values and to ensure that the objectives and goals of the university are being met. A university's core values are usually embedded in their objectives and goals.

Student requirements for admissions: These standards are set by a university but measured by regional and national accrediting agencies. Universities are evaluated as to whether or not their policies and practices are consistent and fair.

Services available to students: Universities provide students with services and experiences to support their overall academic experience. Accrediting agencies evaluate these student support services provided at universities.

Quality of education: Most universities have common core standards to ensure that students are learning while attending the university. Universities use assessment tools where they evaluate samples of student work in targeted courses. Accrediting agencies use the assessment tools and other benchmarks to determine if a university is meeting core standards.

Reputation of the faculty: Faculty members are responsible for developing and teaching courses offered at the university. The quality and reputation of the faculty can weigh heavily in the reputation and overall view of the educational experience at a university.

Accreditation is usually granted by six regional agencies: Middle State Association of Colleges and Schools, New England Association of Schools and Colleges, North Central Association of Schools, Northwest Commission of Schools and Colleges, Western Association of Schools and Colleges, and Southern Association of Colleges and Schools. Online institutions and distance learning programs should have the same standards as "brick and mortar" universities. Students should be weary of online programs that lack accreditation. Some of these schools have been found to make false promises of guaranteeing jobs after graduation. Students later find themselves plagued with very large student loans and the inability to gain employment with their degrees. These schools have been accused of particularly targeting African American students.

ATTENDING COMMUNITY OR TECHNICAL COLLEGES (TWO-YEAR SCHOOLS)

Two-year colleges are attractive to students who may not be ready for a four-year institution. These types of institutions are often less expensive than their four-year college and university counterparts. Primarily, community colleges are state-funded institutions that usually enroll and retain students from their local areas. There are a number of great community colleges throughout the United States, and students may choose to attend these types of schools before they decide to pursue a four-year degree. Many of the community colleges are also technical colleges that allow students to pursue a vocational degree or certificate and move directly into their career after approximately 18–25 months of study in a particular field of study.

Students should consider several important factors when selecting a two-year community college and ensure that the institution is fully accredited by the higher educational agency within the particular region in which they live. Most institutions will list this in their recruitment and promotional materials. Also, students should check to make sure that the particular field of study is offered at the particular school that they are enrolling in. We chat with students who say that they would like to enter a particular profession, for example, forensic science. Some universities do not offer this particular major; however, the student has enrolled into this school that does not offer this major. This student should know that they will have to choose another major if they continue to be enrolled at this school, or they may have to transfer to another college or university that offers that major. Another option would be to enroll in classes and transfer to another institution with the major that the student wants and pursue the forensic science degree at that institution. Students should also check on the number of credits that would transfer when applying to a four-year college. Students should also contact the career and placement office to determine the kinds of jobs and internships that may be available to someone pursuing a degree in the field that they have chosen.

Community colleges usually have certain courses that transfer to four-year colleges, and in most cases, if students obtain the two-year degree, four-year institutions will guarantee transfer to their school. Most community colleges, but not all, have residential halls and facilities for students to live on campus. These types of schools are typically populated by nontraditional students (traditional students are 18–24 years of age), part-time students, and those attending classes in the evening, and may lack residential facilities. Most of these students commute from nearby cities or towns, so there is not a significant need for residential facilities. Community colleges usually offer fewer extracurricular student activities on campus than a four-year university. Cost is a key reason why some students choose to go to community colleges as opposed to four-year institutions. The tuition at a community college is significantly less than that at a residential four-year institution, because most of these schools are nonresidential and a student and their family do not have to pay for boarding. Living at home allows a student to save money. This should be a serious consideration if it is amenable to you and your family. Most community colleges have open enrollment. A community college is an excellent way to begin a college education and transition to a four-year institution or move directly into a career.

FACTORS IN SELECTING THE RIGHT INSTITUTION

When applying for admission into a university, there are many things that potential students and their families must remember in deciding what the best institution is for them, including location, tuition, student life, collegiate athletics, on-campus housing, off-campus housing, and university ranking and reputation. In making their decision, they should consider if they will feel comfortable in a large university or a small university. Does the university have the major that the student intends to declare? Is the university's location somewhere they are comfortable? Does the university have the extracurricular activities in which they are interested? Is the university that they chose affordable for them and their family? There are so many colleges and universities, so how does a student select one that is best for them? That is the intent of this book: to help students choose the university or college that is best for them and to guide them through the maze of the college process.

Most colleges and universities will want to examine a student's official transcripts or academic records before accepting him or her for study there. A transcript is an official record from a student's former high school giving a summary of the courses, grades, and grade point average they have achieved during their high school years. Most universities use these and extracurricular activities to determine if students will be accepted. Some universities will take into consideration only the grades that students obtain in common core classes, which in most cases include English, math, science, and social studies. A transcript can be obtained from your high school, and usually a person such as the guidance counselor would handle such duties. The student should work closely with their high school counselors in evaluating college choices.

One word of advice is to not take counselors' advice as the only source of recommendations. Some counselors may recommend black students attend technical or community colleges, even when they have the grades and test scores to attend very good four-year colleges. The authors recommend this from personal experience while counseling high school students on their college choices. Students should seek college advice from guidance counselors, teachers, community leaders, parents, and also college admissions officers and recruiters.

A certified copy of the transcript will have a special stamp and will have the signature of the appropriate member of the staff at the high school. This will be taken care of by the guidance counselor's office and normally mailed by them to the appropriate addresses. If a student sends the transcripts themselves, they are not considered as official because they were not sent by a person from the high school or school district. All students should look at their high school transcripts to ensure accuracy before they submit them to a university as a part of their application packet. Most colleges and universities are concerned with a student's cumulative grade point average from high school. Admission officers will want to know how students have performed over time, so be sure to have official records sent that describe your academic performance for the past three to four years.

Many high schools require that basic courses be taken for graduation. Most high school curriculums call for completion of basic courses; however, universities expect students to have more than just basic skills and base-level knowledge. Most colleges would like students who have taken college preparatory courses in high school. These include basic- and advanced-level courses in math (e.g., algebra, geometry, and trigonometry), science (e.g., biology, chemistry, and physics), and English. If students have not had these courses, they may still get accepted and admitted to a university; however, students may have to take some remedial courses during their freshman year for further preparation. Having to take remedial courses for better readiness is not the end of the world. Some very successful and intelligent people have had to take remedial courses in college before they became the people who they are today.

Placement tests are exams that colleges and universities use to access students' skill levels in particular subject areas like English, mathematics, writing, and science. These courses assist in placing students in the right level. Depending on a student's placement test score, this may mean that an introductory-level course can be skipped, or it may show that a student needs some remedial courses. Remedial courses assist students in improving their skills in a particular subject area. These courses may show a student what area they need to improve and may also reveal their strengths in a subject area. Students usually do not receive college credit toward graduation for remedial courses, but these courses are still counted into a student's college grade point average. At most universities, placement tests are given during orientation. Each university has their own system of scoring and determining a student's placement in a level of study in a particular course. Community colleges usually do not have placement tests.

Most high schools offer advanced placement exams for top high school students. Advanced Placement (AP) courses are classes in which students can receive college credit while in high school if they make an acceptable score on the AP exam. These courses usually last one academic year and are designed to be college-level courses; however, students must complete the national AP exam in the particular subject that they enrolled in to get AP credit. The exam is scored on a scale from 1 to 5, and there is usually a fee associated with taking this exam. Universities determine if the student will receive college credit for the AP courses taken. Students must typically score at least a 3, 4, or 5 on the exam to receive credit.

STANDARDIZED ADMISSION EXAMS

In the United States, there are two exams that colleges and universities use to measure students' aptitude and learning. The Scholastic Aptitude Test (SAT) and the American College Test (ACT) are exams that most schools use to determine, or as a part of a formula, admission decisions. The SAT is more of an aptitude test for reasoning and verbal abilities and has three components that include Critical Reasoning, Mathematics, and Writing (the writing test was made optional in 2014). The ACT is an achievement test that measures what a student has learned, and has four components—English, Math, Reading, and Science—and sometimes, the writing portion of the test that some universities require. The ACT has about 200 questions plus an essay that is optional, while the SAT has 170 questions. Students taking the SAT find that the questions get more difficult as the test progresses, while the ACT maintains a constant level of difficulty. The SAT has more emphasis on verbal skills. Students who will take the SAT should build their vocabularies. Both exams are multiple choice tests; however, on the SAT, some math questions will have to be worked out by hand. Both exams take approximately 3 hours and 30 minutes. Students are allowed breaks while taking both tests.

One of the major differences between the ACT and the SAT is the science portion of the tests. On the ACT, there are questions from biology, chemistry, physics, and earth science. This portion of the test assesses a student's ability to understand graphs, research summaries, and understand hypotheses. While having taken some of these science courses would be helpful and probably boost a student's score on the ACT science portion, if a student has strong critical reading skills, they can determine the correct answers. The ACT also has questions in trigonometry, while the SAT does not. Students should at least have a basic understanding of trigonometry. Another difference between the ACT and the SAT is that the SAT penalizes students' random guessing. The ACT has no guessing penalty. This does not make one exam better or easier than the other. Being knowledgeable about this penalty may assist students in not being penalized for hapless guessing. The scoring scales for the two exams are different. Each section of the ACT is 36 points, while on the SAT, each section is 800 points. While it is difficult to get a perfect score on both, students are encouraged to do their best because most colleges and universities in the United States have come to rely on the scores of these tests in making admission decisions.

For the SAT, the scores from each section can range from 200 to 800, so the best possible total score is 2,400. The average score for each section is roughly 500, so the average total score is about 1,500. Each category in the ACT receives a score between 1, which is the lowest score, and 36, which is the highest score. Those four scores are then averaged to generate the composite score. The average composite score is around 21. In 2016, the SAT will return to a 1,600 point scale and eliminate antiquated vocabulary words. In addition, the essay section will also be optional. Moreover, the test will no longer penalize students for wrong answers, and the Reading (comprehension) section will incorporate subjects that students typically learn in high school. Below are a few strategies to assist students in maximizing preparation before taking the SAT or ACT.

- Students should familiarize themselves with the exam because this improves their confidence. Students should be familiar with all parts of the exam.
- Students should study unfamiliar vocabulary. Being familiar with words can increase their overall scores. Vocabulary is associated with reasoning and critical thinking. Students and their tutors can create flashcards to aid in remembering words and their usages.
- Students should review math consistently. Reviewing math and the processes of working out several math problems will allow students to focus on mathematical knowledge that are keys to solving math problems.
- Students should remember that practice makes perfect. If possible, students should enroll in preparation courses or, at the very least, buy a study guide book and take the practice exams at the conclusion of the book.
- Students should examine incorrect answers. A lot of information can be gained by studying the answers that they have incorrectly answered on the practice study exams. This also prevents students from making the same kinds of mistakes when they are taking the real ACT or SAT.

It should be noted that African Americans score lower on standardized admission tests, although African Americans whose family incomes are high usually score higher on these types of tests.[1] The reasons cannot be easily explained and have been debated in conversations among African American educators. These standardized tests are not necessarily the best measurement of college success. When these exams became the norm around the mid-1920s, *aptitude* was a code word for intelligence; however, these exams do not measure intelligence. These tests do not measure students' determination and grit in the pursuit of their college education. African American students should choose the exam that best plays to their individual strengths. If a school prefers one test over another, then the student should prepare for the test of that school's preference. The cost to take either the ACT or the SAT is roughly the same, approximately $55.00.

Test scores are critically important and care should be taken about reporting test score results to colleges. Students should not report their test results until after they have obtained the scores they feel are the highest they can achieve. Rather than indicating which colleges to send scores to before they take the test, they should wait until after they receive their scores and then report. Many parents and students do not realize this is a viable option.

NOTE

1. "SAT scores show disparities by race, gender, family income," *USA Today,* August 26, 2009.

STEP TWO

Getting Admitted to College

COLLEGE SELECTION AND APPLICATION

After students have taken either the ACT or the SAT, a formal application to the school(s) of choice must be submitted. Students should construct a list of universities they are interested in attending to which to apply. On this prospective list of schools, students might have some schools that they are almost sure they will be accepted in. These are called "safe schools." Students may also have schools on their list that are fairly competitive in student selection as well as a few elite and highly selective universities, especially if the student has an average to high grade point average and strong standardized test scores. Students should ask other students, alumni, and school representatives about the particular college or university in which they are interested. In deciding where to apply, students should ask the following questions:

What is the overall reputation of academic programs at this university? The reputation of the college is important. Degrees from universities with strong academic reputations are perceived as being able to provide a better education and opportunities. Students indicate that a university's reputation is the greatest influence in their school choice.

Do I want to go to school in an urban or a rural area? Students should choose universities that are best suited for them. If students are accustomed to an urban environment or enjoy the amenities of a major city, then they should choose urban campuses. Some urban campuses have security issues and higher crime rates because of their location. If students enjoy being outdoors and away from metropolitan living, then they should choose a college in a rural setting. Many universities in rural areas have been deemed college towns because most of the activities of the town center on the activities taking place at the college.

Does the school that I am considering have the major that I want? Not all majors, like pre-med, physical therapy, and other professional-type degrees, are offered at some schools. If this is the case, students should major in an area that is close to their field of choice and then attend graduate or professional school to obtain the desired degree. Students could also transfer to a university that has their desired degree. Some students choose to attend certain universities because they want to study under a particular professor. In some scientific and social science fields, particular scholars under whom a student studies can enhance their opportunities for graduate school. Each academic department usually has a page on their university's website with faculty members and their credentials displayed. Students should read about their potential professors, and they should Google them to learn more information about them.

What are the experiences of African American students on this campus? Students should find out if there have been recent racial incidents on campus. This can be accomplished by reading the student and local newspapers in the town in which the school is located.

Are the academic facilities (libraries and computer labs) sufficient? When a student attends a campus visit, they should ask to visit the library. If they are going to major in a discipline that has an extensive lab requirement, they should ask to see the lab facilities as well as learn about the Internet speed and other technology on campus.

What kinds of student support services and tutoring are offered for courses? When students inquire about majors in which they are interested, they should also ask questions about learning supports offered on campus. Many universities offer tutoring or supplemental instruction for some courses. Student-athletes at universities often participate in mandatory study halls.

How much financial aid is this school offering? When a university offers financial aid, the student must be sure that the aid offered covers their expenses. If the aid does not cover all of their expenses, then the student should have a plan of how they will make up the gap between the amount covered and the amount owed.

What are the housing options and what housing is available for freshmen students? Students should make a visit to the campus and see their future living space. Universities and colleges often require that students live on campus during their first year. This allows them the opportunity to meet new people and build community. Students who live on campus their first year usually have better retention rates and return for their second year.

What extracurricular, cultural, and religious activities does the university offer? Most universities have an office of student activities. Students should explore potential activities, clubs, programs, and organizations in which they could become involved. This information can be found in brochures or on the school's website.

What will be my travel time and expense to and from the school? If a student commutes, they may want to consider the cost of the mileage for gas, whether or not they have access to a car, and the weekly or monthly cost of public transportation. If a student chooses to attend a school away from home, they may want to consider the cost of travel to return home for holidays and other visits.

What is the typical class size at your university? Some colleges have 200–300 students in the lower-level courses and 15–20 students in small, upper division classes. It is typically believed that smaller class size is conducive to better learning. Other institutions have small class sizes for all of their course offerings.

How often will I get to interact with faculty members? At some universities, students get very little interaction with professors because research and service duties are their focus and courses are taught by graduate students. Other schools require students to meet regularly with faculty advisors who guide them in selecting courses and graduating on time.

Are the introductory classes taught by professors or graduate students? At some universities, undergraduate courses are primarily taught by graduate students. It is perceived that courses taught by professors rather than graduate students provide students with a richer educational experience.

What kind of equipment or facilities are available for students? Cutting-edge equipment and technology help to better prepare students for their chosen career or graduate school. Prospective students should determine available computer labs, their location on campus, and their hours of operation.

Do career services have a good track record of helping students find employment after they graduate? If a college's career services unit is resourceful in assisting graduates in finding employment, then this provides their graduates easier access to career opportunities after graduation. Prospective students should determine a school's career services options and employment success rates upon graduation prior to applying to school.

These questions will allow students to see if their personal goals match the university's goals and figure out which university is a good fit and choice to attend. Usually, colleges tend to be smaller with smaller class sizes, while universities have larger lower division courses. Faculty members at colleges tend to focus on teaching; however, many of them are highly productive in conducting research. Typically, universities offer master's and doctoral degrees, which require completion of the bachelor's degree and sometimes a master's degree prior to enrolling in a doctoral program. Universities tend to be larger than colleges, and their faculty members divide their time and attention between research, teaching, and service. Some large universities will have divisions of separately named colleges such as "College of Liberal Arts," "College of Fine Arts," or "College of Business."

Universities often promote professor-to-student ratio in recruiting prospective students. Most schools who feature their small professor-to-student ratio believe that a smaller class yields better learning and opportunities to learn. This may not always be the case. Private liberal arts colleges usually have small enrollment and thus small class sizes, usually taught in classrooms with only about 10–15 students. These courses are primarily taught by professors. In this case, the professor may learn students' name and recall some details about each student. Some large state universities can have large class sizes with as many as 200–300 students in a class. These classes are taught in a large auditorium; the professor is often assisted by a graduate student. In large auditorium classes, it is more likely that a professor will not know each student personally. The professor will not remember each student's name or what distinguishes them from any other student. These courses may also have supplemental instruction, so that students can get individual help if needed.

There are many sources of information about colleges and universities to help students in making their school choice. First, the student should request information from colleges and universities they wish to attend. Information is available online, can be picked up from admissions offices, or can be mailed to the student upon request. Second, there are many online resources including the following:

- National Center for Education Statistics—Search for Schools and Colleges, http://nces.ed.gov/globallocator/
- National Center for Education Statistics—College Navigator, http://nces.ed.gov/collegenavigator/
- Peterson's guide to colleges and universities, http://www.petersons.com/
- U.S. News & World Report online annual ranking of Best Colleges
- Forbes *America's Best Colleges*
- The Common Application, http://www.commonapp.org/
- CollegeStats.org, http://collegestats.org/colleges/all/
- Startclass, http://colleges.startclass.com/
- Campus Tours, http://www.campustours.com/
- U.S. College Search, http://www.uscollegesearch.org/

APPLICATION PROCESS

The application process is the most important factor in getting admitted to any college or university. Each application must be completely filled out. Applicants must take care to check their grammar and spelling, and then have their applications proofread by a parent, teacher, guidance counselor, or someone they trust with the skills and experience to give positive feedback. It is best to fill out applications either online or using downloaded applications. This should be the first option before completing handwritten applications. Read all instructions carefully to ensure an understanding of all application requirements and what each line of the application is specifically asking for. If more clarity is needed on any item on the application, call the college's admissions office for guidance.

Students should apply to colleges early. In general, students in their junior year of high school should begin the initial stages of considering what universities they may want to attend. This also takes the pressure of making this decision off of the student during their senior year of high school. "Early action" admission is an accelerated application process where students usually apply in November and receive a college decision by January. This shows that you are highly interested in the university and you are serious about attending the university in which you are applying. Be sure to read the application details carefully as some institutions allow you to apply only to one school for early action. Another option, "early admission," allows students to submit applications by an earlier deadline; this option sometimes gives students a better chance of obtaining financial aid and scholarships. Planning ahead and applying early allows students to have the security of knowing where they are attending and allows them to relax and not continue to stress over an admission decision. It also allows prospective students to weigh other offers and possibly bargain for a better financial package from a competing school. Most need-based scholarships are offered on a first come, first serve basis, and therefore, applying late may limit a student's opportunity to receive a scholarship. Some early action and early decision options provide students with opportunities for competitive merit-based scholarships. As always, for each institution in which students are interested, they should carefully read the instructions for applications and track each deadline.

Some universities use a rolling admission process in which applicants have a large window of time to apply for admission. Most of the elite schools do not use a rolling process. The process usually opens during the fall and may continue up until the summer. In the rolling process, students are usually notified of the admission decision within a few weeks. Universities who use a rolling admission process typically accept students as long as there are spaces available. An open admission process typically allows any student with a high school diploma or a GED to enroll at the university. In an open enrollment process, students may still have to make a minimum score on the ACT or the SAT and have a certain grade point average to gain admittance. Students should start considering college applications roughly 16 to 12 months prior to enrolling in college. Students should write to the universities they have chosen and request application materials, catalogs, and information about financial aid, housing, and fields of study. You can also get this information on the universities' websites. Students should complete their college application in a timely manner and pay attention to prospective colleges' deadlines. These deadlines are listed on the application forms. Colleges and universities receive thousands of applications from students each year. In order to be considered for admission at the college of your choice for the term you want to begin, it is essential that your application and all supporting materials, such as references and personal essays, be received before the deadline. To have a good beginning at the application process, carefully follow the instructions of each school that you are considering. If you have any questions about the application process, call the college's admission office for clarification.

The "common application" can be used by students to apply to institutions in the United States, Austria, France, Germany, Italy, Switzerland, and the United Kingdom. The common application is managed by the Common Application Incorporated, which is a nonprofit organization whose mission is to provide a holistic admission process. This process takes into account both subjective and objective measures by using the applicant's essays, recommendations, standardized testing, and class rank. Students should check to see if their prospective college or university accepts the common application. Even if students do use the common application, most submissions are handled electronically. Before an application is submitted, review all the application materials and proofread the personal statement essay (if this is a part of the application).

A student's personal statement should share their personal and academic experiences. Students should sell themselves and discuss their academic and extracurricular activities. Make those who are making the decision see what an asset you would be to their university and that they would be proud to have you as an alumnus when you graduate. These essays usually ask students questions about their abilities, goals, and talents. They may also ask the reason the students wish to attend college in general and/or specifically their university. The personal essay is very important to the college application. Students should have several readers who can provide feedback on their personal essay.

Some universities will want a recommendation from students' high school teachers, counselors, or administrators. It is an excellent idea to have a teacher in mind to serve as a reference and ask at least three weeks prior to the application deadline. Students should select someone who knows them well and who can attest to their academic ability. Most of all, select someone who is going to write a good recommendation letter.

If universities have a set number of freshman students to be admitted in each class, students may be placed on a wait list. Wait lists are tools to keep a healthy pool of applicants. To be wait-listed does not mean that the student has been formally accepted to the university, but may be admitted if openings become available. This is usually a policy used at highly competitive universities. Some students may be accepted on a conditional basis. Conditional admission means that the university has accepted a student; however, the acceptance status depends on the student completing coursework or meeting specific criteria before enrollment or full acceptance. Conditional acceptance is a way for marginal students to prove that they are college ready. Open admission is a noncompetitive university admission where the only requirement is that applicants have a high school diploma or its equivalent to be admitted. This type of admission is usually used at community colleges or lesser competitive four-year colleges. Some universities use rolling admissions when admitting applicants to the university. Under rolling admission, candidates are invited to submit their applications to the university within a designated period of time, usually about six months. After this period ends, the university reviews applications and then let the applicants know if they have been admitted or not.

If parents want their children to think about and eventually attend college, it is never too early to ask them what college they plan on attending. Students should make the decision to attend college long before their senior year of high school. When a student enters into their freshman year of high school, they should begin to seriously think about what colleges they should consider and what fields they may want to enter. While in high school, students should take challenging courses in core academic subjects. That usually includes four years of English, three years of math and science, and three years of social studies. To become a more attractive college applicant, African American students should become involved in community service, extracurricular activities, and other experiences that demonstrate their ability to succeed in higher education. Students can gain valuable insight through conversations with mentors and college students as well as participating in academic enrichment programs, summer workshops, and seminars to keep their skills sharp and gain new ones. African American students should look at the entrance requirements for schools in which they are interested. Students should narrow down the colleges to the ones they are truly interested in and then make visits to these campuses. Make a list of pros and cons about each school, and then decide which school fits your needs and budget. After a final decision has been made, students should notify the school that was chosen and submit a deposit for a room in a residence hall. Students should also sign up for an orientation session and then attend the designated orientation session. Typically, when students leave the orientation session, they will have registered for their first semester of courses and are official college students.

CAMPUS VISIT AND DELIBERATION

Students deciding which university to attend should make visits to any university under consideration if it is feasible and affordable. A campus visit will allow students along with their parents to gain a better perspective about the university. Students and their parents should start planning their potential college visits early. Most universities have virtual tours on their websites: virtual tours are a very good way of getting a look at what a university has to offer before taking an actual campus tour. This is a good practice especially if the university is a great distance from the student's home. When visiting a campus, students should talk with students currently enrolled at the university being considered. These conversations will allow students to get a clearer picture and gain greater insights that are not presented in brochures or on the university's websites. Students should also research the institution's academic departments, majors, and professors of those departments. If possible, students should sit in on a lecture as well as visit the student union and other support services, student housing, and on-campus cafeteria. Classroom visits will allow students to get a feel of the pace of a college classroom, while visiting the cafeteria and student union will provide them with an opportunity to see what college life may be like.

While on their campus visits, students should inquire about campus safety. Students should ask their tour guide and others about campus safety policies and any incidents that have occurred over the last two years. Students should read the newspapers of the city where the college being considered is located. This will help them understand important issues on campus and in the surrounding area. After visiting all the colleges being considered, students should take notes about each of their visits and make a list of pros and cons to discuss with their parents before moving toward a final decision.

MAKING A FINAL DECISION

Deciding on the college to attend is an important decision that should not be entered into lightly. Therefore, students should discuss the particulars with their parents or guardian. Ultimately, it is the student's decision; it is the student who has to attend and spend the next four or five years at that prospective school. When students begin to narrow down their list of schools, it is best to make a list of pros and cons of each school to make the best informed decision. As a prospective student, you should look at the practicalities of attending each university. A few things to consider: Does this school have the major that will allow you to fulfill your ultimate career goal? Are your high school grades and standardized test scores good enough to get accepted into your school of choice? Can you afford this particular school, or will you end up in debt after graduating? Will this school prepare you for future employment or graduate or professional school after you finish? These are just a few questions that you should be asking and discussing with your parents as you deliberate and reach your final decision about what university to attend.

Finalizing plans for college in terms of academic performance should begin in a student's freshman year of high school. The first step is for parents and their children to schedule an appointment with the school's guidance counselor to have a very detailed discussion about the student's academic performance and potential, and the availability of information about colleges, and to outline a clear plan for the remainder of the student's high school year. Care should be taken to ensure the school counselor has the best interest of the student in mind and is not biased. Too often, African American students who are bright and have potential are steered toward technical schools and trade occupations when they might be better suited for college. An obvious sign that the school counselor is not providing good academic advice is prolonged discussions about what the student cannot do versus what the student can do. School counselors should be but one source of information and decision making. Parents should talk to teachers and also seek advice from sources external to the school. Parents and students should begin scheduling visits to the colleges and universities of interest to the student. These visits should include schools on the student's "wish list" and also those that are backup or "safe schools." The concern should not be on the schools' costs at this point. College visits and website information will include discussions about tuition costs and possible sources of financial aid. Many colleges and universities have specific activities geared toward recruiting students as early as their high school freshman year.

UNIVERSITY AFFILIATION AND DIVERSITY AT INSTITUTIONS

Students might take into consideration universities' affiliations in deciding if a university is a good fit for them. There are some universities that are based on gender like Wellesley College, Spelman College, Judson College, and Smith College. There are some universities with religious affiliations such as Notre Dame, Lane College, Samford University, Boston College, and Baylor University. There are specialized universities such as HBCUs, for example Alabama State University, North Carolina A&T University, Howard University, Morehouse College, and Hampton University. There are Hispanic-serving institutions, such as California State University at Fullerton, Florida International University, University of New Mexico, University of Puerto Rico, and Texas State University, and military-serving institutions, such as the United States Naval Academy, the United States Air Force Academy, the United States Military Academy, the Citadel, and the Virginia Military Institute. Many universities pride themselves on diversity in the composition of their student bodies and their faculties. These schools champion the diversity of their student body and their faculty. Some universities argue that diverse student bodies and faculty members contribute to a better education because students are exposed to diversity of thoughts and wide-ranging opinions and perspectives. Diversity is more complex than just race. Diversity can encompass race, gender, ethnicity, sexual orientation, religion, and political affiliation. By choosing a university that values diversity, students are being better prepared for the workforce that they will face in the future.

DIVERSITY AND MULTICULTURALISM

Often when considering what college to attend, students overlook the issue of diversity and multiculturalism. Diversity is the inclusion of individuals representing more than one national origin, race, color, religion, socioeconomic status, and sexual orientation. Multiculturalism is the preserving of different cultures within an organization or a society. For African American students, the issue of diversity of a university should not be overlooked. African American students should look for universities that celebrate diversity and multiculturalism because these students will more likely be appreciated for their cultural and racial differences. While it is important to be around individuals who look like you and share some of the same experiences, African American students should be on campuses with people from various backgrounds and religions, and socioeconomic status. Even if students choose to attend a historically black university, usually these schools will have other races and cultures represented in their student bodies and faculty members. Students should take advantage of the diverse student population and learning opportunities available at their university. Students who understand and appreciate diversity are better prepared for life after graduation. Interacting with various ethnicities, races, and cultures make students more well-rounded individuals and exposes them to various ideas and philosophies. Diversity prepares students for the world of work. More than likely, newly minted college graduates will work in jobs that have diverse populations. Diversity and various points of view during classroom discussions enrich one's higher educational experience and add to student learning. Every student has something different and unique to contribute to an intellectual discussion. Universities whose value systems do not offer diversity as a central piece of a student's college experience are not offering a first-rate 21st-century college education to their students. When differences arise between a student and someone else, it's important to address the issue. Most universities sponsor common annual events honoring and celebrating diversity, which probably include:

National Coming Out Day: At some universities, National Coming Out Day is celebrated. This is an annual day observed on October 11 each year and recognizes the process of coming out or self-disclosing one's sexual orientation.

Black History Month: This celebration takes place during the month of February. It was started by Dr. Carter G. Woodson as Negro History Week and celebrates the history, heritage, achievements, and contributions of black people to society.

Disability Awareness Month: This national campaign is celebrated every October to raise awareness about employment issues for the disabled.

Hispanic Heritage Month: National Hispanic Heritage Month is observed from September 15 to October 15, by celebrating the histories, cultures, and contributions of American citizens whose ancestors came from Spain, Mexico, the Caribbean, and Central and South America.

International Bazaar: The International Bazaar is an event that gives cultural groups the opportunity to share their history and heritage, while giving individuals the opportunity to learn about many different cultures and traditions.

Women's History Month: This annual celebration highlights the contributions of women to history and contemporary society.

National Science Day: Every year, this day celebrates and spreads message about the significance of scientific applications in the daily life of the people. It also shows the activities, efforts, and achievements in the field of science for human endeavor.

Most universities continue to examine how diversity can affect college experiences of African American students. It is beneficial for African American college students to not isolate themselves and to interact with people different from them. Being in college allows a unique opportunity to interact and live with students from various backgrounds and cultures. Expanding their worldview by learning about each other's differences and similarities will likely enhance their college experience and also prepare them for the environment that they will experience when they graduate and begin their career.

PLACEMENT TESTS, ADVANCED PLACEMENT COURSES, AND DUAL ENROLLMENT

A recent trend in higher education is allowing students to become dual enrollment students and pursue college coursework while completing high school. Some universities and high schools have allowed bright high school students to take classes and earn college credit that can be used toward a degree. This allows a student to prove to colleges that he or she is mature and ready for success in a university setting. It allows students to cut down on the cost of college by getting started early with college and taking a lower course load. A course load determines how much a student pays because base tuition is a fixed cost per credit hour. This option is usually only reserved for those extremely bright students who have a demonstrated history of academic success and high grade point averages. Dual enrollments have also been criticized because high school students who do not do well may choose not to attend college as a result of their experience with dual enrollments. Whether or not to pursue dual enrollment should be determined in consultation with a student's parents, the student, and the school's guidance counselor.

FULL-TIME VERSUS PART-TIME STUDENT

A student's status is based on the number of credit hours that he or she enrolls in during a given semester. At most universities, a student who is enrolled in at least 12 credit hours during a given semester is considered a full-time student. Most full-time students take about 12–16 credit hours, which is about four to six classes during a semester. If a student is enrolled in less than 12 credit hours, which is about one to three classes per semester, then they are considered a part-time student and will take longer to graduate. Most financial aid requires students to be full-time. Federal loans allow students to be enrolled while attending school part-time. Part-time students may choose to attend school on a part-time basis because of work and family obligations that may dictate how much time students can devote to school. Juggling one's schedule to attend school and study, even on a part-time basis, can be difficult.

There are advantages and disadvantages to both full-time and part-time statuses. Full-time status offers more opportunities for financial aid and students can complete their bachelor's degrees usually within four years. Most scholarships and fellowships require that students attend school on a full-time basis. Full-time students can immerse themselves into campus life, and they may enjoy greater access to campus activities and extracurricular activities. Full-time programs often have a greater academic load. It is certainly challenging for full-time students enrolled at a university to also be employed full-time.

Part-time students can usually pursue their education at a slower pace and may be able to continue working, often full-time, and have the time to balance other responsibilities and families. A number of universities offer courses for part-time students during the evenings, weekends, and online to help accommodate the need of these students. Part-time students who are employed can take advantage of employment tuition reimbursement programs through their employers if they offer such programs. However, part-time students can often be overlooked by their universities if they cater mostly to full-time students. Students must decide which status is better for them, going to school full-time or going to school part-time.

NONTRADITIONAL STUDENTS

Various indicators are used to identify nontraditional students, including family's financial status, delayed and inconsistent enrollment patterns, and high school graduation status. Though *nontraditional* is a term often used to describe many individuals enrolled in universities, there is no precise definition of a nontraditional student. Traditionally, a nontraditional student was thought of as any student who was above the 18–24 years old norm and who did not go to college directly after graduating from high school. Students who delayed entering college for at least a year after graduating or those students who completed some certification of completion are considered nontraditional students. The definition for nontraditional students has expanded and now includes those who attend school part-time, work at least 35 hours per week, have dependents other than a spouse, have a single parent, and/or does not have a traditional high school diploma. Students with financial constraints and low socioeconomic status or those who are financially independent are also classified as nontraditional students.

In a college classroom, there is very little that separates traditional and nontraditional students. There are some barriers that nontraditional students may experience that may not be experienced by traditional students. These barriers include negative perceptions about older students' ability to learn, perceptions projected by traditional students, tuition cost, and lack of time.

STEP THREE

Paying for College

TUITION AND FEES

Tuition is the charge for the instruction and services that a college student receives. Colleges charge tuition by the units that make up an academic year, such as a semester or a quarter. Typically, an academic year begins in the fall semester, usually in August or September, and goes through December. The spring semester usually begins in January and goes on through May or June. Increasingly more students are attending courses or enrolling into online courses during the summer. Most public colleges offer discounted rates for students who are residents of their states and who graduated from high schools in their states. Students from other states wishing to attend public universities in states where they are not a permanent resident are charged double tuition: this is called out-of-state tuition rate. Other costs for out-of-state residents, such as student fees and room and board, may be the same as for residents and nonresidents. In some cases, tuition is more expensive based on a student's major.

Tuition can include room and board, laboratory fees, activity fees, and recreational usage, among other fees. Most students do not have enough money to pay tuition outright, so they have to supplement the cost with loans, scholarships, or grants to pay their tuition. In some cases, the fees are itemized and are included with the overall tuition. There have been noted examples where universities have charged fees that students may not have a full understanding of. The most common fee used by most universities is an out-of-state fee. This is a sum of money charged to those students who are not residents of the states where their colleges are located. Other examples of charges that are not so clear-cut are globalization fee, parking and pedestrian fee, student success fee, and the life safety and security fee. Fees charged by universities have been a point of contention for many students since aid to universities began to be reduced in the 1980s.

The cost of a college education is continually rising in the United States. According to the College Board, for the 2014–2015 academic year, the average published tuition and fee prices for full-time in-state students in public four-year universities ranged from $7,142 at bachelor's colleges and $7,968 at master's universities to $10,075 at public doctoral universities. Following are the data for 2014–2015:

- The average published tuition and fee price for full-time out-of-state students at public four-year institutions is about 2.5 times as high as the price for in-state students.
- The average out-of-state tuition cost increased from $13,338 in 2013–2014 to $13,819 in 2014–2015.
- The average published in-state tuition and fee price for students enrolled full-time at public two-year colleges increased by $106 (3.3 percent) between 2013–2014 and 2014–2015.
- The average published tuition and fee price for students enrolled full-time at private nonprofit four-year colleges and universities increased by $1,100 (3.7 percent) between 2013–2014 and 2014–2015.
- The price at for-profit institutions have risen more slowly in recent years than prices in other sectors, but the estimated $15,230 average tuition and fee price in 2014–2015 is more than four times as high as the average price at public two-year colleges and 67 percent higher than the average in-state price at public four-year institutions.[1]

There are ways to deal with these costs. Parents can begin investing in private savings accounts when their children are young. Many states also have tuitions savings accounts. All 50 states and the District of Columbia offer 529 plans, named after Section 529 of the Internal Revenue Code, which established federal tax advantages for qualified college savings plans. There are two types of 529 plans: prepaid tuition plans and college savings plans. These education savings plans allow families to set aside funds for their college education, much like a 401k retirement savings account, except the 529 permits tax-free earnings withdrawal when used for qualified higher education expenses. They also provide tax benefits while parents are investing. Plans have a maximum savings amount. In Virginia, for example, a maximum of $350,000 can be deposited for each student.

For families who do not have the financial means to pay for college out of pocket, there are options to fund a college education. Scholarships are a great way to pay for college if your family cannot finance your college education. There are over a million scholarships awarded each year. There are scholarships provided on the bases of academic merit, disability, race, nationality, and religious affiliation. In some cases, scholarships are not awarded because no one applies or those who apply are not eligible for scholarships. Federal Pell Grants are another way for those who cannot pay for college out of pocket. Grants are awarded to students who have not earned a bachelor's degree. Students can receive up to $5,550 for the award year for up to 12 semesters. Institutional grants are financial aid sponsored by the institution, and merit-based grants can also cover the gap of tuition that is not covered by federal financial aid. Students may also apply for loans to pay for school. Some of the most popular loans are the Parent PLUS Loan (parents take out loans on student's behalf), Federal Perkins, Direct Subsidized (the federal government pays the interest while student is in school), and Direct Unsubsidized loans. Federal work-study programs, military service, and employee assistance are other sources to pay for college.

Student fees are various charges that can range from laboratory fees to parking fees if you own a car and intend to park on campus. Universities usually provide a student fee total; however, they may itemize only the most significant fees. There may be student identification card fees, health insurance fees, gym facility usage fees, athletic activity fees, diplomas and graduation expenses, computer access fees, local bus service fees, and student activities fees. The most common fees assessed are those associated with a lab for a course in which the student is enrolled. There are fees usually associated with science, technology, and engineering courses. Students and parents should contact the registrar's office, campus cashier, or financial aid office to get a better explanation of any charge or fee assessed by a university. Students should examine their student bills and check for fees that may be charged. Students must make sure that any fees have been rightly charged to them.

FINANCES AND FINANCIAL AID

Students may also hear various terms associated with student financial aid. Financial aid is monetary assistance that students and their families receive in the form of scholarships, grants, work-study, and education loans. Many terms are used in determining the type of financial aid provided to students. Merit-based aid and scholarships are funds that are available based on academic performance, leadership, community service, and other factors. Need-based aid is based on the student's or family's financial needs. Some universities use a need blind policy to determine admissibility of applicants. A need blind admission policy is when a university does not consider the financial needs of the applicant when determining admissions. In contrast, a need aware policy is when a college or university does take into consideration the financial needs of the applicant when determining admissibility. Students should consider these policies when making their final decisions about the university to attend.

Several types of financial aid are offered to students who meet certain financial criteria. Grants are financial aid that does not need to be repaid. Grant decisions are based on family income, household size, reported assets, and the number of children in college. To receive aid from federal programs, a student must:

- qualify for financial need (except for certain loans);
- have a high school diploma or a GED certificate, or pass a test approved by the U.S. Department of Education;
- be working toward a degree or certificate;
- be enrolled in an eligible program;
- be a U.S. citizen or eligible noncitizen;
- have a valid Social Security number;
- maintain satisfactory academic progress once in school.

The most common grant is Pell Grant, which pays for tuition, fees, and books, and refunds to the student unused money. If students take out loans to pay for college, they must pay back the lender along with the interest on the debt taken for their college education. African American students should know that they have the power and control over how much money they borrow and spend. They should be fully aware of the responsibility, repayment, and interest rates. Historically, the interest associated with students loans were fixed, but now these rates can be adjustable and could increase. Scholarships do not require repayment. These are the most underused in financial aid categories because each scholarship and its funding agency have established their own criteria for their scholarship. They can be based on academics and various other categories. There are many scholarships that have been designed specifically for African American students. Most universities will have applications for all internal scholarships. Various civic groups and organizations will offer scholarships, and they should be contacted directly for their scholarship applications and requirements. Finally, colleges and universities offer on-campus employment to students qualifying for work-study.

SCHOLARSHIPS AND FELLOWSHIPS

Scholarships are financial aid awarded that do not have to be repaid. Scholarships are awarded based on numerous factors, such as cultural background, academics, extracurricular participation, sports, and other activities. A separate application process is usually required. The Free Application for Federal Student Aid (FAFSA) application for financial aid is a form that students fill out to be considered for both state and federal financial aid. This application becomes available in January of each year. The government must receive a student's application before March of each year to be considered for the state portion and the FAFSA form must be renewed each year. After submitting the form, the student will receive award letters or notifications from schools where the student has been accepted. This letter outlines the student's financial aid award package. Students may also finance their college education through loans. Loans can be from the government or private lenders with varying interest rates and terms.

Fellowships are financial awards usually awarded to graduate and postgraduate students. The financial awards usually have requirements associated with receiving them. They may require a student to conduct research under the guidance of a professor, or students may also be employed in an office on campus. Fellowships may have a tuition waiver, and they may have an additional stipend associated with them. Grants are financial aid money that does not have to be repaid to their funding sources. Grants are available through many different sources such as the federal government, state agencies, and individual universities and provide students with financial aid that they are not required to repay. The funds are applied to school expenses in the same way student loans are applied. Tuition, books, housing, and other costs associated with postsecondary education are paid for by grants.

FEDERAL WORK-STUDY PROGRAM

Work-study is a federal program in which colleges and universities receive a certain amount of money to pay out in student wages. This program is designed to assist students who are in need of financial assistance while pursuing their degrees. Determination of financial need is based on several factors including a student's income. If the student is not independent, then need is determined by the parents' income, assets, family size, and family members also enrolled in college. Students will need to verify their enrollment at a university and have a valid Social Security card. Under this program, students are obligated to work 15–20 hours per week. With this program, students cannot work as many hours as they would like. Employers take into consideration the student's class schedule and maintain time sheets usually in the department where the student is employed. Federal work-study programs allow students to learn about their schools from the inside out. Approximately 3,400 universities receive funds to employ work-study students. All funds earned through federal work-study are considered taxable income, and it is in the students' best interest to file a tax return with the Internal Revenue Service (IRS).

With the federal work-study program the hourly wage paid to students cannot be less than the federal minimum wage. According to the Department of Education, students can be employed by the institution itself; a federal, state, or local public agency; a private nonprofit organization; or a private for-profit organization. Institutions must use at least seven percent of their work-study allocation to support students working in community service jobs. These employment opportunities could include jobs such as reading tutors for preschool age or elementary school children, mathematics tutors for students enrolled in elementary school through ninth grade, literacy tutors in a family literacy project performing family literacy activities, or emergency preparedness and response. In order for a student to receive federal work-study, they must complete and submit a FAFSA. These funds are limited, so it is best to pick up an application and complete and submit it as quickly as possible. If students need more information, they can visit the www.fafsa.gov website and download a PDF. Below are the steps for applying for federal financial aid.

1. Complete the free application for federal student aid. Deadlines are usually from January 1 to June 30. Some states may have earlier deadlines.
2. Review the student aid report (SAR). This contains the information that you reported when you completed the application.
3. Review your SAR and make any changes if necessary.
4. The universities that you list on the FAFSA form will get your SAR data electronically.
5. Contact the school or schools being considered. Make sure the financial aid office at universities has all the information needed to determine eligibility.

It is federal law that all males attempting to obtain federal financial aid must be registered for the selected service. Under federal law, persons who have been convicted under federal or state law of the sale or possession of drugs are not eligible for federal student aid.

TUITION REIMBURSEMENT

Some companies offer tuition reimbursement or tuition assistance. This is a great benefit that can greatly cut down on a student's cost of college. This is usually a contractual agreement between the employer and the employee, which lays out the terms and conditions to receive this benefit. Depending on the company, the conditions of the contract will vary. One of the conditions that has become standard in these kinds of contracts is that most companies will reimburse tuition only for a grade "B" or better. It is typical that if the employee makes below this grade, the company will not reimburse money spent for tuition. Some companies pay for the course at the time the student registers. Others pay tuition only after successful completion of coursework in a given term. Students should inquire about the timing of reimbursement when utilizing a tuition assistance program. Initially, students who are employed at a company may not be immediately available for this benefit. Companies want to know that students are not employed with them just to get their tuition paid. At most universities, employees, their spouses, and children can receive reduced tuition or tuition waivers depending on the particular university's policies.

The billing and receivables office is responsible for collecting tuition and fees that are due. This office may also be called the office of the bursar. The staff in billing and receivables can answer billing questions, process refund requests, review transcript exceptions, and process approved short-term loans. This office may also perform collection efforts for Federal Perkins Loan, return checks, and past due receivables. Some students participate in internships and cooperative education programs while they are in college. Internships are apprenticeships or temporary employment programs where students gain experience in exchange for working at a business or government. Internships may be paid or unpaid, but both allow students gain valuable experience usually in a field they wish to build a career. Unpaid internships usually have more stringent labor guidelines. Federal law prohibits unpaid internships from being used to displace paid employees. Co-operative Education is often referred to as co-op programs. Co-op programs are academic-focused programs that allow students to obtain professional work experience while they are in college. Co-op programs provide students with the chance to combine classroom study with periods of paid professional employment directly related to their major and career goals.

RESIDENTIAL HOUSING AND MEALS

The cost of room and board depends on the housing plan and food plan a student chooses. There are various types of on-campus housing for students. There are dormitory-style housing, apartment-style housing, and suite-style housing. The cost of college housing for most campuses average about $10,000 for most universities. Some students may choose to live off-campus; however, they still may be required to choose a meal plan. Most suite-style rooms usually have a common area where students can congregate or cook small meals. It appears that most students have become accustomed to suite-style rooms. Housing and meals are usually charged together; it is the policy at most universities that if students live in university housing, they have to buy a meal plan that can vary from a set number of meals per semester to unlimited meals. Meals are planned to be nutritionally balanced. At most universities, there are several options for each meal including vegetarian and vegan options. Universities also work with students who have documented food allergies.

BOOKS AND SCHOOL SUPPLIES

Most universities provide estimated costs of books and other supplies for their schools. In most cases these are woefully inaccurate because textbooks for each class are chosen by the professor who is teaching a course. There is not a systematic way of determining which textbook will be chosen by a professor. Some professors choose one textbook for a course while others choose multiple textbooks and supplemental books. Also, professors do not determine the cost of textbooks; the publishing company does. In most cases, a professor may not know the exact cost of a textbook because they are provided with free desk copies of the textbook that is being used in their class. Most textbooks are found in the campus bookstore, but there may be a slight-to-moderate markup on these textbooks. Students who purchase textbooks online or at local used bookstores may find savings when purchasing their textbooks for class. Other supplies may be needed for school such as pens, pencils, file folders, flash drives, notebooks, computers, and computer accessories. Students can sometimes rent books from independent bookstores or the university bookstores. Typically, renting books are cheaper than buying them. If the book is needed for a student's major, it may be wise to buy it.

There are schools where the professor has no input into the textbook being used. For-profit colleges and universities may develop the course syllabus and select the course textbook for each course. This is done by a central office or department chair to maintain control and uniformity of all the course material for each class, regardless of the instructor or whether the course is taught online or in a classroom setting. Students have access to the course syllabi through a central repository. Textbooks can still be purchased through an online campus bookstore or from such sites as Amazon.com. Alternatively, some for-profit schools include the cost of textbooks in students' tuitions. Once a student signs up for a course, the textbook is available for download electronically to a computer, laptop, cell phone, or tablet for use.

Students today must have a personal computer and printer to effectively perform in college. Assignments, readings, and even correspondence with instructors require each student to have their own computer. Some schools include the cost of computers in student tuitions. Regardless of whether they do or not, students should make a reasonable investment in a high-quality computer or tablet and also a high-quality printer for their personal use. Those available in school libraries and computer labs tend to be limited in access and printing.

APPLICATION FEES, ADMISSION ESSAYS, AND INTERVIEW QUESTIONS

College admission applications usually consist of completing an application, writing an essay (if required), and possibly an interview with a representative from the admission office at a prospective school. Most universities have application deadlines. Most students apply to several schools, so it is important to keep track of the universities in which you are applying. Colleges have an application processing fee, which is usually between $50 and $90. These fees can add up, so it is best for students to find out as much information as they can about the schools in which they are interested. If you have financial hardship, you can ask if the application can be waived. Make sure that all information on the admission application has correct grammar and spelling and is carefully proofread. If an essay is also required for application, students should make sure that the essay answers all parts of the questions being asked. Like the application, students should make sure that the essay is coherent and free of grammatical and spelling errors. Importantly, make sure that the information presented in the essay is a true reflection of your high school and life experiences. If the university that you are applying to is your first choice, indicate this within your essay. There are a few topics that students should refrain from writing about in their essays. If a student has had problems with drug abuse, they should avoid mentioning this in their essay. Students should also refrain from discussing how active or inactive their sex life is. Evaluators of admission essays do not want to read about something that may be embarrassing or too personal. If a student has a criminal history, they may mention this in their application; however, they should not draw undue attention to this in their essay. Student essays should also not overly stress information about their heroism. This can be interpreted as arrogant and narcissistic. Students should also avoid essays with controversial topics because the evaluators may be offended by the position taken in the essay. These types of topics also may make the applicant appear narrow-minded. Students should also not use their admission essay as an opportunity to work through some traumatic life event. Discussing negative events in an admission essay may cause doubt about your readiness for college.

When writing an admission's essay, students should discuss their backgrounds, especially if this is central their story. Students may also want to write about an instance where they failed and what they learned from this failure. This will probably impress the evaluator that a student has shown the maturity to learn from a failure or bad decision. Another great essay topic for students' admission essay is discussing their transitioning from childhood to adulthood. This will showcase a high point in a student's personal development and also show their maturity. Students should attempt to show their character through the words in their essay. Regardless of a student's grades and standardized test scores, universities want people of character and good citizens on their campuses.

Some universities require interviews as a part of the application process. Though this process is somewhat dated, it is still used to help competitive institutions select their incoming freshmen class. These interviews can be somewhat intimidating, but their intent is to assist the student and interviewers determine if the university is a good match for the both of them. The questions that are asked during these interviews are not meant to put the applicant on the spot. The university is attempting to get a sense of the applicant, which may not be possible by reading an admission application or essay. Although each university has created questions to ask applicants, there are usually some universal questions that students should be prepared to answer. Students are usually asked some variation of these questions:

- Tell me about yourself or tell me your story?
- What do you do best?
- Why do you want to go to college?
- What is your biggest weakness?
- Why do you want to attend this college or university?
- Who have been the biggest influences on you?
- What do you do in your free time?
- Tell me a challenge that you have overcome?

- What do you see yourself doing 10 years from now?
- What was the last book that you read that was not associated with a class assignment?

Last but not least, students should make sure to add at least two safety schools on the list. Safety schools are those universities in which students are almost certain their application will be accepted. With safety schools, students must make sure that this is a school that you are interested in attending if you are not accepted to the other schools on your list or if you have a change of heart about your top choice school.

The next section of this book introduces students to policies and procedures used on many campuses. Among the topics discussed in the section are classroom etiquette, how to interact with professors, how to appropriately attire, how to practice time management, and how to combat procrastination. The section provides information to students on how to become a successful college student.

NOTE

1. https://www.collegeboard.org/.

FURTHER READINGS

Baron's College Division Staff. *Profiles of American Colleges 2015*. Hauppauge, NY: Barron's Educational Series, Incorporated, 2014.

Brooks, F. Erik, and Glenn L. Starks. *Historically Black Colleges and Universities: An Encyclopedia*. Santa Barbara, CA: Greenwood Press, 2011.

Cohen, Harlan. *Naked Roommate: And 107 Other Issues You Might Run into in College*, 5th ed. Naperville, IL: Sourcebooks, 2013.

Emmert, J. M. *HBCU Today: Your Comprehensive Guide to Historically Black Colleges and Universities*. Newtown, CT: BEE Publishing, 2009.

Gasman, Marybeth, and Christopher L. Tudico, *Historically Black Colleges and Universities: Triumphs, Troubles, and Taboos*. New York: Palgrave Press, 2009.

Hilton, Adriel, and J. Luke Wood. *Black Males in Postsecondary Education: Examining Their Experiences in Diverse Institutional Contexts; Contemporary Perspectives on Access, Equity and Achievement*. Charlotte, NC: Information Age Publishing, 2012.

Kinjufu, Jawanza. *Black College Student Survival Guide*. Sauk Village, IL: African American Images, 1997.

Princeton Review. *The Complete Book of College*, 2015 ed. (College Admission Guide). Denver, CO: Princeton Review, 2014.

PART II

Navigating through Campus

STEP FOUR

Adjusting to College Life

Many universities operate under either a "semester" or a "quarter" system. These may also be called terms. Generally, academic years are divided into two periods. The fall term usually begins in August or September for most schools, and the spring term usually begins in January. Semesters can last from 12 to 20 weeks. Under the semester system, summer terms usually have a shorter number of weeks. Under a quarter system, there are four grading periods all treated equally. Quarters are usually 11 or 12 weeks and are the equivalent of two-thirds of a semester. The exception is if a college offers quarters where each course lasts for three or more hours per week. For example, some schools may hold 11-week courses where each class during the term meets for four hours. Each university has an academic calendar that is set by the university registrar in consultation with administrators and other units on campus. The academic calendar lays out all of the important dates during an academic semester or quarter. These dates usually include the registration period, the opening day of classes, midterm and final exam schedules, and all breaks that will occur during the academic year. This calendar also lays out when grades are due and special events such as convocations and graduations.

Many students who leave for college are both excited and fearful about entering a new environment. The college life and the many aspects of a university can be very complex. There are many policies and procedures used at universities. Students should obtain a copy of the Student Handbook on their first day on campus and spend some quality time becoming familiar with all of its contents. The handbook will cover all facets of the university, from academic issues to residence life. There will be supplemental and more specific information on each area of the university on the school's website. If there are areas that need clarification, the best way to navigate some of the procedures is to ask questions. There are various reasons why students do not ask for help. Some students find it difficult to ask questions; they feel that they must go through the school of hard knocks to become a college student. Other students do not ask for help because they do not want others to think that they are uninformed about college or do not want to appear as weak. Some students simply do not know that they need help. Asking for help from the appropriate resources is not only smart but can assist students in having a productive time on a college campus. There are many programs such as orientation and first-year experience programs set up to assist incoming students in adjusting to new expectations and life on campus.

It is very important that African American students take advantage of talking personally to admission officers, deans of students, student advisors, and counselors as soon as they start college. Many students may be first-generation college students, with no prior exposure to college life. Students will find most of those they talk to very open and willing to answer any questions asked in providing guidance.

Freshman orientation is an overall introduction to the university that a student has chosen to attend. It is the first step in actual college experience. When you have reached the orientation stage, you are officially a college student. College orientation usually lasts about two days; however, some colleges also sponsor one-day orientations, which are also called drive-in orientations. Before attending orientation, students should read information that the university sends them about the activities that will take place during the orientation session. This information will be mailed as soon as the student signs up for orientation, so sign up as early as possible. Since there are multiple orientation sessions, students must make sure that they are showing up on the correct dates. These events usually occur over one to three sessions and give incoming freshmen and transfer students an idea of what to expect as a college student at their university. Orientations are filled with academic and nonacademic activities and provide incoming students with an opportunity to see the campus, visit resident halls, and meet academic advisors, professors, and department chairs. Most college orientations are aimed at the entire family and are filled with activities for parents accompanying incoming or transfer students. At the conclusion of the orientation session, students usually receive their class schedules for the upcoming semester. While orientation may appear to be fun and games, students must remember that this is the official beginning of their college career.

PLACES AND SPACES ON CAMPUSES

There are various places and spaces on campuses that have specific purposes: academic, residential, and recreational buildings located on a campus. Academic buildings are those dedicated to instruction and academic pursuits of a university. These buildings may include classrooms, studios, scientific and technological laboratories, and other research facilities. At most colleges, academic buildings are named after former presidents of the university or significant individuals who were instrumental in the university's academic history. Departments, professor offices, and classes are held in these buildings, and they may also house administrative offices. Recreational buildings have stadiums, gymnasiums, and recreational centers, or health and fitness facilities where students can exercise. Some university's recreational facilities offer indoor and outdoor swimming pools, state-of-the-art fitness machines, racquetball and basketball courts, rock climbing walls, and indoor and outdoor tracks. Student unions, also called student commons or activity center, are community centers where students can meet and gather. The student union is a place where you can go to meet friends for lunch, meet with a student organization to plan the next great event, or gather with your study group. The student union provides food, fun, relaxation, meeting space, and much more and is a common space to connect the campus community. On most campuses, the student union includes a food court and convenience store, meeting and banquet rooms, a bookstore, check-cashing and cashier services, and ATM machines. The student union usually holds offices such as student activities, student government, union boards, and various other programs. The university union board provides campus-wide, student-focused programs to meet the entertainment needs of students on social, recreational, educational, and cultural levels. Membership is open to all students. The residential facilities are student housing provided by a university. Residence halls are also called dormitories or dorms, although this term has fallen out of favor with student affairs professionals.

Campuses usually include student health centers that provide efficient medical care for students who are enrolled in the university. The health center's staff includes physicians, mid-level practitioners, and medical support personnel. Students may schedule an appointment or a walk-in to receive services such as consultations, x-rays and lab services, psychiatric care, pharmacy immunizations, allergy injections, tuberculin testing, gynecological services, HIV and STD testing, student insurance information, health education resources, and alcohol and other drug evaluation and referrals. Students are usually charged a fee that allows them access to medical services from the facility. Student health center services and schedules may vary depending on the university.

ADJUSTING TO THE UNIVERSITY ENVIRONMENT

There are steps that one can take as a first-year student in college. First-year students should be patient. This is a new experience, and they will not master every aspect of university life quickly. The campus atmosphere will be new, and this may be overwhelming for some students, but as soon as they become more familiar with the campus and the people that they meet, they will become more comfortable with navigating their new surroundings. It is important to connect with other students on campus. If students talk with fellow students, they will most likely discover that others have the same concerns and questions about being a first-year student. Professors, counselors, academic advisors, and resident assistants are equipped to help solve problems and direct students to appropriate resources where they may find the answers. There are also numerous offices and programs on university campuses created to enhance students' college experiences. Often, these resources go underutilized.

African American students should take advantage of the many sources of support such as counseling centers, career centers, financial aid programs, mentoring/tutoring programs, diversity offices, and academic advising offices. They should get involved in various activities on campus. Some African American students get involved with only those activities and events that they believe are directed at African American students. While taking part in these activities is great, limiting their participation to these events and activities limits their cultural horizons and opportunities to learn about themselves and others.

While in college, African American students must not neglect their needs and must grow both intellectually and creatively. They must take time to develop themselves and their talents. This begins with making sure they follow habits of good nutrition, regular exercise, and adequate sleep. Most university campuses have a recreation center that can be instrumental in assisting students in alleviating the stress associated with being a college student. The campus recreational center usually provides programs that promote healthy practices and various health topics. Students should not overdo it with extracurricular activities, and they must find a balance between academics and extracurricular activities and hobbies, especially in their freshman year. A student's time at college should be viewed as an opportunity to develop independence and to learn to take care of their own physical and emotional needs. Students should avoid merely vegetating or becoming a couch potato. Students should not passively deal with negative situations that they may encounter, but deal with them actively and seek assistance if needed. Recognize that there are many creative and enjoyable ways to use your time in college. African American students should explore opportunities and engage in various activities. They should not predetermine if they are going to dislike activities prior to engaging in them. Keep an open mind about all activities that take place on campus. They should remember it is okay to explore doing things by themselves from movies to sporting events or plays at local theaters. College students must recognize that their college years could be a period of growth and self-development.

THE FIRST-YEAR EXPERIENCE PROGRAMS

The first-year experience is a form of extended orientation for new students at colleges to help them transition from high school to the university setting. Some of these programs last a few weeks while others extend to an entire semester. Some have official ceremonies such as convocation that bring the entire group together to mark the completion of the orientation process. Some religious schools require students to attend such activities as weekly mass. While the transition experience is unique for each student, the first-year experience program is designed to help freshman students get comfortable with their new surroundings and connect with the university. These programs are aimed at incoming students and are also an attempt to build community within the university. By offering activities through a concentrated first-year experience, universities believe if students connect with their universities through targeted programming, they are more likely to return for the sophomore year. Some colleges even offer college credit for completing the first-year experience program.

African American students should take advantage of their first-year experience in order to avoid the isolation that can sometimes be experienced on some college campuses. Depending on the campus, the first-year experience may also provide referral services to students about academic and personal opportunity and conduct interviews as a proactive measure to address students contemplating withdrawal from the university. They may also act as an emergency contact for students experiencing immediate health or personal problems that may affect their academic performance and class attendance.

LIVING IN A RESIDENCE HALL

Most campuses have an office of student affairs or student life that is responsible for advising students and providing support services. This office may also oversee student government, clubs, and other activities. Usually located in the Student Affairs division of a university, residential life has support staff. These positions range from the director of housing to resident advisors or assistants (usually called RAs or community leaders). These are student positions, usually junior and senior students, who are trained to assist other students with their needs while living in a residence hall. At most universities, these are coveted positions because they usually have free room and board and other financial benefits for students who hold these positions. Resident directors, or area directors or area coordinators, are also employed in residential life. These administrators, who often live in the residence halls and are trained to assist students with personal, academic, or social needs, including emergency situations, lead and supervise resident assistant staffs. Some universities may employ older graduate students to fill these positions. With residential life, student may hear the terms *on-campus housing* and *off-campus housing*. On-campus housing is available to students on a university or college campus and is often referred to as dormitories, residence halls, or on-campus apartments. Off-campus housing is available to students off the university or college campus. Most universities have relationships with area realtors and can recommend rental properties for students. Some universities own off-campus housing spaces and may make these available as well.

Residence halls usually include student rooms, bathrooms, common areas, and possibly kitchens or cafeterias. Occupancies range in resident halls from single rooms up to multiple-person suites. Residence halls may be segregated by sex or may be co-educational. Universities have strict policies on residents hosting guests. Students are held responsible for their guests and their actions when they visit students in residential housing. Fraternities and sororities may also have housing. This housing is usually open only to members of their organizations. These organizations' housing facilities may also be used for hosting parties and other social gatherings. Most universities also offer married student housing. Within these forms of residential halls and facilities, university dining services provide meals for residents. These services serve nutritious, well-balanced meals. At most universities, the meal plans are required for on-campus students and may be available for students living off-campus. Typically, students pay for the food they eat and are refunded the balance at the end of the year; some universities bill students a set fee for unlimited dining for each semester or quarter. Students access food service facilities through a student's campus identification card that is provided to them at no charge. They are intended for permanent use through all continuous periods of enrollments.

Students who move to campus may experience a culture shock. Living away from your parents for the first time may be a very exciting time; however, living away from one's parents and assuming more responsibilities may also be a frightening and challenging task. Living in a residence hall can also be a new and exhilarating experience. Building a community in a residence hall is important, and establishing ground rules with a roommate or roommates is a very important start. Some of the typical disputes are over room cleanliness, noise complaints, and personality clashes. In most residential hall living facilities, resident assistants, usually a second- or third-year student, is responsible for providing leadership for various areas in the living facilities. Students should establish roommate agreements to help guide behaviors and actions while living in the same living area. Items that could be listed in the roommate agreement may include rules for entertaining visitors, personal space, use of each other's items, and privacy. Living in a residence hall can be a big adjustment for students who are used to their own living space and not used to having to share with others. Social skills and getting accustomed to living with others must be learned if students are going to be happy living in a residential hall.

Many factors contribute to the relationship between roommates: family background, personality traits, and cultural beliefs are some of the major factors. Recognizing these factors may assist students in establishing a good relationship with their roommate. Roommates with different living habits and lifestyles are the most common source of roommate conflict. Failure to communicate your expectations with your roommate about living together can lead to tension and an unbearable living arrangement. During a conflict with a roommate, you should communicate your needs and expectations respectfully. You should also take ownership of your contributions to the conflict.

Disputes between roommates will arise. When there are disputes, how should roommates settle them? When issues with one's roommate begin to distract a student from studies and day-to-day living environment, it is then time to attempt to resolve the problem. Settling disputes with your roommate may call for mediation by a third party. Residence assistants are trained in handling these situations and have had live simulation of possible scenarios in settling minor roommate disputes. Below are a few reminders in avoiding disputes between roommates and having to call for the intervention of a resident assistant:

- Be patient and live by the golden rule. Do onto others as you would have them do unto you.
- Privately approach your roommate with issues.
- Keep calm and express the key issues that may be causing problems.
- When a student feels threatened, it may warrant a room change.
- Communication is the key.
- Try to settle the dispute on your own. If this cannot be accomplished, then seek out your resident assistant.
- Know your resident assistant's on-duty hours. Residence assistants are full-time students and some even hold other part-time jobs, so they may not always be available.

In residential housing spaces, occurrence of theft may also be common. In order to avoid thefts, students should remember to always close and lock their doors when they leave their rooms and keep personal belongings out of sight and in a safe place. Students should lock their doors, even if they go down the hall or to the bathroom. If property is stolen, contact the campus police, and complete a police report.

MAKING NEW FRIENDS AND CREATING FRIENDSHIPS

During their time in college, students will gain new friends and friendships. Some of these friendships will last a lifetime, others will not. There are a number of ways to meet new friends on campus. Students can meet people while doing ordinary things during the course of their daily routines. African American students should look for ways to get involved with other people and develop friendship. For example, they can:

- Sit with various groups of people in the cafeteria during lunch and dinner
- Change where they sit in class to get to know a variety of classmates
- Find a few study partners; they do not have to be African American
- Find exercise partners to work out with (this allows students to remain physically and emotionally active)

African American students must put themselves in situations where they will meet new people. If students engage in activities, especially those about which they are passionate, they will likely meet like-minded people and develop friendships. Students should allow friendships to develop naturally. Close friendships evolve over time. Usually, people begin to share their inner feelings after they have developed trust; therefore, it is not a reasonable expectation that people who you just meet share feelings quickly. Clubs, churches, part-time jobs, and volunteer work are great opportunities to meet new people and make friends. Most importantly, African American students should work at developing their social skills and expand their network of friends.

PERSONAL SAFETY

All students contribute to making sure their campuses are safe spaces. There are some effective strategies that students should employ to help them remain safe while on campus. Students should use good judgment, trust their instincts, and use common sense. Students should avoid being alone with someone that they do not know. They should always let someone know where they will be going and the person or people who will be accompanying them. When possible, students should travel in groups and in well-lit areas. Students should not leave backpacks, books, purses, or personal property unattended. When possible, students should use their university's transit system. Lastly, students should avoid the use of alcohol and drugs because they impair good judgment, and big mistakes can occur while intoxicated.

DYSFUNCTIONAL FAMILIES AND ABUSIVE RELATIONSHIPS

Everyone has faced problems, regardless of their race, gender, and socioeconomic status. Many African American students believe that once they leave home and their old neighborhoods, they will leave any problems behind them. On their college campuses, they may discover that they are experiencing the same problems they encountered at home. While it may be ideal for students to grow up in a two-parent home with loving and supporting parents who have helped them established high self-esteem, this may not always be the case. Students who have grown up in supportive homes feel valuable and confident and do better in college. For students who did not grow up in this kind of environment, all hope is not lost. Becoming a college graduate may give some students opportunities to correct family mistakes and make better lives for themselves. There are various examples of types of dysfunctional families. The following are some illustrative instances of behaviors that often transpire in dysfunctional families:

- Family members may have addictions or substance abuse, which adversely affects the entire family.
- Family members may intimidate and use physical violence as a means of control.
- Family members may force children to watch violent behavior or force them to take part in admonishing and beating siblings.

- Family members may exploit children. Children may take on the primary role of responding to the physical and emotional needs of their parents or other adults.
- Family members may threaten to withdraw financial or basic physical care from their children.
- Family members may fail to provide their children with adequate emotional support.
- Family members may be overbearing, and children may have excessive demands placed on their time, choice of friends, or behavior.
- Family members may not provide children with rules, guidelines, structure, or other parameters.
- Children may be prohibited or restricted from direct communication with other loved ones.
- Children may have been slapped, hit, scratched, punched, or kicked.

Dysfunctional family structures may make it difficult for students to concentrate and function in college. Students who are experiencing the effects of a dysfunctional family should seek counseling at their university's counseling center. Students growing up in dysfunctional families are likely to develop low self-esteem and feel that their needs are not important or not being met. Dysfunctional families may fail to provide for many of their student's emotional and physical needs. Students from dysfunctional families may experience problems in their coursework, friendships, and romantic relationships. Dealing with dysfunctional family members causes stress, especially for those attempting to get a college education.

RELATIONSHIPS, RESPONSIBLE ACTIONS, AND SEXUAL VIOLENCE

Sexual violence is a wide-ranging group of unwanted physical sexual acts committed against a person's will. This includes acts in which a person agrees to the sexual encounter but is unable to give legal consent or changes his or her mind. Regardless of their sex, gender, or sexual orientation, any person can commit sexual violence. Similarly, any person can be a victim of sexual violence. Rape, sexual battery, sexual assault, and sexual coercion are all examples of sexual violence. Each state's legal system defines sexual violence differently. While sexual violence is a criminal act, it may also create a hostile environment, which is a violation of state and federal laws, under Title IX. Various definitions of sexual assault include all practices of sexual violence, which encompasses rape, sexual assault, sexual battery, and sexual coercion. It is important for students to receive and give affirmative consent before engaging in any sexual or intimate acts. Either party can withdraw consent to sex at any time, even during a sexual act. Sexual violence can result in suspension, expulsion, termination of student employment, criminal charges, and imprisonment. Drugging a drink is also a serious crime. At parties and other social gatherings, students should keep control of their drinks at all times. This is a good way to help prevent date rape drugs from being added to drinks. Sexual violence often has long-term and negative repercussions. Common effects of sexual assault are depression, academic decline, abuse of drugs and alcohol, posttraumatic stress disorder, trauma-induced neurobiological changes, and contemplation of suicide.

Sexual harassment is illegal and includes unwelcome sexual advances, demands for sexual favors, or other sexual verbal or physical acts that seriously interfere with a student's learning atmosphere. Sexual harassment can transpire in various ways. Harassment can include comments about an individual's body, physical touching, sexual stories, sexual comments, and sexually explicit posters, calendars, cartoons, or other materials that may create a hostile environment. Many factors are used to determine if a hostile environment has been created by unwelcome conduct. Conduct will be evaluated from both a subjective and an objective perspectives. All relevant circumstances will be considered, including:

- The number of individuals involved and the degree to which the conduct affected education
- The type, frequency, duration, location, and context of the conduct
- The age and sex of the alleged harasser and the subject or subjects of the harassment
- The nature of the conduct and whether the conduct is gender-based

Students who have experienced such incidents can take the following actions:

- Individuals can file a Title IX complaint with the Office of Civil Rights (OCR) either along with or instead of filing with their school.
- Survivors of sexual assault should consider seeking immediate medical assistance and take actions to preserve evidence, even if only to have the option to use it in the future.
- Targets of stalking can seek restraining orders and take other actions to help stop the stalking.
- Survivors of harassment or sexual violence can seek help from their school's Title IX coordinator as well as from police and private organizations dedicated to providing support.

Here are some ways that bystanders and friends can help prevent sexual violence on campus. Some tips apply to everyone; others are more applicable to students.

- Do not leave someone alone if they are unconscious, drunk, or high on drugs.
- Never allow people you do not know and trust into your home or housing.

- Do not let anyone engage in sexual activity with someone who is unconscious, drunk, or high on drugs.
- Remain with friends during parties and leave with them.
- Hire a designated driver who will stay sober at parties.
- Offer help, including help calling the police or help making a report.

The bystander effect is when people prevent crimes from happening by intervening or acting to protect a victim. Bystanders often think that they should not act when they see sexual violence because they do not want to get involved in the matters of others. A growing kind of sexual violence is sex trafficking. College campuses have become productive recruiting grounds for sex traffickers and can involve other students or college-aged individuals. Sex trafficking is where people are forced, coerced, or tricked into the sex industry. Students are targeted through social media. They are kidnapped or lured at clubs, bars, malls, or on campus. They may be enticed with the promise of money or tuition payments. Those who traffic in sex may also use modeling, faux romantic interest, or other opportunities to bait students into the sex industry.

Intimate partner violence is also called domestic violence, dating violence, or relationship violence. Intimate violence is a form of abusive behavior acted out by one partner to sustain control over the other. Intimate partner violence can be physical, psychological, or sexual and can also include threats of physical or sexual violence. Intimate partner violence can be between same- or different-sex partners. Individuals who stalk a partner are more likely to perpetrate physical or sexual violence. Intimate partner violence does not require sexual intimacy. Stalking includes repeated harassment or threats that cause fear in a person. Intimate partner violence is any pattern of abusive behavior against a current or former partner used to maintain control over that person. Ending all contact with someone who engages in stalking behavior is usually best. Students should seek help from the university's or college's counseling office, campus police, or the city's police department.

Colleges and universities must act on reports of sexual violence (including sexual assault), dating violence, stalking, and domestic violence. They are required to follow policies regarding confidentiality in handling sexual violence complaints. Federal law requires that universities receiving federal funding have policies against sex discrimination and sexual violence. They must designate a Title IX coordinator. This individual is required to adopt and publish grievance procedures, and they must respond to complaints. Universities must use the preponderance of the evidence standard to resolve complaints and notify both parties of the outcome.

MANAGING STRESS WHILE IN COLLEGE

Stress is the mental and emotional strain or tension that comes from being involved in very demanding situations or circumstances. College students must adjust to the ever-changing environment of academic life, and this can cause a great deal of stress. Stress has both physical and emotional effects on African American students, and it can create positive or negative feelings and experiences. On the positive side, stress can sometimes help students realize their full potential and strength after overcoming a stressful situation. On the negative side, stress can turn into feelings of distrust, rejection, anger, and depression. If stressful feelings are left unchecked, stress can lead to various health problems such as headaches, upset stomach, rashes, insomnia, ulcers, high blood pressure, heart disease, and stroke. Stress is a natural occurrence in life, and no person can eliminate all of the stress from their lives. Therefore, African American college students must learn to manage the stress in their lives. Deadlines, assignments, midterm examination and final examinations, competitions, studying, extracurricular activities, leadership and membership in organizations, and other obligations can lead to stress. All students have different stressors and find various ways to relieve stress. Students must find positive means to alleviate their stress. Stress can help or hinder us depending on how we react to it. In combating stress, students must become aware of their stressors and their emotional reactions to these stressors. Students must take notice of their distress and determine what has caused stress for them. Students must take their problem seriously and deal with it through the appropriate stress relievers.

In life, people cannot avoid stress. Students should concentrate on those things that they can change and then begin making those changes. In coping with stress, students should learn to moderate their physical reactions to stress and then utilize relaxation techniques such as deep breathing exercises, yoga, meditation, and other techniques to relieve muscle tension. Put all stressful situations in perspective. Students should not dwell on the negative aspects of the stressful situation.

Students should build up their physical and emotional reserves by participating in a regular exercise program. Students should exercise for cardiovascular fitness three to four times a week. Moderate, prolonged rhythmic exercise is best, such as walking, swimming, cycling, or jogging. Students should also attempt to establish a well-balanced, nutritious meal plan and attempt to maintain their ideal weight. Students should avoid or limit nicotine, excessive caffeine, and other stimulants. In stressful situations, students should remember to get proper rest by getting enough sleep. African American students should pursue realistic goals that are meaningful to them. Students should not pursue unrealistic goals that others may have set for them or that they do not share or have a genuine interest in. In pursuing a college degree, students should expect some frustrations, failures, and sorrows. By identifying unrelieved stress and learning how to effectively combat stressors, students can reduce the negative effects of stress.

STUDENT CONDUCT AND JUDICIAL HEARINGS

Student judicial programs promote responsible individual and group behavior. This office informs students and organizations of their rights and responsibilities for preparation and dissemination of the code of student conduct. Typically, student judicial program staff coordinate the disciplinary review process in response to allegations of misconduct and offer mediation services to students in conflict. The office maintains student disciplinary records and completes transfer applications and other background clearance forms. Students may be referred to a disciplinary program for academic dishonesty and other instances of personal, physical, and sexual misconduct.

RACE, STEREOTYPES, AND RACISM

There are many forces that cloud the educational experiences for African Americans on college campuses. Some African American students can experience stress because they are stereotyped, or they may even feel guilty because they have advanced to better opportunities than their friends and family members. African American students may be judged by racial or ethnic stereotypes. Stereotypes are widely held but overly generalized beliefs. There is usually very little basis or truth to stereotypes; many negative stereotypes are erroneously associated with African Americans. Some of the negative stereotypes about African Americans include being loud, obnoxious, rude, athletic, violent, and dropouts and having a bad attitude and low job expectations. One of the most widely held stereotypes is that African Americans are always late for events. This is often called "C.P. Time" or "colored people's time." Other stereotypes include being less intelligent, lazy, and less sophisticated than whites. In stereotyping, individuals do not see people as individuals but as an entire group and tend to generalize negative behaviors as representative of an entire racial or ethnic group. Some African American students may feel like they carry the burden of the entire race on their backs and must stand as a representative for all African Americans. All of the above stressors may cause some African American students to have less than positive experiences at the universities that they attend. African American students must learn to cope with racism to reach their full academic potential. Racism is prejudice, discrimination, or antagonism directed against someone of a different race based on the belief that one's own race is superior. People not recognizing what they say or do is a racist behavior. Others may very well understand that their actions or behaviors are racist. Racist actions usually involve some form of racial prejudice and discrimination. Discrimination is the act of treating someone less favorably because they are affiliated with a particular group. This could be based on race or ethnicity or on some political affiliation, religious affiliation, Greek organization, sexual orientation, socioeconomic status, age, or gender. Prejudice that is based on an individual's race or ethnicity is "racial prejudice." On college campuses, discrimination may occur when student organizations refuse to accept potential members of particular racial or ethnic groups.

African American students may experience race-related stress and additional frustrations. Race-related stress refers to the psychological and emotional distress associated with experiences of racism. Students can experience race-related stress even through the perception of a racist behavior. Race-related stress can conjure up emotions such as anger, anxiety, paranoia, fear, frustration, and depression. It is best for African American students to realize and understand when they are experiencing such an event and use effective life skill strategies to combat any feelings triggered by racism. Effective coping mechanisms include counseling and developing a support group that may assist in combating the effects of racism. Students should not internalize racism. Students also should not turn to drugs, alcohol, or acts of violence to soothe the pain associated with racism or racist acts. Race-related stress can affect the body negatively and cause health concerns. Just as with other stress, internalizing racism and racist acts can cause hypertension, heart disease, muscle tension, and digestive problems.

Racism may be the source of some African American students feeling like they are less intellectually capable than other students. This is called the "imposter syndrome." This causes African American students to believe that they do not have what it takes to complete college. The imposter syndrome may also cause some African American students to feel inadequate based on their race and socio-economic status or to discount or downplay their intellectual abilities and accomplishments. They may believe that they have achieved success through sheer luck, quota systems, or networking. This phenomenon may be present among other minority groups and white women as well. Students should be rest assured in the fact that many successful African Americans have felt inadequate at some time or another and advanced to complete their degrees and achieve great accomplishments in many fields of endeavor. The imposter syndrome can lead to overextending one's self and to feelings of guilt, shame, fear, anxiety, and dissatisfaction.

ACTING WHITE

On some college campuses, African American students are accused of "acting white." Although many have different definitions for acting white, most definitions include reference to situations where African American students are teased and ridiculed by their peers and others for being involved in activities perceived as being the characteristics of whites. Behaviors of acting white might include reading books, speaking standard English, enrolling in advanced courses, making good grades, dating someone from another ethnic group, or wearing conservative clothes. The acting white phenomenon is rooted in ignorance and has prevented some African American students from doing their best in college. Students should not worry about the perception of acting white and take every opportunity to excel academically. There have been numerous examples of African Americans who have been accused of acting white but have been at the forefront of intellectual movements in the United States. Some African American students underperform to fit in with groups. In underperforming, students not only hurt themselves but also confirm negative stereotypes that others may have. There are a few strategies that can be employed to assist in combating race-related stress:

- Students should know who they are culturally and historically.
- Students should build support networks. Students must realize that they are not the only person dealing with racism and race-related stress.
- If students believe in spirituality, they should use prayer and meditation to aid themselves in combating stress associated with racism.
- Students should become involved in organizations or causes that combat racism.

In challenging racism on their campuses, African American students should document any incident of racism, and they should report these incidents to the appropriate authorities. Students should not tolerate acts of injustices and should challenge others when witnessing these types of acts. Most campuses have an equal opportunity action officer or another high-level individual who handles these types of complaints. In discussing the incident with this person, students should make sure that they are clear about what it is they want to see changed and be clear about how they would like to see that change. When attempting to get a policy changed, students must not let their emotions take over; they should be very strategic in attempting to rectify a racist incident or when attempting to get a policy or procedure changed. Students should make sure to talk to the department that will most likely be able to assist them the most in combating or correcting the racist incident. Students should always follow up with any meetings that are scheduled after their initial report of the incident. Combating racism begins with everyone; African American students should not underestimate the power they have to change things. In U.S. history, African American students have been at the center of protest movements. Their involvement has been instrumental in starting several major movements, particularly the Civil Rights movement in the American South during the 1960s.

EXTRACURRICULAR ACTIVITIES AND GREEK LIFE

In broad terms, extracurricular activities are activities that are not part of the academic curriculum or paid employment. Participation in extracurricular activities benefits African American students and those from low socioeconomic backgrounds because these activities usually help students connect to a university. It is important not to underestimate the importance of extracurricular activities in the college experience, but it is also important to understand that extracurricular activities are not the most important aspect of a student's college experience. Involvement in extracurricular activities should reflect a student's true interest and passion. Most universities like to see students involved in and committed to one or two extracurricular activities rather than being involved in several extracurricular activities only superficially.

On most university campuses, various extracurricular activities are offered. These activities range from clubs and organizations to intramural sports; students may find several activities to get involved with on campus. For most African American students and students of color, most college campuses have an organization called the Black Student Association (BSA) or a similar named organization. This organization and those like it were established to promote better scholastic, cultural, political, and social experiences for the African American student communities at universities. Many students also get involved with the Student Government Association (SGA) or serve on other department or university committees. On most campuses, the SGA is recognized as the representative entity for the student body and involves students who may have questions, ideas, and suggestions for the betterment of the university as a whole. By gaining experience with student government or serving on a committee, African American students can gain better insights into how the university functions and the governing policies and procedures. By becoming a leader in organizations such as fraternities, sororities, clubs, teams, and choirs, students can gain important leadership skills. It also shows a student's dedication, balance, and leadership. Some African American students find it difficult to balance academic and extracurricular activities. They forget to prioritize their activities and become consumed with extracurricular activities instead of their studies. It can be difficult for students to determine if they are involved in too many activities, but students should ask themselves these questions in determining if they are:

- Do I have enough time to keep up with my readings for classes and complete assignments?
- Can I get the proper amount of sleep at night (8 hours)?
- Can I still hang out with my friends on occasion?
- Can I still make time to talk with my family and friends on occasion?
- Am I struggling with or failing exams and assignments?

One of the biggest mistakes that an African American student can make is to let extracurricular activities take priority over their academic studies. Gaining time management and preventing procrastination will greatly help students balance their academic activities and extracurricular activities. There are many extracurricular activities that infringe on students' study time. Students' overinvolvement in organizations such as fraternities and sororities can be detrimental to their success in college.

While black Greek-lettered organizations do not discriminate and people of all races are free to become affiliated with these institutions, these organizations have maintained a predominately black membership. Black Greek organizations have a long and storied history at both historically black colleges and predominately white campuses. There are nine recognized organizations under the guide of the National Pan-Hellenic Council. Alpha Phi Alpha, the first black Greek fraternity, was founded in 1906 at Cornell University. Later, Kappa Alpha Psi was founded in 1911 at the University of Indiana, and Omega Phi Psi was founded in 1911 at Howard University. Phi Beta Sigma was founded in 1914 at Howard University, and Iota Phi Theta was founded in 1963 at Morgan State University.

Black Greek-lettered sororities include Alpha Kappa Alpha, which was founded in 1908 at Howard University, and Delta Sigma Theta, founded in 1913 at Howard University. Zeta Phi Beta was founded in 1920, and Sigma Gamma Rho was founded in 1922 at Butler University. Some people are critical of black Greek organizations believing they are elitists and have drifted from their traditional missions. For the most part, all of these organizations began as academic support groups for African American students during their college experience. These organizations were formed to help uplift African Americans and address the issues within the African American community. Unfortunately, some contemporary members have joined organizations only because they wanted to be popular or perform at a step show. African American students who are considering joining one of these organizations should weigh the pros and cons of this decision. As with other extracurricular activities, overindulgence in Greek life can be detrimental to a student's academic career.

African American students are more likely to join historically black fraternities and sororities, whether they attend a predominantly black or white institution. The following are the histories and details of the nation's leading black fraternal organizations.

Alpha Phi Alpha Fraternity, Inc.

Alpha Phi Alpha Fraternity is the first intercollegiate Greek-letter fraternity established for African Americans. Seven college men recognized the need for support for African American men and formed this organization at Cornell University in Ithaca, New York, in 1906. Some of its founding members wanted to establish a literary society while others wanted to form a fraternity. The fraternity's headquarters is located in Baltimore, Maryland. The fraternity's colors are black and old gold and the organization's official flower is the yellow rose. The fraternity's motto is "First of All, Servants of All, We Shall Transcend All" and its symbol the sphinx. The organization's official publication is also called *The Sphinx.*

The founders of the fraternity are known as the "Jewels" and were Henry Arthur Callis, Charles Henry Chapman, Eugene Kinckle Jones, George Biddle Kelley, Nathaniel Allison Murray, Robert Harold Ogle, and Vertner Woodson Tandy. Founder Eugene Kinckle Jones proposed the Greek letters for the group, while founder Harold Ogle proposed the fraternity's colors. After being established at Cornell University, other chapters were then established at Howard University and Virginia Union University a year later. Alpha Phi Alpha was the first black fraternity to become international when the organization chartered a chapter at the University of Toronto (this chapter later transferred to Huston-Tillotson University).

Alpha Phi Alpha offers outreach through its national programs that include World and National Affairs; Continuing the Legacy; Leadership Training Institute; Got to High School, Go to College; Alpha Head Start Academy; and Economic Development. It is also instrumental in fundraising for the Dr. Martin Luther King Jr. memorial monument that is being placed on the national mall in Washington, D.C.

Notable members of the fraternity include Thurgood Marshall, Charles Hamilton Houston, Dr. Martin Luther King Jr., W. E. B. Du Bois, John Hope Franklin, Rayford Logan, Eugene Jones, Maynard Jackson, T. J. Jemison, Edward Brooke, Willie Brown, John Johnson, Frederick D. Patterson, Whitney Young, Duke Ellington, Fritz Pollard, and Cornell West.

Kappa Alpha Psi Fraternity, Inc.

Ten college students founded Kappa Alpha Psi on the campus of Indiana University in Bloomington, Indiana, in 1911. The fundamental purpose of this fraternity is "Achievement in Every Field of Endeavor" and its official colors are crimson and cream. The fraternity's official flower is a red carnation, its symbol is a diamond, and its official publication is the *Kappa Journal*. The organization is headquartered in Philadelphia, Pennsylvania.

The fraternity's founders were Elder Watson Diggs, John Milton Lee, Byron K. Armstrong, Guy Levis Grant, Ezra D. Alexander, Henry T. Asher, Marcus P. Blakemore, Paul W. Caine, Edward G. Irvin, and George W. Edmonds. They were part of a small minority population of students at Indiana University and were discouraged from participating in campus activities. Blacks were denied joining all organizations and activities except participation in track and field. To fill this void of educational and social support, these young men formed an organization. The organization was originally chartered and incorporated originally under the laws of the state of Indiana as Kappa Alpha Nu. The name of the organization was subsequently changed in 1915 after some white students referred to the organization as "Kappa Alpha Nigger." After the initial chapter was established, other chapters were established at the University of Illinois and the University of Iowa. The first two chapters established at black colleges were at Wilberforce University and Lincoln University in Pennsylvania. Its first chapter established in the South was at Morehouse College. The fraternity's national initiatives include the Guide Right Programs, Kappa League, Student of the Year Competition, and the Kappa Alpha Psi Foundation.

Nicknames for members of the fraternity are Nupes, Pretty Boys, or Kappas. Notable members include Ralph D. Abernathy, Cedric "the Entertainer," Bill Russell, Wilt Chamberlain, Tom Bradley, Arthur Ashe, Whitman Mayo, Carl Stokes, Mike Tomlin, Johnny Cochran, Tavis Smiley, John Singleton, Oscar Robertson, Gale Sayers, Lem Barney, Horace Mann Bond, Daniel "Chappie" James Jr., Montell Jordan, Donald Murray, Louis B. Stokes, Lerone Bennett, Walter Fauntroy, John Conyers, and Willie Davis.

Omega Psi Phi Fraternity, Inc.

Omega Psi Phi Fraternity was founded at Howard University in 1911 by three liberal arts undergraduate students, Edgar A. Love, Oscar J. Cooper, and Frank Coleman, and their faculty adviser, professor Ernest Everett Just. It was the first predominately black fraternity founded at an HBCU. The fraternity was organized in Just's office in the campus's biology building. The fraternity's motto is "Friendship Is Essential to the Soul," and its cardinal principles are "Manhood, Scholarship, Perseverance and Uplift." The fraternity colors are royal purple and old gold, its symbol is the lamp, and its official publication is the *Oracle.* In 1914, the fraternity was incorporated in Washington, D.C., and by 1920 the fraternity had established 10 chapters. The second chapter was established in 1914 at Lincoln University in Pennsylvania.

The fraternity's headquarters is located in Decatur, Georgia. Its national programs include Achievement Week, Scholarship, Social Acton Programs, Talent Hunt Programs, Memorial Service, Reclamation and Retention, College Endowment Funds, Health Initiatives, and Voter Registration, Education, and Motivation.

Members of Omega Phi Psi are referred to by the nicknames the Ques, Q-Dogs, Omega Men, and the Sons of Blood and Thunder. Famous members include Bill Cosby, Carter G. Woodson, Roy Wilkins, L. Douglas Wilder, Vernon Jordan, Jesse Jackson Sr., Benjamin Hooks, William H. Hastie, Michael Jordan, Shaquille O'Neal, Vince Carter, Earl Graves, Tom Joyner, Rickey Smiley, and Steve Harvey.

Phi Beta Sigma Fraternity, Inc.

A. Langston Taylor, Leonard F. Morse, and Charles I. Brown wanted to organize a Greek-letter fraternity that would exemplify the ideals of brotherhood, scholarship, and service when they founded Phi Beta Sigma Fraternity, Inc. at Howard University in 1914. The fraternity was incorporated in 1920. Believing that the other black fraternities had become too elitist in their views and practices, the founders of Phi Beta Sigma desired to create an organization that viewed itself as "a part of" the general community. After the first chapter was established, two other chapters were established at Wiley College and Morgan State University in 1915.

The fraternity's colors are royal blue and pure white, its symbol is a dove, its official flower is a white carnation, and its official publication is *The Crescent.* The fraternity's motto is "Culture for Service and Service for Humanity," and its headquarters is located in Washington, D.C. The fraternity has a constitutional bond with a sorority when they assisted with the founding of Zeta Phi Beta Sorority, Inc. in 1919. Phi Beta Sigma's national programs include Bigger and Better Business, Education, Social Action, and the Phi Beta History Museum.

Notable Phi Beta Sigma members include James Weldon Johnson, George Washington Carver, Huey P. Newton, Jerry Rice, Ryan Howard, Randolph, Emmitt Smith, Blair Underwood, Hosea Williams, James Forman, John Lewis, and Rod Page.

Iota Phi Theta Fraternity, Inc.

Iota Phi Theta was founded at Morgan State University in 1963 by 12 students: Albert Hicks, Lonnie Spruill Jr., Charles Briscoe, Frank Coakley, John Slade, Barron Willis, Webster Lewis, Charles Brown, Louis Hudnell, Charles Gregory, Elias Dorsey Jr., and Michael Williams. The group's stated purpose is "The development and perpetuation of Scholarship, Leadership, Citizenship, Fidelity, and Brotherhood Among Men." Nicknames for members of the organizations are the Outlaws and the Iotas.

The fraternity's colors are charcoal brown and gilded gold, and its motto is "Building a Tradition Not Resting on One." The fraternity's symbol is the centaur and its official flower is a yellow rose. The fraternity is headquartered in Baltimore, Maryland. The fraternity's national programs include the Iota Foundation, the I.O.T.A. Youth Alliance, the Digital Heritage Initiative, the Afya Njema Program, the Developing Fatherhood Project, the IOTA Political Mobilization Campaign, Community Reclamation Initiative, and Cultural Education Movement.

Famous members of the fraternity include Elvin Hayes, Calvin Murphy, Spencer Christian, Tommie Frazier, Larry Johnson, Terrence "T. C." Carson, and Bobby Rush.

Alpha Kappa Alpha Sorority, Inc.

Alpha Kappa Alpha Sorority was founded at Howard University in 1908. It is the oldest Greek-lettered organization established by African American women. The sorority's colors are salmon pink and apple green, its symbol is an ivy leaf, and its official flower is the pink tea rose. The sorority's official publication is the *Ivy Leaf*, and its headquarters is located in Chicago, Illinois.

In 1907, Ethel Hedgeman began recruiting young women who were interested in forming a sorority. In the fall of 1908, she began writing the sorority's constitution and created a motto and colors. Hedgeman also named the sorority in 1909. Seven honors students expressed interest and were accepted into the sorority. The first initiation of members occurred at Howard University in 1909. In 1912, some members wanted to change the name and colors of the sorority. Nellie Quander, a former president of the Howard chapter, found out about these plans and informed other founders and members. A division in the sorority resulted, leading to some members leaving the sorority and founding their own, Delta Sigma Theta, in 1913.

Alpha Kappa Alpha's national programs include Advocates for Black Colleges, the Howard University Fund, Chapter Scholarships, Ivy Acres, Ivy Reading AKAdemy, Leadership Fellows Program, PIMS Partnerships in Mathematics and Science, and the Young Authors Program.

Notable members include Sonia Sanchez, Toni Morrison, Wanda Sykes, Star Jones, Stephanie Elam, Ada Lois Sipuel, Pauline Redmond Coggs, Ella Fitzgerald, Maya Angelou, Bebe Moore Campbell, Mae Jemison, Phylicia Rashad, Coretta Scott King, and Bernice King.

Delta Sigma Theta Sorority

The founders of Delta Sigma Theta were initially members of Alpha Kappa Alpha Sorority. However, in 1912, they decided that the scope of that organization was too narrow and the sorority was too closely aligned with the Alpha Phi Alpha Fraternity. Their efforts to change Alpha Kappa Alpha led to them leaving the sorority and founding their own.

Delta Sigma Theta Sorority was founded in 1913 by 22 students at Howard University: Osceola Macarthy Adams, Edna Brown Coleman, Pauline Oberdorfer Minor, Ethel Carr Watson, Margurite Yound Alexander, Jessie McGuire Dent, Vashti Turley Murphy, Wertie Blackwell Weaver, Winoa Alexander, Frederica Chase Dodd, Naomi Sewell Richardson, Madree Penn White, Ethel Cuff Black, Myra Davis Hemmings, Mamie Reddy Rose, Edith Motte Young, Bertha Pitts Campbell, Olivia Claire Jones, Eliza Pearl Sippen, Zephyr Chisom Carter, Jimmie Bugg Middleton, and Florence Letcher Toms. The first public act performed by the founders involved their participation in the Women's Suffrage March in Washington, D.C., in 1913. The sorority's second chapter was formed at Wilberforce University in 1914 and a third chapter at the Virginia Union University in 1907.

The sorority's national headquarters is located in Washington, D.C., its motto is "Intelligence Is the Torch of Wisdom," and its symbol is fortitude. The sorority's colors are crimson and cream, and its official flower is the African violet. The sorority is usually referred to as the Deltas or DST. The organization's official publication is the *Delta Journal*.

The major programs of the sorority are based on the organization's Five Point Programmatic Thrust: Economic Development, Educational Development, International Awareness and Involvement, Physical and Mental Health, and Political Awareness and Involvement. National programs include Delta Gems, Delta Days, Empowering Males to Build Opportunities for Developing Independence (EMBODI), the Delta Research and Educational Foundation, Mission Hospital, and Voting Rights.

Notable members include Betty Shabazz, Shirley Chisholm, Dorothy Height, Alexis Herman, Merlie Evers-Williams, Elaine R. Jones, Darlene Clark Hines, Ruby Dee Davis, Barbara Watson, and Barbara Jordan.

Zeta Phi Beta Sorority, Inc.

Zeta Phi Beta Sorority was founded in 1920 at Howard University. The founders were Arizona Cleaver, Myrtle Tyler, Viola Tyler, Fannie Pettie, and Pearl Neal. They are collectively known as the "Five Pearls." From its beginnings the sorority chose not to engage in elitism and also believed that socializing should not overshadow the mission of their organization. The sorority aimed to address societal mores, ills, prejudices, poverty, and health concerns of the day. The founders sought to establish an organization that rested the precepts of its motto, "Scholarship, Service, Sisterly Love and Finer Womanhood." The sorority's colors are royal blue and pure white, and its symbol is a white dove. The sorority's official flower is a white rose and its official publication is *The Archon*. The sorority is headquartered in Washington, D.C., and they are referred to as the Zetas or Sisters of the Dove. The sorority has a constitutional bond with Phi Beta Sigma Fraternity. A. Langston Taylor and Robert Samuel Taylor, two members of Phi Beta Sigma, were instrumental in helping form Zeta Phi Beta.

The sorority's programs include the National Educational Foundation, the Stork's Nest, Zetas Helping Other People Excel (Z-H.O.P.E.), and Zeta Organizational Leadership Program (ZOL). The official auxiliary organizations of Zeta Phi Beta include Amicae, Archinettes, Amicettes, Pearlettes, and the Zeta Male Network.

Notable members include Zora Neal Hurston, Ester Rolle, Dionne Warrick, Tonea Stewart, Sarah Vaughn, Cheryl Underwood, Elizabeth Koontz, Minnie Ripperton, Violette Anderson, Ja'net DuBois, Melba Moore, Jane Kennedy, Syleena Johnson, Bernice Donald, and Wendy Palmer.

Sigma Gamma Rho Sorority, Inc.

Sigma Gamma Rho Sorority was organized in 1922 at Butler University in Indianapolis, Indiana. It is the only predominately black sorority that was founded on a predominately white campus. The founders were Mary Lou Allison Little, Dorothy Hanley Whiteside, Vivian White Marbury, Nannie Mae Gahn Johnson, Hattie Mae Dulin Redford, Bessie M. Downey Martin, and Cubena McClure, and all were educators.

The organization became an incorporated national collegiate sorority on December 30, 1929, when a charter was granted to the Alpha (i.e., first) chapter at Butler University. The sorority's aim is to enhance the quality of life within the community. The organization also aims to provide public service, leadership development, and education of youth and to address the concerns that impact society. The motto of the organization is "Greater Service, Greater Progress," and their colors are royal blue and gold. Its symbol is a poodle and its official flower is the yellow tea rose. The organization's official publication is the *Aurora* and the organization is headquartered in Cary, North Carolina.

Sigma Gamma Rho's national programs include the National Education Fund, Project Reassurance, the Mwanamugimu Essay Contest, Project Africare, Project Wee Savers, Operation BigBookBag, the Sigma Youth Symposium, the National Marrow Donor Program, the Cancer Awareness Program, and Sigma Public Education and Research Foundation (SPEAR). National affiliate organizations include Philo Affiliates and Rhoer Affiliates.

Notable members include Vanessa Bell Armstrong, Eugenia Charles, Louise Beavers, Kelly Price, Victoria Rowell, Tonya Lee Williams, Hattie McDaniel, Marilyn McCoo, Maysa Leak, Anna Maria Horsford, Ellia English, and Lana Michele Moorer, better known as MC Lyte.

NAVIGATING THE ACADEMIC CULTURE

The academic culture of a university is extremely important, so it is important for students to understand this culture. It is often the case that students have the intelligence and the will to graduate; however, sometimes they lack the ability to navigate the academic culture, which causes them to be unsuccessful in a university setting. Frankly, many students penalize themselves by not exercising the proper etiquette in a classroom and not knowing how to properly conduct themselves in a college classroom setting. An academic culture is an atmosphere where faculty and students are intellectually curious about a variety of topics and subjects. It is an atmosphere where faculty and students think critically and beyond what is obvious. The atmosphere in a college classroom is one where ideas are examined and discussed and arguments are supported by facts. It is an atmosphere of self-discovery where students are evaluated by their professors, who are experts in the courses that they teach.

Within a university, there is an academic culture with its own language, assumptions, and acceptable behaviors. Each university has a set of rules, protocols, and traditions. Some are universal to college, and some are specific to the university that a student attends. If students aim to be successful in an academic setting, they should honor the rules, protocols, and traditions of the university. The language, assumptions, and acceptable behaviors may vary from university to university, but for the most part, some universal principles are expected in an academic setting. It is important for students to know what is acceptable and unacceptable at the university that they attend. Mastering and understanding an academic culture will make your time in college enjoyable and less frustrating and will improve your chances of graduating. In the classroom, students should come to class early. If a class is going on in the classroom in which their class is to meet, students should remain quiet outside of the classroom until the professor has dismissed the class. Students should not enter the classroom until the professor using the classroom has finished packing up or until they state that it is okay to enter the classroom.

STEP FIVE

Getting to Know Campus Personnel

UNIVERSITY PERSONNEL

Most universities are operated by a governing body usually called the board of trustees or the board of regents depending on the structure of the university's system. In a regents system, several universities may operate under one governing board. The regents system's head may also be called a chancellor. The university's president usually reports to the board of trustees who usually have the authority to hire and fire the president. The president is the top administrator at a university, and the academic provost is the second in leadership. The provost is the senior academic officer of a university and reports to the president of the university. The provost typically oversees all academic policies and curriculum-related matters and acts in the stead of the president in his/her absence at certain events. Academic deans are senior administrators of an academic division or college. There is usually an associate dean or deans who support the academic dean in managing the departments and programs that operate in that college. Some students confuse academic deans and the dean of students. The dean of students is an administrator chiefly responsible for student judicial affairs. The dean of students may also supervise other units on campus such as the office of the University Counseling Center, Multicultural Student Affairs, Veteran Student Affairs, International Student Affairs, Student Organizations, Career Center, and Student Activities. Chairs are responsible for leading departments. A department chair is usually a faculty member assigned by the dean to handle the administrative duties of a department. A chair's duties range from completing work orders to fix things in classrooms to handling student complaints. Another important administrator is the university registrar. Most students do not know what a registrar does and what their job entails. The university registrar is the official who handles student records such as transcripts and student verification. The registrar is responsible for distributing student grades after professors submit them.

Students may hear references to faculty and staff in the university setting. While both are essential to the function of a university, they are distinctly different. Faculty members are those people who teach at the university, while staff are all those people who provide administrative support. There are various support staff who are employed at universities. They range from the university president to the custodial staff. After graduation, many African American students appreciate the relationships they have formed with support staff. The mentorship that some of these staff members have becomes just as important as the mentorship they received from their professors. An advisor helps students by giving them advice on what classes they should take and helping them set up their class schedules. Advisors also help students keep track of the classes they need in a particular curriculum to receive a degree. While advisors are responsible for assisting students to select classes, it is ultimately the student's responsibility to know what courses are needed for graduation.

PROFESSORS AND ACADEMIC PERSONNEL

The basic duties of a professor are to excel in three phases: teaching, research, and service. The importance of these may differ depending on the mission of the university. At most research universities, these professors usually focus on research, and they are expected to produce studies, articles, books, and various other types of material. At teaching universities, professors focus on teaching and still may produce research, but usually they do not have the same research expectations as those employed at research universities. Both research universities and teaching universities have service expectations, but these expectations may vary in priority depending on the type of university. Types of service might include reviewing and editing peer papers, moderating conference sessions, or participating on committees.

Most students do not recognize that there are various classifications of people who teach courses at universities. A visiting professor is a person who is hired on a temporary basis for one to two years to cover a vacancy in a department. Lecturers are those who primarily teach at universities but do not have any research obligations. Lecturers may be employed part-time or full-time and may hold some administrative duties such as student advising. An adjunct professor is usually a part-time instructor, although there are some who may teach on a full-time basis. Because they are part-time instructors, this does not mean that they are any less important than full-time instructors. Adjunct professors must meet basic educational requirements such as having a graduate degree or substantial experience in a particular discipline or subject matter before they can teach at the college level. Because of decreased funding, many universities are moving to a model where they are using more adjunct professors to teach courses.

Assistant professors are tenure track entry-level instructors. Specific tenure track procedures and requirements depend on the university and the field. It usually consists of professors meeting certain established criteria, which are usually set by a department or college. When granted tenure, professors can be fired only if there is due cause and a justifiable reason. The tenure process may consist of a combination of student evaluations, department head evaluation, research articles, research presentations, and service acts. Usually, assistant professors have not obtained tenure. It usually takes about five to seven years to obtain tenure. After assistant professors obtain tenure, they become ranked as associate professors.

Usually, associate professors are also tenure track instructors. They have met all of the requirements to become an assistant professor, and they have a regional and national reputation as a scholar or professional. They have solid teaching reputations and have performed excellent public and professional service. After associate professors obtain tenure, they move on to the rank of professor. At some universities, they may also be referred to as "full professors." To rise to the level of professor, the instructor must have met the qualifications for tenure, demonstrate expertise in the field, and have a distinguished record of research. They must have established a national and international reputation. After retirement, a professor may be awarded the title of "emeritus," which indicates a position of honor.

TEACHING ASSISTANTS, GRADUATE RESEARCH ASSISTANTS, AND TUTORS

Teaching assistants are also called TAs. They are usually full-time PhD students who are assigned teaching duties for introductory courses. Teaching assistants can also serve as liaisons between students and professors. Among the numerous duties that teaching assistants may take on are lectures, grading, leading study sessions, and constructing exams. Teaching assistants are usually students who are pursuing graduate degrees. Graduate research assistants may be different from teaching assistants. Graduate research assistants are also called GAs. They usually assist professors in conducting research and scientific research projects. Teaching assistants and graduate research assistants are usually compensated with paid tuition and receive a small stipend for their services. In athletics, graduate assistants may serve on the university's coaching staff for the various sports teams.

There are also tutors who serve as student support. Tutors may be undergraduate or graduate students whose primary role is to assist students in retaining material in a particular course or discipline. Each department usually has tutors. Tutors are excellent students in the particular subject matter, and they provide one-on-one instruction to students having trouble in a course. The term *coach* is also used to describe individuals who provide student support. The term is more commonly used at online universities; a coach can serve in a wide range of roles from advisor to tutor. Coaches are mentors, and they provide academic mentorship to students who enrolled in online programs. Most universities offer support services to students in the form of psychological counseling as they pursue their academic and personal goals and to enhance the quality of each student's experience. Counselors at most universities are credentialed and hold appropriate licenses to provide counseling and psychological services. Counselors are bound by law to maintain confidentiality of students under their services and care, and the cost of counseling is usually covered by a student's tuition and fees.

Universities have campus police. They are sometimes called campus security; however, this term is appropriate for many of them who serve in this role. Many of these individuals have completed the police academy and the same training as local law enforcement. Campus police may also be called public safety. They are a multifaceted organization providing police, safety, and parking services to campus communities. These services usually include criminal investigations, traffic enforcement, medical transport and care, fire and crime prevention, safety programs, escort services, key control, motorist assistance, and other miscellaneous activities related to the safety and well-being of university students, faculty, staff, and visitors.

STEP SIX

Supporting Successful Habits

COLLEGE CLASSROOM ETIQUETTE AND POSITIVE INTERACTIONS WITH YOUR PROFESSOR

Some behaviors are unacceptable in a college classroom setting. Students should attend all classes and should not be late to class. Coming to class late is an unnecessary interruption to the professor's lecture. Chronic tardiness shows a professor that a student may be uninterested in learning and not taking their college education seriously. Students should use decorum in dealing with their professors and treat them like they are their future bosses. Students must take ownership of their actions. When students screw up, they should be honest with their professors and admit their mistakes. Professors have much more respect for students who admit their mistakes; however, these issues cannot be everyday occurrences.

Students must remember to avoid using unprofessional communication with their professors (profanities). It is not the norm for students to use profanities in a classroom discussion. Even if your professors use profanity while teaching and during class discussions, you should not do so. Students should listen intently to lectures and participate in all activities during the class. You should read the syllabus. On the first day that a class meets, the professor will read the syllabus for the course and discuss any questions that students may have. This is the time to get any needed clarification about assignments or rules of the class. Students miss valuable lessons by not paying attention to the syllabus. There is an old saying, "There are no stupid questions." However, yes there are stupid questions, especially if they can be found in the professor's syllabus for a course. Students should check the syllabus first before asking questions about readings or assignments. Asking questions that are clearly mentioned in the syllabus may indicate that a student may not be totally invested in the course. Professors usually take notice of those students who are engaged in learning during their teaching.

Students discredit themselves by looking disinterested by slumping in chairs or sleeping during a class or using a smartphone. Professors can serve as a wonderful resource for students especially when students need recommendations.

Some college students fear their professors because they do not view them as approachable. This may be particularly intimidating for African American students who may have had little or no interaction with people of other races. Most professors want all students to view their classes as interesting, and they want students to have a genuine interest in the courses that they instruct. Professors are human beings, and they are susceptible to the same emotions and feelings as others. With this in mind, professors sometimes make judgments based on assumptions. The way a student interacts with professors and perform on assignments may correctly or incorrectly feed into this judgment. Students should be conscious of how they are perceived on campus. Many professors read the student newspaper, and they make note of stories about students. Some professors are members of various social media outlets, so do not put questionable or embarrassing information on social media. This is also good advice even after graduation.

Students should remember that professors are not available 24 hours a day. Professors have other interests and obligations besides work. Many students e-mail professors during early mornings or during late night expecting an immediate response. This is not a reasonable expectation from your professor. Students make the assumption that professors know everything and have made "A's" in all of their undergraduate and graduate courses. Professors may only be tangentially knowledgeable about subjects that are not their field of expertise. It is also important for students to note that professors are professionals who should judge all students impartially. Students sometimes misinterpret professors' professionalism and politeness as "softness."

There are a few strategies that will help students develop positive interactions with their professors. Honesty is the best policy when dealing with a professor. Students should be honest with their professor in all situations. The professor is more apt to give students a second chance if they are honest. Students should not pack up their things before the class is over. This is not only rude, but a professor might think that they are not truly interested in the class. Students should not take critical feedback personally when a professor returns assignments or exams. Students should think about how they performed in a class before asking a professor to serve as a reference. Students should also notify their professors if they are going to miss a class, especially for an extended period of time. One of the most annoying questions for professors is, "Did I miss anything important when I was absent." Questions like these do not show forethought and may cause a negative encounter with professors.

Students can buy or rent required textbooks for all classes and stay on top of their studies from the beginning of the semester. To prepare for classes, students should consider getting a dictionary and a thesaurus. These two items will come in handy with writing papers. Here are additional tips on what students should do when interacting with their professor; these may help students to have positive interactions with their professors:

- Students should use supplemental instructional labs and writing centers. Using labs and other services will improve student papers and assignments. It also shows that students are willing to do extra work to get a good grade.
- Students should not stare at their laptop or phone during the entire class. This behavior is an indication that they are not paying attention.
- Students should not say to a professor, "I missed class, can I turn my assignment in late?" This statement indicates to a professor that the student is poor at time management or not serious about his or her education.
- Students should never say, "I do not have a pencil, do you have extra pencils?" This action shows that they are not prepared for class and may not be serious about pursuing a college education.
- Students should not ask the professor, "Can we get out of class early?" This question may indicate that the class is not a priority and they are not serious about graduating.
- Students should never say, "I stayed up all night to get this assignment finished, and I just finished before class." This statement shows that they did not put significant time in completing the assignment.
- Students should not say, "Is this going to be on the exam?" This statement can be very disruptive and show the professor that they do not have a genuine interest in the course.
- Students should never say, "I took this class for an easy 'A.' " This statement is an insult to a professor.
- Students should not go to a professor during office hours expecting to change a professor's mind about a grade on an assignment or examination.
- Students should not go to class in pajamas or any other inappropriate dress. Students should view their time at college as preparation for the world of work.

PARTICIPATING IN CLASS DISCUSSIONS

There are proper and improper ways to express yourself during class discussions. The goal of a class discussion is to present and examine course information and elaborate on key points of the information. Class discussions also allow students to ask questions and get clarification about information that may be unclear. By participating in class discussions, students show professors that they are receiving and understanding the information being presented in class. Students should maintain eye contact with the professor during lectures and practice active listening. Eye contact should also be maintained when participating in class discussions with your professors and other students. Looking directly but comfortably at the person with whom you are talking helps communicate your genuine interest. Looking away or staring too intently can be uncomfortable for the other person. Staring at your computer, cell phone, or electronic tablet during a lecture is also an indication that you may not have a genuine interest in the course. Students should maintain good body posture while in the class session and engage in class discussions. When students are engaged in a discussion with professors or fellow students, they should turn toward them. This positioning makes an interaction with an individual much more personal than turning away or to the side. Students who exhibit poor posture by slumping down in their desk are perceived as passive, and it may give the perception that they are weak and timid. While participating in class discussions, facial expressions and gestures are just as important as what students are saying during the discussion. Students' expressions should match what they speak in the discussion. When angry, the most effective way to deliver the information is to speak with a straight, nonsmiling facial expression. On the other hand, if the information being delivered is lighthearted, a big smile and jovial gestures may be appropriate. Students must control the tone of their voice. They should use a level and even tone of voice in class discussions. Consider your tone, inflection, and volume when speaking to professors and fellow students. This tone should be clear and convincing.

As African Americans, what you say in class discussions may be intimidating to some because it differs from their worldview. But a well-thought-out response is much better than a poorly-thought-out response. It is probably best to respond in the moment during a class discussion. However, it is also okay to think about a topic or an issue brought up in a class discussion and return to a person at a later time to share your thoughts about an issue. Self-discovery and revelation are cornerstones of higher education and the university experience. The most important thing in all class discussions is to actively listen. Listening reflects a commitment to learning and understanding the information presented in a course. During class discussions, African American students should attempt to provide content keeping in mind that classmates will not only hear them but more likely receive the information. In some courses, discussions may turn to controversial racial topics. Some students who may not have had close interactions with African Americans may say things that you do not agree with and even make you angry during these discussions. During these times, some African American students may choose not to express their views on these topics for fear that what they say in a discussion may be misconstrued. Other African American students may express themselves. If students choose to express themselves and their feelings, they should make sure that they use tact and well-thought-out responses during these discussions while challenging their classmates. They must avoid putting students down while expressing views. It is okay to feel uncomfortable and even angry during class discussions. Below are a few suggestions to help students gather their thoughts and express themselves clearly during a class discussion:

- Students should be as specific and clear as possible about what they are attempting to express. Being vague in speaking might lead to misinterpretation.
- Students should take ownership of what they are attempting to express in the discussion. It is best to note during the discussion that the information that they are expressing comes from their frame of reference and perceptions.
- Students should ask for feedback and listen to others' perspectives. Ask follow-up questions like, "Am I being clear? Does that make sense?" Listening to their feedback and engaging in a discussion can correct any misperceptions either party may have.

The lecture and discussion model of teaching is a common practice in the university setting. If students master how to clearly and appropriately express themselves during classroom discussions and effectively master taking notes during lecture, then they are well on their way to becoming an excellent student and graduating from college.

APPROPRIATE STUDENT ATTIRE IN CLASS

What students wear to class says a lot about them and how they think of themselves. Students send out messages by their attire and carry themselves on campus. African American students send out positive or negative messages with their clothing; others can make judgments about them based on their attire, and this remains true on a college campus. Does your attire convey a lack of focus? Does your attire convey intelligence? Does your attire convey professionalism? Does your attire convey mediocrity? A student's attire should convey confidence and show that you have high self-esteem; it can also set you apart from other students in your class. Students have only one opportunity to make a first impression and few other chances to make a lasting impression.

There are three basic categories of wardrobe for students: business, business casual, and casual. For men, business attire may consist of single-breasted suits in blue, gray, or black (with only two or three buttons). This may appear conservative, but flamboyantly colored suits are not acceptable in the business arena. There is a difference between dressing sharp and dressing business appropriate. Male students should wear ironed white-, blue-, or pastel-colored shirts with their dark business suit, and they should always wear a t-shirt under their dress shirt. This prevents the dress shirt from becoming stained in the armpit area of the shirt. In business attire, male students should wear ties with small prints or striped design and the tie should stop at the top of one's belt. Belts and shoes should match, and shoes should be polished and well maintained. Bow ties are acceptable, especially on a university campus. Business casual for men usually consists of a dress shirt, pants, and blazer. It is important that clothes fit properly. Some African American students have a tendency to want their pants to sag.

When wearing business attire or business casual attire, pants should not sag. Sagging mimics prison culture. Sagging pants developed when prisoners were not allowed to wear belts for fear that belts could be used by prisoners to hang themselves. The prison policy and the lack of proper sizing and ill-fitting prison uniforms brought about the phenomenon of sagging, which became popular in hip-hop culture. Male students should wear their pants at their natural waist or just below their belly button and their underwear should not show above their pants. For casual wear it is appropriate for students to wear khakis, jeans, or other pants with golf shirts, button-down shirts, and even t-shirts. Any t-shirt worn should not have profanity or inappropriate messaging on it. Even if it is meant to be humorous, African American students should remember it could be misinterpreted and send the wrong message to the larger campus community. It is better for African American students to overdress rather than underdress. If a student goes to see a professor during their office hours, students should wear presentable clothing. In discussing appropriate attire, it is of little importance how much a student's clothing costs. It is more important that students wear appropriate, proper-fitting, and clean clothes to class rather than attempting to buy expensive clothing.

African American female students also convey various messages by the way they dress and carry themselves on campus. As with male attire, there are three basic categories of wardrobe: business, business casual, and casual. Appropriate distinctions should be made between the appropriate attire for class, work, church, business and formal affairs, relaxation, and play. Female students should refrain from wearing sheer garments unless they wear proper undergarments to obscure their transparency. Females should also refrain from micromini skirts or shorts. Females should wear clothing that covers enough of their thighs while they are standing or sitting. Like with males, females should refrain from wearing t-shirts with profanity or questionable messages on them. Females should not wear ripped jeans or torn jeans to class. They also should not wear bedroom slippers, pajamas, and hair rollers to class.

Female students' business attire should consist of navy blue, black, or gray pencil skirt or pants. Their blouse must be appropriate in style and color (solid), or a solid dress and jacket should be worn. In business attire, females should wear closed-toe shoes with heal heights no more than two inches and the shoes should be polished. Females should limit themselves to three pieces of jewelry (watch, ring, necklace, or earrings). If female students wear bracelets with their business wear, they should not jingle. Female students' nails should be neatly trimmed and polished in natural tone or clear polish, and they should make sure they have the appropriate tone of lipstick and makeup. Females may carry a small handbag and wear neutral or dark hosiery.

Students should attempt to wear attire that is appropriate for the climate where their university is located. All students should make sure clothes fit properly by getting pants hemmed and jacket sleeves tailored. Students have only one opportunity to make a first impression. Some majors will require you to wear uniforms such as scrubs for nursing or dental majors, or police uniforms. Nontraditional students who leave work and come directly to class or leave class and go to work may come to class in their uniforms. Students send a message with their attire. African American college students should start dressing for success and the job that they want while they are in college.

TIME MANAGEMENT AND PROCRASTINATION

Time management is one of the most important aspects of becoming a successful college student as well as in life. If students do not master time management, they may feel frustration and even anger because they did not complete tasks that they wanted to accomplish. African American students must identify and discover techniques to help them manage their time efficiently. In developing good time management techniques, students learn to identify goals they wish to accomplish and then prioritize study activities and assignments. Some students make daily lists of activities, tasks, and assignment due dates. This information can be kept on an electronic planner on your computer or smartphone. If the student is old school, they can write these things down on a note pad, three by five cards, or day-planner. It is the student's responsibility to organize their list and keep track of the things that need to be done. African American students can control many aspects of their lives by the choices they make. Students must anticipate future external events and control those things that they can. African American students' lives are not controlled by outside events. Things happen, but they must be strong enough to move past these events. If students understand that they control their circumstances instead of their circumstances controlling them, it will be easier for them to prioritize and develop a plan, and determine in what time frame their goal must be accomplished despite outside circumstances.

African American students should also understand that they cannot meet everyone's expectations. Attempting to fulfill everyone's expectations creates unnecessary pressure on a college student. Unreasonable demands and the expectations of others may be inappropriate for their lifestyle as a college student. By trying to meet the expectations of others, they may be shortchanging themselves and their needs. African American students must determine their needs and what others expect of them, especially if their goals and priorities are different from others. African American students should also realize that they are not perfect. Perfectionists are often frustrated people. This does not mean that there should not be standards in academics and in living life. It is good to have standards and high expectations, but it is important to not become perfectionistic in expectations. Perfectionists also tend to be especially prone to procrastination because the perfection they demand is impossible to achieve. This may also cause anxiety because perfectionistic goals are impossible to reach.

Procrastination is a key culprit in some African American students being unsuccessful in graduating from college. There are many types and causes of procrastination, and it can take many forms. African American students should not allow procrastination to rob them of an opportunity to receive a college degree. There are many reasons why some students procrastinate while in college and not complete the tasks needed to obtain a degree. Some students may simply be genuinely disinterested in obtaining a college degree. If that is the case, they should go and pursue their passion, whatever that may be. Some students find it difficult to begin tasks no matter how simple they may be. Other students are fearful of having their assignments graded, which creates anxiety. Some African American students may have fallen in to peer pressure from those who did not attend college, and they overvalue what these people think of them. Being a college student has a great deal of uncertainty associated with it, and some students find it difficult to deal with this uncertainty. Lastly, some students procrastinate because they have low skill sets and procrastination allows them to have an excuse for failing a particular course or assignment. African American students must acknowledge their procrastination and identify what has caused them to procrastinate. Poor time management, anxiety, guilt, and low self-esteem may be the causes of procrastination. Students must determine what caused their procrastination and then employ effective strategies to combat it. The following are just a few behaviors associated with procrastination:

- Students ignore tasks, assignments, exams, and term papers, believing that they will be able to simply get away.
- Students underestimate how long it will take to complete a task or overestimate their abilities to complete the task.
- Students believe that mediocrity and poor grades are okay as long as you pass the course with a "C" or "D" grade.
- Students substitute activities that are not associated with the task of studying when it is study time, that is, cleaning up the bathroom as a substitute for studying.

Effective planning is an excellent tool in combating procrastination. African American students should make long-term and short-term plans but should avoid over planning. Students must take ownership and make sincere decisions about their work and how they work. Students who choose to spend a minimal amount of time on their schoolwork have no one else to blame but themselves and should admit this if results are not up to standard. If students want to devote only small amounts of time to tasks like studying and reading textbooks, that is their choice, but they must be willing to deal with the consequences of this action.

There are strategies that students can employ to prevent procrastination. Students can break down larger tasks into smaller ones. Students should also determine a reasonable time frame to complete assignments and study. Oftentimes, students underestimate the time required for an assignment or believe they can do more than is humanly possible. Students should also realize that relaxation is needed, especially after long periods of work. There is time for relaxation while accomplishing tasks associated with school. It is a good practice for students to monitor their progress on the small tasks, and when problems occur, address them early to avoid these problems from becoming bigger in the future. African American students must be reasonable about the expectations of themselves, their abilities, and the college experience. Most of all they should not sabotage themselves when they are making progress toward obtaining a degree. Students should remember that they are college students and the responsibility is solely theirs to graduate. College is not like high school, days are less structured, and students cannot get away with only marginally studying. In college there may be days where students have three to six classes per day with heavy reading loads and assignments for each class. A college student must negotiate their time between many competing interests. Students must realize that procrastination will help end their time on a university campus very quickly, and they should never be afraid to ask for help.

NOTE-TAKING, LISTENING, AND READING STRATEGIES

Note-taking, listening, and reading strategies are skills that can be learned and honed. Students should keep all of their notes for various classes organized. This can be done by keeping a separate notebook for each class. Students should write their names and date of the class when they are taking notes. The date when a note is taken will help provide a logical flow of the notes taken and better organization when studying for a unit exam, midterm exam, or final exam. Students should use standard paper to take notes. Using smaller pieces of paper forces some students to attempt cramming too much information on the paper. This will make it more difficult to decipher the notes when studying. Students should also write notes clearly. They should utilize a system of symbols when taking notes to save time. When professors write information on the board, this is a signal to take notes on the information presented. Usually when professors stress an idea or ideas during their lectures, this is a signal that this information may be used as an exam question. If they also use examples to emphasize various points, these examples should be written as notes and reviewed when studying for an exam.

Listening and note-taking skills go hand in hand. Both activities are essential to students in a classroom. Before students go to each class session, they should check the course syllabus. This will show what activity or lecture will take place and on what day. Read the assignment and write down any questions to ask the professor. Students should get mentally prepared for class and free themselves from mental distractions. When taking the notes, do not try to write everything down. The point of taking notes is to understand and remember the information, not to write down everything the lecture says.

Professors usually give signals about what they believe are important points during their lectures. These important points made during lectures usually translate into exam questions. Students should try to summarize the speaker's words by paraphrasing the information provided. By paraphrasing, students will gain a better grasp of the information being delivered. When taking notes during a lecture, students should make sure to listen for verbal and nonverbal cues. Most professors use signal words. These are clues to the information they believe is important. Professors use phrases like "the main points are . . ." or "you should remember. . . ." Signal words usually are indicators that these will be exam questions. Some just boldly say this will be an exam question. During the lecture, a professor's voice may change. The change in speaking pattern and the rate of speech are indicators of important points in the lecture. The professor may speak louder or slower to make a point. They may speak higher or lower to emphasize important points. Students should watch for a professor's nonverbal cues during the lecture. Hand gestures, steps toward the audiences, or the pounding of a fist on a podium are indicators that the points being made are important. In some cases, professors lecture on subjects and topics that are not in the textbook. Students should write these down because more than likely this information will probably be an exam question and the professor may be the only source of the information provided. While taking notes, students should clear themselves of mental clutter by not shutting down when hearing information that they do not agree with or may not understand. Note-taking is a central student activity during a lecture and essential to becoming a great college student.

Reading textbooks, listening, and note-taking are skills that students can use in all courses and are great skills to have in general. How well a student reads is probably a strong indicator of how well they will do in college. Some would say that it is the most important skill a college student needs to graduate and succeed. Reading a textbook is not like reading a novel and other popular books. In reading material for class, students should start by looking at the book title and the title of the chapter. This gives the student an indication of what the reading material will be about. Students should scan the assigned book or chapter to see how the material is organized. In scanning the material, students should examine the subheadings, topic sentences, charts, graphs, and chapter summaries to gain an understanding of how the information is organized before heavily delving into the reading material.

It is best to read textbook chapters multiple times. On the first read, students should just try to get a good idea and a general understanding of the material. On this read, students do not need to take notes or look up words that they do not know. Concentrate on the first sentence in the paragraph because this indicates what the entire paragraph is about. The important point during the initial read is to separate the information that is understood from the information that is not understood. Students should pay attention to all bold or italicized printed words or phrases. This indicates that the words are important.

On the second read, students should reread difficult passages. Rereading the passages several times improves the chances of gaining an understanding of the information. During this read, students should also look up any words, definitions, or phrases that are not understood. Students may understand some words as they are used in the context of the material. They should write down the main ideas of the chapter while reading. After the chapter material has been read twice, students should read the information again. If students are having difficulties after reading the information twice and taking notes on the reading material, then they should discuss the information with their professor.

STUDY HABITS AND MASTERING EXAMS

Some students entering college may have to adjust their approaches to studying and test-taking to become successful college students. Some students find that the study habits and techniques that were used in high school are inadequate for college courses. College can be strenuous, but by becoming skilled at note-taking and studying, students can help improve their chances of making good grades and completing their degrees. Study skills entail learning how to study. Because these skills can be learned and improved, with enough hard work, anyone can succeed in college.

While it is important for students to develop their own style of studying, they may want to consider the time of the day in which they work best and are the most alert. Students must identify the times of the day when their energy levels are at their highest; this is the optimal time to attempt to complete assignments and term papers. If a student works best in the morning, they should not plan all of their study time for the evening. On occasion, it can be okay to still do work at the last minute, but this is not a good habit for successful African American college students to form. It is a good idea to have a special productive space and time for students to study. It is very important to schedule study time and determine a special place to study.

African American students should also optimize their work environment by making sure that their physical environment is conducive to concentration and studying and free from distractions. They should also guard their time by blocking off periods of time that are dedicated for studying. This may require students to say no to various activities and to people requesting services or attention. To avoid interruptions while studying, students may arrange their work area and sit with their backs to the traffic flow of the study area. Students could also simply close the door to the area where they are studying and not respond to any visitor that may knock on the door. Students may also find it useful to find and use a special space such as a library carrel or an office where others will be unable to locate them. Students should also turn off their cell phones while studying and listen to messages or return missed call during a study break. During the period that is blocked off for studying, students must *study*. Do schoolwork and refrain from checking e-mail and social networking sites, watching television, and surfing the Internet. Students can also incorporate studying into their daily routines by taking schoolwork with them and studying while waiting for events to start, while riding the bus, or during downtime at work. They can use flash cards or begin work on assignments in between breaks and other spare moments at work.

Students should not study too long at one session. Studying too long will exhaust even the most intelligent student, so one should take short breaks in order to not tire oneself out. Students should also study difficult subjects first. This is suggested so that if students become tired and have not completed other subjects, they will have tackled the subjects that are the weakest. If students do their studying the other way around, then it may be more difficult later into the study session. Students should work on assignments and other term papers in stages. When students step away from assignments and then come back later, they may see mistakes and corrections more easily. Being away from an assignment allows students to see projects, assignments, or papers with objectivity. Students will only be able to work on papers and assignments in sections if they begin early and allow themselves plenty of time to complete the work.

TEST ANXIETY AND TEST-TAKING STRATEGIES

Many people do not do well when taking exams. Exams are not the sole indication of the information that an individual knows and it is certainly not an indicator of intelligence. Yet exams are widely used as a method at universities to determine course grades for students. Like note-taking, listening, and reading, test-taking is another skill that can be developed and improved. Some people suffer from test anxiety. Test anxiety is excessive nervousness or panic that people experience in testing situations. It can actually impair learning and negatively affect test performance.

While most students experience some test anxiety during exams, but when it becomes debilitating, then students should seek assistance and employ some test-taking skills that can assist them. Test anxiety can be caused by a lack of poor time management, cramming the night before the exam, poor study habits, and poor organization. There are both mental and physical symptoms of test anxiety. Mental symptoms include mental blocks and mental distractions. During mental blocks, students cannot remember the information that was learned before the test was taken. Mental distractions deal with students becoming easily distracted by the environment while taking an exam. Physical symptoms include sweaty palms, headache, perspiration, increased heartbeat, butterflies in the stomach, muscle tension, upset stomach, and nausea.

There are strategies to combat test anxiety. Students can reduce test anxiety by studying the material well enough so that if they become stressed, they can recall the correct answers and perform well. Students must get enough sleep the night prior to the exam. Sleep is very important to a positive mindset and outlook. Having sufficient sleep allows the brain to function properly, which improves a student's chances of performing better on exams. Students should also eat properly. Eating too little or too much prior to an exam can effect mental functioning. Eating "junk food" prior to an exam may overly increase energy or lower energy if the student crashes from the junk food. Students should avoid alcohol and drugs before taking an exam because these will negatively affect your test performance. The following are recommendations for taking tests:

- On the day of the exam, go early to the exam venue and take a moment to relax.
- Listen carefully to the professor's last-minute instructions. Most professors give some useful information just prior to the exam begins.
- Read and follow the directions very carefully and then develop a strategy of how to proceed with taking the exam.
- Determine the difficult and easier parts of the exam. Those that are easier should be done first and then tackle the more difficult parts.
- Keep a steady pace. Do not spend too much time on one question because time may run out at the end.
- Students should trust their knowledge and not rely on patterns or guessing. Guessing should be saved when time is running out and if there is not a penalty for wrong answers.
- Students should make sure that they have completed all sections of the exam. Sometimes people fail exams because they do not complete the entire exam.
- Students should answer the questions that are on the exam and not those that they wish were on the exam.
- After the exam is completed, students should use their remaining time wisely by checking answers. Students should change answers only if they are sure that their initial answer is wrong and a change is needed.
- Students should learn from exams. If students are allowed to keep their graded exams, these can be used to learn a professor's testing style and prepare for the midterm and final exams.

VARIOUS TYPES OF EXAMS

Various types of exam patterns are used in college, and depending on the design of the exam, a particular strategy is required to score well on the exam. Testing is the method that most professors choose to see if students are learning and retaining information being transferred in class. Professors must assess and find out what students actually know. Tests are used as a method of providing overall grades for students at the end of each term. Finally, tests hold professors accountable for the courses they are responsible for teaching. Some types of exams are true/false, multiple choice, matching questions, essay, and open book.

True/False Exams

When taking true/false exams, students should make sure that all parts of the questions are true. Professors use these types of questions to test knowledge of details and to make sure that all parts of particular information are known. On this type of exam, it is important to note that all parts of the question must be true for the answer to be correct. True/false questions created using absolute words such as always, never, none, every, entirely, and only are often false. However, questions that us qualifiers such as sometimes, often, usually, frequently, ordinarily, and generally are more likely to be true. True/false questions with words like *not* and *never* may require a little more thought than simple true/false questions. Double negatives used in questions create a positive statement, so students should remember this when answering true/false questions.

- Read the exam questions carefully before beginning the exam.
- Keywords such as always, never, none, every, entirely, and only are often false.
- Keywords such as sometimes, often, usually, frequently, ordinarily, and generally are more likely to be true.
- When in doubt guess "true" as the answer. Exams tend to have more true answers than false answers.

Multiple Choice Exams

Multiple choice questions can be very difficult because there are many possible answers to the question. If students do not know the correct answer outright, they should use the process of elimination and rule out two incorrect answers and then focus on the remaining two choices. This can make it much easier to choose the correct answer. Another strategy students should use is to read the question and use each answer as a separate true/false question. After reading each potential as a true/false question, look for the correct answer as it pertains to the question being asked. This maneuver also helps to eliminate incorrect answers. Lastly, students should choose answers that are grammatically correct. Correct grammar that matches the question and the answer can provide students with good clues of what answer may be correct or incorrect. Students should also:

- Read the exam directions carefully and correctly. Students may be asked to select either correct or incorrect answer.
- First, eliminate any obviously wrong answers and strike them out to avoid confusion.
- Choose the best answer and do not succumb to second guessing.
- If the answer is unknown and there is an "all the above" choice, select it.

Matching Exams

Matching exams are also used in college to test students' identification skills and their ability to make connections. Matching exams usually have two columns or lists of words or terms that students have to match correctly. Students should begin by examining both columns and then look for relationships between the words on the two lists. This will help in the matching process. Students should use one list as a base and search matches in the other list; this process allows the two lists to remain clear while taking the exam. Students should be sure to look through both lists in their entirety before beginning the exam. There will probably be more than one match for some words or some words that may match better than others. Students may lose points on the exam by not choosing the best possible matching answer. After all of the known answers have been chosen, students should then guess at the answers that they do not know.

- Read the exam instructions very carefully.
- Look through the entire list before beginning the exam.
- Use one list as a baseline and make matches from the other list.
- There may be more than one correct answer, so choose the best possible answer.

Essay Exams

At most colleges, essay exams are the typical type used to test students. Essay exams involve writing a lengthy response to a question or several questions. When taking an essay exam, it is important to read all of the directions very carefully. There are many possible ways to respond to essays; therefore, it is imperative that students recognize if their professor has specific guidelines for essay exams or a way they want students to respond. If the essay question has several parts, students should respond to all parts of the question. In writing an essay exam response, students should search for key words. Words like analyze, evaluate, explain, summarize, discuss, compare, and contrast are all terms used in essay exam questions. Knowing these terms and how they are used will help students provides professors with the type of information and responses they are seeking.

Students should organize their thoughts and take time to write an outline before starting the essay. This will allow better organization of the essay and allow for more efficient use of time during the exam period. In the first paragraph of the essay, students should restate the question because it provides a clear thesis statement and allows the professor to understand how the question was interpreted.

Students should also write legibly and double space their essay because it provides room to make corrections. It is best to write on only one side of a paper. Papers can become quite messy and difficult to read, which may result in the professor missing pertinent information in the essay. Essays are subjective. The appearance of the essay may influence the professor grading either negatively or positively. Use examples to explain points made in the essay. This shows accurate comprehension of the question and information. After completing the essay, students should proofread and polish their essay. Lastly, students should always use standard English and good grammar in their essays.

- Consider exactly what the question is asking.
- Think and organize thoughts and make an outline before beginning the essay.
- Answer all parts of the essay question.
- Check spelling and grammar. Proofread the essay before turning it in.

Open-Book and Take-Home Exams

Open-book exams are sometimes given in undergraduate courses. These are exams where students are allowed to use their textbook or a portion of their textbook to answer questions. Students make the mistake of thinking that open-book exams are easier because they can use their books during the exam. This type of exam is usually given when there is a need to refer to charts or graphs. When preparing for an open-book exam, students should prepare for the exam just as if it were any other kind of closed-book exam. When taking an open-book exam, familiarity with where the information is located in the textbook will greatly help complete the exam in a timely fashion.

Take-home exams are sometimes used in place of the other types of exams. Students also make the mistake of thinking that these exams are easier because they can complete them at home. This type of exam usually has a specific date when they are due. Professors usually grade them harder because the student has the opportunity to complete the exam at home. Collaboration is not permitted on take-home exams. Students usually have approximately a week to work on take-home exams; however, some professors have shorter periods to take the exam. This type of exam is basically a short research paper that a student is expected to produce in a short period of time.

FURTHER READINGS

Bragg, Debra D., and Elisabeth A. Barnett. *Academic Pathways to and from the Community College: New Directions for Community Colleges*, Number 135. Hoboken, NJ: Jossey-Bass, 2006.

Brown, Cecil. *Dude, Where's My Black Studies Department*. Berkeley, CA: North Atlantic Books, 2007.

College Board. *Book of Majors 2015: All-New Ninth Edition*. New York: College Board, 2014.

Covey, Stephen R. *The 7 Habits of Highly Effective People*. New York: Simon & Schuster, 1989.

Cushman, Kathleen. *First in the Family: Your College Years: Advice for College from First Generation Students*. Providence, RI: Next Generation Press, 2006.

Gasman, Marybeth, Benjamin Baez, and Caroline Sotello Turner. *Understanding Minority Serving Institutions*. New York: SUNY Press, 2008.

Jones, Lee. *Making It on Broken Promises: African American Male Scholars Confront the Culture of Higher Education*. Sterling, VA: Stylus Publishing, LLC, 2002.

Palmer, Robert T., and Adriel Hilton. *Black Graduate Education at Historically Black Colleges and Universities: Trends, Experiences, and Outcomes*. Charlotte, NC: Information Age Publishing, 2012.

Peterson, Marvin W. *Black Students on White Campuses: The Impacts of Increased Black Enrollments*. Ann Arbor: University of Michigan, Institute for Social Research, 1978.

Tanabe, Gen, and Kelly Tanabe. *501 Ways for Adult Students to Pay for College: Going Back to School Without Going Broke*. Belmont, CA: SuperCollege LLC, 2015.

PART III

Learning the Language and Lingo of Higher Education

Course catalogs provide full details on all degree programs and associated class offered by a college. This includes all majors and their associated minors and concentrations. For each degree program, the catalog outlines all classes required to complete the degree program. It outlines prerequisite courses, core classes required for each degree, and electives that may be taken as part of each degree program. While some universities have gone to an online format for catalog, it still may be helpful for students to get a hard copy to keep abreast of the university's policies and regulations.

The course catalog is the most important document a student is given. Each student must carefully follow the course outline to ensure they are taking all required classes and also taking them in the order recommended. The course catalog identifies classes required during each student's year of college, from their freshman year through the end of the senior year. Any deviation from the schedule of courses should be approved by the student's advisor, department chair, and the registration/academics office. The advisor should also be consulted when the student is selecting electives. These should be directly associated with the student's major or minor.

A student's classification is based on where they are in their degree program. Student classification refers to the familiar categories for the four undergraduate years. The undergraduate classifications are freshman, sophomore, junior, and senior. A student's classification is not based on how many years a student has attended a university. It is based on the number of courses passed and the number of semester hours earned. Not pursuing enough credit hours during a semester may delay graduation for the student. There are other classifications of students such as post-baccalaureate students, nondegree students, and graduate students. Nondegree students work for college credit but are not enrolled in a degree-granting program.

Post-baccalaureate students have received an undergraduate degree but take courses beyond their bachelor's degree. These students are not enrolled in a particular degree program and may be taking classes for self-development. Usually, nondegree students must meet all of the requirements of those seeking a degree. If a nondegree student would like to change their status to degree-seeking student, each school has specific policies and process to do so.

STEP SEVEN

Signing Up for Courses

MAJORS AND MINORS

Most college degrees require a major. A major is a set of courses in a specific subject that leads to a college degree. Typically, about half of the courses a student takes in college are major courses or are related to major courses. Choosing a major will lead to a career in a particular field. While some students know exactly what they want to major in when they first enroll in college, most students enter college undecided. Some universities allow students to become "undeclared" or "undecided" majors until they have selected their major. Most students have decided their major by the completion of their sophomore year. Majors should match a student's career goals, and students should choose majors as soon as they are sure that their choice is right for them. Choosing a major can reveal what a student is truly passionate about. Sometimes, students choose to double major. Double majors are usually reserved for those who are the brightest and who are driven to complete two undergraduate degrees.

A minor is a set of courses leading to a secondary course of study during your undergraduate study. It is usually less credit hours than a major. Minors are subcategories that allow students to explore additional fields of study that they may have personal interest in and want to learn more about. Minors allow students to gain training in a certain field of study and can be a great addition on a resume and can complement your major by providing some exposure to another field. One's minor can show that you have some additional skills; for example, a law enforcement or criminal justice major may minor in Spanish, which could make them more attractive to potential law enforcement agencies.

GENERAL STUDIES COURSES

Many colleges require students to take a set of courses referred to as general studies courses or the core curriculum. The core curriculum covers a broad range of subjects that provides a student with a good knowledge base. These courses are a set of common courses required of undergraduates regardless of the major a student chooses. These courses are usually heavily based in the liberal arts and usually consist of courses such as history, literature, performing arts, philosophy, religion, social sciences, economics, geography, political science, natural sciences, mathematics, and applied sciences. These courses assist in developing a student's mind and cultivating critical and creative capacity, which students can use in everyday life. These courses serve to cultivate an intellectual curiosity that fosters life-long learning. These courses are usually taken before beginning major courses; however, some cores can be taken simultaneously with major courses, but this is not always ideal. Course numbers usually are sequenced. Any courses beginning with 100 are usually a freshman-level course, for example, psychology 100, English 101, history 100, and sociology 100. Courses beginning with 200 are usually sophomore-level courses. Junior-level courses usually begin with 300, and senior-level courses with 400 or above. Freshmen and sophomore students should not take 300- and 400-level courses unless they have completed lower-level courses because many of the upper-level courses have prerequisites. Prerequisites are prescribed courses that should be taken before enrolling in an upper-division course. Prerequisites are a way of making sure that students have the necessary knowledge base to complete the 300- or 400-level courses. General studies courses are designed to make students appreciate the intellectual and learning process and prepare them for study within their majors.

Supplemental instruction is a means of getting the assistance needed in courses. Supplemental instruction sessions are regularly scheduled informal review sessions where students can compare notes, discuss readings, and predict things that may be on an exam. In supplemental instruction, students learn how to integrate course materials and study skills with a leader who has previously done well in the course. Supplemental or tutorial sessions are a good tool to use to get individual instruction, which can be lacking at some large universities. Students must determine which size university is the best fit for them. No matter the size, building a relationship with your professors and/or their graduate assistants can be key in getting the individual instruction and successfully completing a particular course with an acceptable final grade.

COLLEGE CLASS SCHEDULES

High school course schedules are not like those in college. In high school, students keep the same schedule. Classes are often the same Monday through Friday. In college, each class has its own schedule. A student's schedule may be different on each day. A lot of students opt for a Monday, Wednesday, and

Friday schedule or a Tuesday and Thursday schedule. In high school, most courses are usually offered between 8:00 am and 3:00 pm. In college, some classes may be offered during the evenings, weekends, and over the Internet. Students have the choice of when they take their classes. In consultation with an academic advisor or a faculty member, students also have the option of choosing the particular classes that they would like to enroll in. Most universities have degree plans, which are semester-by-semester course planning sheets to show a student which classes are needed to complete their degree by a particular time period. Of course, the completion date and graduation depend on the students ability to pass courses without having to repeat them. Ultimately, it is the students' responsibility to take the courses needed to graduate.

A typical first-semester schedule usually consists of a total course load of 12–15 credit hours. At most universities, 12 credit hours are considered full-time status. Fifteen hours is suggested during the first semester because a student may have a difficult time adjusting to college life, and this will allow them to drop a course and remain a full-time student. This is important because if a student is receiving federal financial aid, they must be a full-time student to receive this benefit.

Students are encouraged to see an academic advisor early and often and ask a lot of questions. Advisers are there to help students succeed and adjust to college. There are three primary resources that students should use to determine what courses to take and whether they are taking the right courses needed for their major's degree requirements. Your academic or faculty advisors are great resources in making the correct course choices. Students should always keep a copy of their university's undergraduate catalog. The catalog will specifically lay out which courses are needed to complete a degree for every major offered at the university. Students should also obtain a degree completion plan, which also lays out courses needed to complete a degree in a given major. Students should meet with their academic advisor at least once or twice a semester to ensure that they are on track and enrolling in the correct courses for their major. Academic advisors usually do not keep a record of your grades. University officials cannot release any information about students to anyone including their parents if they have not authorized them to do so. The Family Educational Rights and Privacy Act of 1974 prohibits releasing information about students. Therefore, advisors and university administrators will release only general information about policy and procedures.

COURSE SYLLABUS

The course syllabus outlines the requirements of each individual course listed in the course catalog. It outlines the purpose of each course as well as all requirements to complete the course. The plural form of the word *syllabus* is syllabi. Your professor will usually hand out a syllabus on the first day of class. In most cases, the only information that a student may have about a course is the information found in the course catalog. The syllabus functions as a guide throughout the course in which you are enrolled. It provides more specific information than a catalog. In the syllabus, the professor provides the conception of the courses, assignments, examinations, due dates, grading scale for the courses, and other pertinent information about their expectations for the course. It also gives the student the structure of how the course will be taught and how examinations will be structured, that is, multiple choice, short answer, essay, or a combination.

In the syllabus, the professor provides all of the course policies, and this can pertain to attendance and missed assignments. The consequences of violating policies are also provided in the syllabus. The syllabus usually contains a list of tentative dates of readings and examination and assignment due dates. The most prominent mistakes students make regarding the syllabus is they lose the syllabus and fail to obtain another copy or they fail to keep up with the assigned readings. Sometimes due dates on a syllabus may change depending on the flow of a class discussion or other circumstances that interrupt the pace of teaching and learning in a class. The syllabus can be viewed as a contract with both parties; the students and professors agree to uphold the contract. The syllabus is not written in stone, but the only person who can change the syllabus is the professor. A syllabus also provides students with an indication of a professor's personality and how tough they may be in instructing the course. Professors sometimes come across extra tough in their syllabus; sometimes they do this to scare off students who are not serious about the class. Some students who do not want to work really hard may use the drop/add process to change classes to avoid difficult or stern professors.

While it is important to understand all assignments in each course, the most important are the midterm and final examinations. Midterm examinations are given at the midpoint of a semester. These exams are given to students to assess their knowledge of course material up to the middle of the semester. Dates for midterms are determined prior to the semester and are usually listed in a professor's syllabus that is distributed during the first week of class. In some cases, the midterm exam can be up to 50 percent of a student's overall semester grade. The actual exam may be objective, that is, multiple choice, matching, and true or false exams, or they may be subjective essay, short answer, or oral interviews. Some exams may be a mixed form of exam that uses both objective and subjective methods, where the first part may be multiple choice and the second part may consist of three or four essay questions. Final exams are given at the end of a semester and they test a student's knowledge of course material over the entire semester. Like in a midterm examination, a professor may use subjective, objective, or mixed method form of exams. In some cases, a professor may choose to test students only on information covered since the midterm exam. Depending on a professor's discretion, final exams can count a large portion of a student's overall semester grade; students may experience great stress during midterm and final exam periods.

Many functions and order at universities are based on the concept of time. The academic calendar and year are both built on time. Universities follow an academic year. The academic year is the annual period during which a student attends and receives formal instruction at a college or university. At most universities, the academic year typically runs from August or September to December (fall semester) and then from January to May (spring semester). Most universities and accrediting agencies have crafted policies that require a specific number of contact hours for students.

STUDY ABROAD PROGRAMS

Although the benefits of studying abroad are well documented, many African American students do not take advantage of study abroad opportunities. Students who study abroad can gain a global perspective and better understanding of economic issues. Studying abroad can also help students to learn about different cultures by immersing themselves in that culture. Global exposure may prepare an African American student for an international career and for future leadership positions. There are great economic and political advantages for African American students who study abroad. African American students may find it more intellectually liberating to study abroad, and they may return to the United States as better students because of this international experience.

Students studying abroad attend a university in another country and receive credit at their prospective university. While the majority of foreign students who study in the United States are pursuing a full degree, most outgoing students from the United States study abroad for one or two academic terms. The majority of U.S. students who study abroad choose short-term programs. Although few African American students participate in study abroad programs, most universities have established study abroad programs on their campuses. These programs should be undertaken by students who are mature and who are able to adjust to living in another country and experience a different culture for an extended period of time. A study abroad experience can enhance the academic experience of not only African American students but all students in general.

Many terms are commonly used at universities, and if African American students are unfamiliar with these terms, it may be as difficult as learning a new language. There are many reasons why students should learn acronyms and other terms commonly used at a university. Not grasping these terms can make navigating the college experience difficult and graduating even more difficult. The mastery of the university's language and lingo increases a student's awareness and the possibilities to converse with the faculty and staff. Knowing the university's language provides students with a greater understanding of policies and procedure and how the university functions as a whole. It also gives students an understanding of the roles and responsibilities of offices and administrators employed by the university. While the hefty fees associated with studying abroad may deter some students from attempting to study outside the country, some countries' tuition and fees are much cheaper than tuition in the United States; for example, Germany does not charge tuition fees.

STEP EIGHT

Knowing Your Options

COUNSELING AND ACADEMIC ADVISORS

Most universities have counseling centers that provide counseling services with professional counselors who listen and are concerned about students' mental health needs. These counseling professionals listen and attempt to make students' college experiences productive and rewarding. Most university counseling centers offer numerous programs to assist students in adjusting to college and any other problems they may be experiencing. They usually provide crisis and psychological counseling to students who need these services. These services are designed to help students overcome any obstacles to life goals or traumatic situations through customary methods of problem solving and traditional counseling. In the case of extreme psychological problems, most universities either have an on-campus psychologist or have contracts with mental health professionals to assist. University counseling centers help students learn how to cope with their personal problems and assist students with other behaviors such as building communication skills, developing assertiveness, developing test-taking skills and time management, and building stress-coping mechanisms. University counselors also assist students working through difficult situations such as sexual assault, relationship abuse, date rape, HIV and AIDS, and alcohol and drug abuse. University counselors help students with personal growth through individual and group counseling sessions, which provide opportunities for students to participate with peers and professionals in exploring feelings, behaviors, and other common concerns in a supportive atmosphere and to gain clarification and feedback. These counseling sessions allow students to develop a plan and take appropriate actions. Ultimately, the university counseling center's mission is to help students learn to cope, identify choices, make better decisions, and turn problems into learning experiences.

Academic advisors assist students in selecting the correct courses for their majors and in keeping on track for degree completion and graduation. Universities have different policies and procedures that address many of the more difficult questions that a student may have. Universities usually have academic advising services as well as a counseling center to address specific questions such as:

- How do I drop a course?
- When can I drop a course?
- How do I go about dropping a course?
- How can I add a class?
- How do I withdraw from the university?
- How do I preregister?
- Where can I go to discuss my academic difficulties?
- Where can I go for academic advisement?
- What if I just do not know what to do with my future?
- With whom can I talk if I am not sure what to major in?
- How do I change my major?
- Who can help me improve my study habits?
- Where can I go for tutoring?

A university's counseling center and the academic advisement center are fantastic on-campus resources for African American students.

When many students start college, it can be an exhilarating but frightening time. Many of these students fail to ask for assistance and take advantage of the resources available to them. Students must recognize that everyone was a new student at one time, and no one becomes a guru of life as a college student in a few weeks or months. Feeling uncomfortable when one first comes to college is a natural occurrence. Now that you are on campus, you should remember to ask questions.

CONTACT HOURS AND COURSE LOAD

Contact hours are the number of hours that a student is actually in class receiving instruction. Contact hours and credit hours are terms that are closely related. Credit hours are the number of hours that students are given credit for receiving a passing grade in a course. Credit hour can differ from contact hour. Typically, credit hours range from 3 up to 12. The typical number of credit hours for one class is 3. There are a certain number of credit hours needed to receive a degree. Each school defines the total number and types of credits necessary for degree completion, with every course being assigned a value in terms of "credits." The number of credit hours taken by a student builds his or her course load. Course load is the number of courses or credits a student takes during a specific semester. Students may be asked the question, "How many hours are you taking this semester?."

Faculty members are required to hold office hours. Office hours are the hours of the day that professors are in their office so that a student can go and ask for assistance. Office hours are underutilized by most students. Professors expect students to use their judgment to decide when to come for office hours. Professors usually announce their office hours during first few sessions of classes. On Web-based courses, office hours are also posted on the first few sessions of the course opening. During online courses, office hours may be conducted through chat functions, Skype, or telephone.

Students are classified into either full-time or part-time. Full-time students are enrolled in 12 credit hours of courses, while part-time students are enrolled in six credit hours or less.

DROPPING AND ADDING COURSES

Every university has a procedure called the "drop and add" process. This procedure may differ from university to university, but the principle of allowing students to change their schedule underlies the process. This process may be completed by using a paper form or online depending on the university. Usually during the first 10 days, students are allowed to add courses to their schedule or switch times and days of classes to the schedule. At most universities, students may drop or add classes for the first 10 days of a semester, but after the 10th day of the semester, students may only drop courses. Only in exceptional circumstances are students allowed to add courses after the official drop-and-add period ends. Any addition after that period usually requires permission from the professor, dean, and registrar. Any changes to a student's schedule should be approved by an academic advisor or a faculty advisor. In general, a course dropped during the first four weeks of classes is not entered on the student's record. At most universities, students are responsible for the accuracy of their registration and any changes that they make to their schedules. Students should keep up with the accuracy of their course schedules through their university Web accounts.

TRANSFERRING

On occasion, students may find that they may want or need to transfer to another university. There are many reasons why students may transfer from one university to another. Some experience social or financial problems, which may lead to a decision to transfer. Some students may have trouble adjusting being away from home. Some students may realize that the school that they presently attend is not the right choice for them. Some students may not like the climate or the city where their university is located. Some students may not like the food, residence hall, or their roommate. Other reasons that students transfer include the need for spiritual enlightenment or political consciousness and to find their identity. Each academic year there are many students who transfer or consider transferring, so students should not be ashamed if they are considering transferring.

There are many factors that students should consider when making the decision to transfer. Students should determine why they want to transfer. They must determine if it would be an advantage or a disadvantage to transfer. Weighing the pros and cons of transferring will assist students in making the right decision for themselves. After deciding that transferring is the best option, there are several things that must take place such as researching potential four-year universities or whether a two-year school may be a better option. It is routine for students to transfer from a two-year college to a four-year university. However, there are instances where students transfer from a four-year institution to a two-year institution. Students may also want to consider if they will lose credits by transferring and if the university being considered offers the same major or a newly chosen major. When transferring to another university, students must present their college transcripts and in some cases their high school transcripts as well. The presentation of high school transcripts usually depends on the number of hours the student has completed in college.

Generally, grade "C" is the lowest course grade acceptable in a transfer. Some universities will sometimes accept a C or a D grade if the transfer student is from a university in their higher education system. Usually, remedial or development courses are not transferable. It is often difficult for transferring students to find on-campus housing, so it is best to do this early in the transfer process. Students should make sure that transferring does not become a pattern of moving from university to university. Students should also make sure that they have a solid plan of how a transfer fits into their long-term plans because a degree will be harder to obtain if there is not a plan for their academic career.

There are common types of transfer students. Students who have experienced academic trouble at one institution may decide to transfer to another. These students have not performed academically and may need a new environment to restart their higher education experience. They may not have been prepared for college because of poor study habits, or they may not have been emotionally ready and found the pace of studying, reading, and assignment too difficult to follow. These students may have been placed on probation or suspended from a particular university. In other cases, some students decide to drop out of college not because of grades but because of other circumstances, and years later, they return but enroll into another school.

Another type of transfer is students who have completed a two-year institution and wish to continue their studies at a four-year institution. This is probably the most common type of transfer. With this type of transfer students should make sure that all of the credits earned at their two-year institution will be counted at the four-year institution. In some cases, depending on the university's policy, they may have a limit on how much transfer credit students can be granted. If all credit will not be counted, then students should inquire about how many credits will count toward the degree they would like to pursue. Sometimes transferring students do not mind if they lose a few credits or even a semester because they believe the benefits outweigh the liabilities. When students transfer from one university to another, usually the university receiving the transferring students wants a letter of good standing or official indications from the former university. Students should also check to see if there are any residency requirements associated with transferring to the new school. Some universities may have a transfer residency requirement, which requires a student to take a certain number of courses and credits they must complete on campus to earn a degree. In some cases, students find themselves doing very well at the university they initially selected, and they decided that they may want to receive a degree from a more prestigious university. Sometimes the students realize that the academic challenges at a particular university are too great and they may choose to transfer to another college. Students should consider the following when thinking about transferring to another university:

- The school that is being considered is a good choice and fit. Students must do their homework.
- The school that is being considered has a comparable major or the new major the student desires.
- Whether the school being considered will accept transfer students who are on academic probation if that is the case.

It is probably not a good idea for a student to transfer if they are merely experiencing the freshmen blues and finding it a little difficult to adjust to college. If a student's loneliness is greater than that experienced by most students, then transferring may be an option. Students should not consider transferring if they have completed two years of study or if they are really close to completing their bachelor's degree. Many time students may receive bachelor's degrees in fields in which they have lost interest during their junior or senior year, but it was too late to switch majors or transfer. They then find it advantageous to obtain a graduate degree in another field. Students should not transfer if they do not have a well-thought-out plan with definite goals that are also reasonable. Lastly, students should probably not transfer to be closer to a boyfriend or girlfriend. Young students in particular should not make life decisions based on another individual. On many occasions, these relationships are temporary and it would be a bad practice to make a decision based on someone that is not your life partner. Students must make sure that whatever reason they want to transfer is the real reason and not a fictitious one.

ACADEMIC STATUS, PROBATION, SUSPENSION, AND READMISSION

One of the most important aspects of college is establishing a good grade point average. A student's grade point average is determined by the grades that they receive in individual courses and are tabulated over time. In general, a cumulative grade point average is determined by dividing the total number of points earned by the total number of grades or hours not passed satisfactorily. Grade point values per semester hour of credit differ slightly depending on school. Some universities utilize a plus/minus system in grading. If students maintain exceptional academic standing and excellent grade point average or above, they may receive specific designated honors such as magna cum laude, cum laude, and summa cum laude. If students fail courses, they may be placed on academic warning, academic probation, and academic suspension. When a student is placed on academic probation, their grade point average has fallen under a 1.00 for a particular term. If a student's cumulative grade point average has fallen below a 2.00, then they may be placed on academic warning. Students placed on academic warning may not enroll for more than 12 hours. By taking a limited number of hours, students should be able to improve their grades and avoid being placed on academic probation or academic suspension. Usually students placed on academic probation are limited in the number of hours they may enroll. A student on academic probation must achieve at least a 2.0 each grading period until good academic standing is reached or they could be academically suspended. After a student has been placed on academic suspension, he or she will have to reapply to be readmitted into the university and meet the conditions defined under the suspension.

Students who do not meet the normal standards of progress may be placed on probation. When a student is placed on probation, restrictions are placed on the students that may consist of a limited number of courses that a student may enroll in and involvement in extracurricular activities. Academic probation is a notification that a student's performance falls below a university's requirement for good academic standing. Students can avoid academic probation by keeping a grade point average above 2.0. At some universities, a student can be placed on academic probation because they have withdrawn from too many courses during a given semester. Standards for probation may be different depending on the policies set by the university. These requirements can be found in the university catalog. If a student is on probation and their grades fall below the required grade point average, he or she may face suspension from a university. At most colleges, if students are suspended, they will have to sit out for a designated time. This designated time can be from one semester to two semesters. If a student is suspended, they must apply for readmission before they can enroll in classes again. When students apply for readmission from suspension, there is no guarantee that they will be readmitted. The process varies depending on the university, but a student usually has to meet with an advisor or approach a committee to gain reentry. Once students gain readmission, they may have to meet certain requirements or conditions such as not enrolling over a certain number of hours or keeping a certain grade point average.

During a student's college career, they may find a need to withdraw from school. Withdrawal means that a student drops out of all courses during a current semester. Universities have a process that students must follow for official withdrawn from their classes. Simply choosing to not attend classes is not withdrawing from school. During a semester, a student may want to withdraw if there is an emergency, serious illness, or military duty. A student's financial situation may be affected if they choose to withdraw. A student's federal aid is awarded based on the percentage of time enrolled in courses for the semester. Depending on the date that a student withdraws, their student aid will be adjusted. The federal aid received during the semester is subject to the federal return calculation based on the effective date of withdrawal or the student's last documented date of attendance. The withdrawal date is determined by the instructors of your course. When a student withdraws, the grace period prior to repayment begins.

Students can use a nine-month grace period for Perkins Loan and a six-month grace period for Federal Stafford Loans. If a student re-enrolls before their grace period ends, he or she will have a new grace period when they leave school. Some students may choose to drop out of college. Dropping out of college is enrolling in college with the intent of pursuing a degree and the failure to complete a college education. People drop out for many reasons, and just because people drop out of college does not mean that they cannot become successful. If a student chooses to drop out of college, they should make sure that they have a career plan to pursue. While some students drop out, others may stop out. To stop out is to withdraw temporarily from higher education or employment in order to pursue another activity. With the rising cost of college, it is not so uncommon for students to stop and then return at a later date to continue pursuing their degrees. Just as when to drop out, students should have plans in place to determine how they will return to school after stopping out. After dropping out and stopping out, many students drift away from pursuing college education and never return.

DEAN'S LIST

The dean's list is a registry of students who have obtained excellent grades during a semester or term. The standard for making the dean's list varies among universities, but they all recognize high-achieving students and quality academic work. Typically, at least a grade point average of 3.5 is needed to be listed on the dean's list. Usually the dean's list applies only to undergraduate students, and the names of the students who made it to the dean's list are announced after each term. At some universities, the dean's list may also be called the president's list or the chancellor's list. If a student makes it to the dean's list for several consecutive terms, he or she will likely be selected for an honor society. Honor societies are groups that recognize excellence. Various honor societies have been established by various disciplines. Honor societies invite students who meet their requirements to join their membership. The organization usually has an induction ceremony to take in new members. Most of these organizations invite students to become members and do not accept unsolicited members. Observers at graduation ceremonies can distinguish honor graduates because each organization offers something that signifies membership like honor cords, medals, patches, or hoods to decorate the graduate's cap and gown. The oldest honor societies in the United States are the Golden Key, Phi Beta Kappa, and Phi Kappa Phi.

The Latin term *cum laude* means "with praise. Those who graduate with honors will be classified as cum laude, magna cum laude, or summa cum laude. At most universities, a cum laude graduate typically holds a grade point average of 3.5–3.7. A magna cum laude graduate usually means that a student got the second best category of grades with a grade point average of 3.8–3.9. The highest student honor is a summa cum laude graduate. A summa cum laude graduate usually holds a grade point average of 4.0.

TRADITIONS AND CEREMONIES

Most universities and colleges have time-honored traditions that help create the culture there. Many of these traditions and rituals add to the folklore associated with the school. Some of these traditions may be confusing and downright strange. Some traditions may be as simple as learning and singing the school's alma mater or school's fight song to camping out in tents to get prime seats at the basketball team's games to students being tossed in the university's fountain on their birthdays. These traditions should not be rooted in hazing, and students are urged to not participate in university traditions that involve hazing. Many universities have a ritual of passing through the school's main entrance or gate after graduation as a symbolic entrance into the real world.

Homecoming

Homecoming is a tradition at universities where alumni are welcomed back to campus. Homecoming usually offers events aimed at students and alumni. It is usually associated with sporting events, traditionally football games. If a university does not have a football team, then some schools build homecoming activities around a basketball game. If the university does not offer any sports programs, homecoming is billed as an event such as a picnic or some other social event. There is normally a parade and a competition for homecoming queen. This may be a pageant, or it may be simply an election where students vote for a queen and their attendants who represent the three classifications such as Miss Freshman, Miss Sophomore, Miss Junior, and Miss Senior. Other organizations and residence halls may also have representatives in this contest.

Founder's Day

Most universities and colleges have founder's day. This day is usually an annual event that entails a ceremony or university-wide programs that commemorate the beginning of the university. Many universities take this occasion as an opportunity to reflect on their histories and to connect their students with the traditions and history of the university. They also use this time to look toward the future and address the state of the university. At some universities, founder's day is a formal event, while at other universities, it may be a formal speech by a dignitary or distinguished alumnus; at other universities, founder's day is celebrated with carnival rides and vendor food and may have a homecoming-like atmosphere.

Convocation and Commencement

The term *convocation* literally means "calling together." Most universities have a convocation ceremony or university-wide program at the beginning of the fall semester. Some universities have more than one convocation per year. At some universities, convocations are public ceremonies at which all graduates are individually recognized and hooded by the dean of their academic college. At the type of convocation where students are hooded, this should not be misconstrued as conferring degrees.

EDUCATIONAL RECORDS, TRANSCRIPTS, GRADUATION, AND COMMENCEMENT EXERCISES

Students' education records are official and confidential documents protected by one of the nation's strongest privacy protection laws, the Family Educational Rights and Privacy Act (FERPA). An education record is information about any student that is maintained by a university and can include handwritten, printed, or digital content including birthdates; addresses; grades, test scores, courses, activities, and official school letters; disciplinary content; medical and health records; and other personal information.

Personal notes made by teachers and other school officials are not considered educational records. The most common educational record requested in higher education is a student's transcripts. Transcripts are records that are an inventory of grades, courses, and credits earned that a student has taken during their academic career. Transcripts also include records of all awards earned and the date when a student's degree was conferred. There are two types of transcripts: official transcripts and unofficial transcripts. Official transcripts are those records that are maintained and held by the university registrar. Unofficial transcripts are those records that can be made by the student. If a student wants to transfer or verify their graduation for a potential employer, official transcripts will be required.

Graduation is when a student has successfully completed all of the academic requirements in a degree-granting program. The student receives their diploma at a commencement ceremony. Graduation is the term used when a university awards students the actual degree. Many students who may be close to completing the number of hours in a particular degree-granting program may participate in the commencement ceremony, and their name may appear in the official program; however, this does not mean that they have graduated. Graduation is not completed until all degree requirements are recorded on the official transcript.

At a commencement exercise, faculty members wear colorful academic regalia. This regalia is steeped in tradition, which dates back to the Middle Ages. European universities began this tradition as they adopted them from church traditions. University faculty and students began to wear robes for distinction and warmth. American colleges began to wear these robes during the late 1800s. Graduation robes are traditionally black in color; however, universities have adapted the colors of robes according to their school colors. Bachelor's gowns may have pointed sleeves, while master's gowns have long closed sleeves that have an arch near the bottom and an arm opening. Doctoral gowns have wide velvet panels and bello-shaped sleeves with three horizontal bars on each arm. In addition to the graduation robes, mortar boards or doctoral tams are worn.

The color of the lining of the hood represents the university awarding the degree. The color of the facing of the hood reflects the academic discipline of the wearer's highest degree. The colors awarded for graduate degrees are light blue, gold, sapphire blue, white, gold and white, pink, and brown depending on the degree granted. At most university graduations, each school is noted by a procession of people carrying banners. These banners represent the university and other academic colleges. At commencement ceremonies, several categories of students are recognized. Magna cum laude are graduates who have achieved cumulative grade point averages of 3.60–3.74. These students have achieved grade point averages of 3.8–3.9 The summa cum laude are graduates of "highest distinction." They are graduates who have achieved a grade point average of 4.0 throughout their time in college.

The college experience affords students the opportunity to meet new people and learn in a wide range of disciplines. Some people may not see the value of a college education, but college graduates have more career opportunities and usually have larger salaries than high school graduates. The college experience is an excellent place for African Americans to establish networks with a variety of people and assist students in building social capital. College also helps students to learn formal and informal codes of conduct and standards of behavior established in the larger society. A university is a place where students can learn how to work, appropriate wardrobe selections, and suitable behavior. Many African American students state that their parents inspired the goal of going to college. Other African American students state that it was a high school teacher who motivated and encouraged them to go on to college. The college experience allows students to engage in self-exploration and discover who they truly are. Parts I, II, and III of this book have prepared students for things that they may face on campus. Part IV provides numerous vignettes of successful African Americans in various fields who provide their personal stories of how they navigated college and reached their goal—graduation. Their stories should serve as motivation and inspiration for African American college students.

FURTHER READINGS

Bradbury-Haehl, Nora, and Bill McGarvey. *The Freshman Survival Guide: Soulful Advice for Studying, Socializing, and Everything in Between.* New York: Center Street, 2011.

Henderson, C. W. *Open the Gates to the Ivy League: A Plan B for Getting into the Top Colleges.* New York: Penguin Publishing Group, 2013.

Jacobs, Lynn F., and Jeremy S. Hyman. *Professors' Guide to Getting Good Grades in College.* New York: HarperCollins Publishers, 2006.

LaVeist, Thomas. *Daystar Guide to Colleges for African-American Students.* New York: Kaplan Publishing; 2000.

Myers McGinty, Sarah. *The College Application Essay*, 6th ed. New York: College Board, 2015.

Orr, Tamara. *America's Best Colleges for B Students: A College Guide for Students Without Straight A's.* Belmont, CA: SuperCollege Publishing, 2013.

Walker, Sheryl. *The Black Girl's Guide to College Success: What No One Really Tells You about College That You Must Know.* Bloomington, IN: Authorhouse, 2007.

Wilson, Erlene, B. *100 Best Colleges for African-American Students.* New York: Plume Publishing, 1998.

PART IV

This Is How We Did It: Our Undergraduate Experiences

In this section, various individuals who have obtained undergraduate and graduate or professional degrees provide advice for African American students seeking higher education. All participants believe that college years are a critical time for African American students. The participants' demographics and backgrounds are varied. Participants are both male and female and come from large families and small families. Some attended predominately white colleges and others historically black college and universities. They have varied majors that range from business to social work. While in college, participants were involved in various extracurricular activities. Some participants were members of Greek-lettered organizations while others were not.

Each participant was asked to respond to 15 questions about their undergraduate experiences in college. There were a few common themes that emerged from the participants' responses. It is apparent that most of the participants' motivations to enroll in college were their parents or the opportunity to have better lives. They found that having strong support systems were important to their success, and this support came from their family and friends. Participants also discussed their campus resources and how they took advantage of those resources in adjusting to college life. All of these graduates found that they needed some guidance, but they also believe that it is important for students to have the ability to figure some things out on their own as well. The graduates also found that they had to adjust to their college environment and different living arrangements. All participants found time management as one of the most important skills and a key to college success. For the most part, all participants found that professors and staff were helpful in navigating college. Participants found their undergraduate experience rewarding and urged African American students to stay focused on getting their degrees.

Laurian Bowles

Undergraduate Major: Journalism and African American Studies
Highest Degree Obtained: Doctorate of Philosophy in Anthropology
Parent(s) Occupation: Registered Nurses (both parents)
Current Occupation: Assistant Professor of Anthropology at Davidson College

It was a combination of my parents and the personnel at my high school who were the driving force in my decision to go to college. I went to a college prep high school in Philadelphia. There the expectation was that students were going to attend college and that was the primary reason why students were enrolled there. My family was always forward thinking and going to college was a goal that they expected of me. I chose my undergraduate institution, a public institution, due to affordability. I was not really aware of the funding that was available for private institutions. So, I looked for a school that was fairly affordable. I did not transfer to another institution, and part of the reason why I did not transfer is that I had a good scholarship. I had a good support network at home. I had lots of friends from my high school who attended my college, Penn State University. So I did not see the need to think about transferring.

The transition from high school to college was very different and I might even say challenging because I went to a very diverse and multicultural minded high school with kids from the city of Philadelphia. My high school was very urban, very cosmopolitan kind of high school. I found the university setting more difficult because it was more segregated. It was a little bit different for me. I find it important not only to take courses with people but also to engage with them in a social setting. There were some difficulties because there were so many cultural backgrounds and in some cases this can be a combustible mix. When there is diversity, including differing opinions, philosophies, and political beliefs, it can be difficult. This also holds true when there are people from rural backgrounds mixing with people from northern urban, cosmopolitan backgrounds. It was not until I went to college that I realized how much my high school experience really informed my outlook about things like race and gender. It was when I spent time with people who were very different from me and had different politics that I realized how different my experiences were. There were some students not truly used to dealing with difference. This experience was my education beyond the classroom.

In college, I did not know that I would immediately succeed, but I knew that I had to succeed. The demands and expectations that I had for myself were high based on my educational experience. I was very confident in my abilities. My confidence stems from the confidence my parents' had in my ability and had instilled in me since childhood. My mantra is "If everyone else believes that I can do it then I'm sure that I can do it!" Coming out of high school, I always felt smart, but I do not believe that I had a good understanding of the tools or the tricks that were required to be successful in college. I did not realize that college was not just about being smart, but it was also about having good study skills and about going to talk to your professor, and that there are certain rules of higher education that one needs to follow in order to be a successful student beyond just being able to take exams well. So it took me a little bit of time in my freshman year to really realize the institutional demands of school and not just the academic demands of being at school. Mentorship played a role in my successfully completing college. There was a minority advisor in my major; having this person as a contact person contributed to my success as an undergraduate student. Every college at Penn State had a diversity or minority advisor whose job was to make contact with students of color and talk to them about their success and challenges.

I financed my college education from varied sources. I received a scholarship. I also received a grant, and I supplemented my tuition by employment on campus to help reduce costs. I did not take out student loans for my undergraduate schooling because in my sophomore year I signed up to become a resident assistant, which provided free housing, meals, and even a stipend for students at Penn State. My tuition was covered by a scholarship and I was able to work as a resident assistant at the university to cover the rest of my academic financial needs. The friendships and relationships I gained in college were very valuable. The most important relationships I had as an undergraduate were mostly with friends and not so much with staff. I had some really great professors who became mentors and later friends.

I believe that race and gender identity affected my experience as an undergraduate student. Being an African American student at a predominately white institution in a rural community in Pennsylvania was very difficult and very challenging because of the cultural shock that I experienced. I remember the first day of class as an undergraduate; my friend (who is also African American) and I went to have lunch at a restaurant to celebrate being college students. This was the first negative experience in college. As three white students exited the restaurant, they yelled, "Hey you black nigger bitches go home." This was my first experience of racism at my undergraduate institution. I had been in school only for about a week, and this incident really set the tone for my freshman year narrative. I quickly realized that I was in a different atmosphere, and I was going to have to deal with outright racism and those fears associated with it. I drew on my inner strength and the teachings of my parents. They told me from a very early age that sometimes I will have to work twice as hard to get half as far because I am a black woman. I recognized that as early as I faced this notion as my reality, the quicker I could get over my sense of unfairness. I believe this helped me quickly recover from that experience.

I do not have many disappointments that I directly can attribute to my undergraduate experience. I do regret that I did not apply to an Ivy League institution. If I had to do it all over again, I would have applied to more heavily endowed private institutions. This might have expanded my economic and social network after graduation. It is a small regret and I do reflect on this from time to time.

I used several strategies to successfully complete my undergraduate degree. I always talked to my graduate professors even if I just went by their offices to introduce myself to them. I believe this is so important for African American students. I also took advantage of the writing center and the math center and the psychology center and all of the other types of centers that were available. I made appointment with those folks at the beginning of the semester before I even turned in my first assignment just to get a sense of the services offered and talk to tutors in those centers. I asked questions like, "Hey this is what this assignment says and this is what I'm thinking is how I will complete it? Am I on the right track?"

Good time management is essential to being a great student. As an undergraduate, I lived by a calendar; I always used the calendar to keep up with assignments and events. During my sophomore year, I did not always schedule study time, but I always scheduled writing time in my day because I had a very writing-intensive major. I was focused and made statements like, "After dinner, I am going to work on 'X' no matter what." I did schedule that in a formal way and it helped keep things organized.

My advice for current or future African American undergraduate students to be successful is to at least once engage with all of the student support services that might be available at your institution and see whether or not it works for you. African American students must have several mentors instead of just one. Everyone thinks about having a guru mentor, but this might not be as effective as calling upon the expertise of multiple mentors. In using multiple mentors, students use the expertise of one person about specific topics and another about other topics. I believe that students should have at least three or four mentors. I have discovered that some people ask for a mentor and do not know exactly what they want to get from the mentoring relationship. It is best practice to think about what that person can add to your knowledge, skills, and abilities before you ask them to become a mentor because not everyone is going to be helpful in everything. Also seek out upper-class students who are studious and very successful, and talk to them about what are some of the things they did regarding study skills, habits, etc.

I was not religious or spiritual in college. I did not attend church when I was in college. I did not engage in any type of religious fervor during my undergraduate career nor was I part of a sorority as an undergraduate, and neither these institutions shaped my views of masculinity or femininity. As an undergraduate, I started paying closer attention to how patriarchy our society is and the unfairness of views and double standards in regards to men and women. I believe that it is quite unjust for college-age males to be able to do certain things or engage in certain activities and not be seen as problematic. However, when a female engages in the same activity, it becomes highly problematic in the social scene especially with the types of sexual relationships that people are allowed to have and not be seen as a "slut" or a "ho." People are socialized differently and I believe that these double standards are unfair.

I believe students should have an acute level of awareness of institutional racism; they should not personalize an individual experience, but see it as a structural phenomenon. Depersonalizing racism can help African American students avoid internalizing the challenges that they can face as undergraduate students. I believe looking at racism structurally helps students navigate racism and racist spaces. I also believe that thinking about it in terms of structure and not taking it personally is what makes people successful. I advise students to seek out good mentors who are also African American, so they can talk to them about some of the issues of race, class, and gender that they may be facing. African American students should surround themselves with other proactive and productive classmates and they should be forward thinking. Students should take a wide range of classes in terms of not just what they like or the easy classes, but the ones that can help them build a diverse skill set so that it could be used for a variety of different arenas.

Christina Calloway

Undergraduate Major: English with a minor in Public Relations
Highest Degree Obtained: Juris Doctor
Parent(s) Occupation: Father—retired military (Army) personnel; Mother—Counselor (MA in Social Work) with a religious, nonprofit organization for girls
Current Occupation: Attorney with Georgia state government

My mother motivated me to apply to and attend college. My mother was not raised with an understanding that you could attend college after high school; however, as she grew into adulthood, she understood the importance of education and its effect on one's life. She always stressed to my siblings and me that in order to be better (than her and have a better life) we would have to have a post-secondary education. Due to her influence, I was raised thinking that there was not any other option after high school but to go to college.

Due to the military family lifestyle, my father was stationed to another installation in another state the summer before my junior year of high school. I had planned to go to college in the state where we were previously living; however, upon moving to Georgia, my mother researched the educational opportunities and learned about the H.O.P.E. scholarship, which pays for Georgia students to attend state universities and colleges. I applied to the University of Georgia because I was influenced by so many students at my high school who were applying to that school. Once I was accepted, I did not even think about whether I would like the school, the campus, the atmosphere, etc. I just understood that it was one of the best (if not the best) universities in Georgia. Once I began attending, I realized the University of Georgia was not the best fit for me and I transferred within the first semester of freshman year to Georgia Southern University. I knew about this university only because I had an older cousin who was attending Georgia Southern and it turned out to be the perfect fit for me.

As you can see, most of my decisions about choosing schools were influenced by others. As stated above, I knew that I had to attend college after high school, but I had no understanding about what I was looking for in choosing a school that would suit my needs. As a cheeky aside, I guess it is good to know my "influencers" had great educational options!

The transition was more uncomfortable than difficult. I have a really close-knit family, so throughout high school I was always touting how I was so ready to leave home and get some space. When I finally attended the University of Georgia (living on campus), I was incredibly lonely and homesick. This speaks to the fact that I did not research the size of the student population, housing options, and class size. The class sizes were intimidating and I found it difficult to make friends with such a large student population. These feelings helped influence my decision to transfer to another university (Georgia Southern University). Although I did not do any research of Georgia Southern, besides knowing that my cousin was attending there, I felt more comfortable with the student population, class size, the city it is located in, etc. Surprisingly once I got adjusted, the transition into postsecondary academia was seamless. My only struggle was the discipline of actually attending classes; once I discovered that no one could tell you to go or get up and be on time, I thought that was one of the greatest things in the world and that realization almost threatened my focus.

I believed I knew I would immediately succeed in my coursework; I have always been a diligent, focused, and determined student. I also did not want to disappoint my parents and family as one of the first in my family to go to college right after high school and start the path toward getting a college degree. It took a little time for me to become confident socially. In college, mostly everyone is extremely intelligent and talented, which may seem intimidating when you are trying to develop and establish yourself in the campus community. Through joining organizations and becoming an active member of my campus community, I was able to become more confident in my social skills.

As an undergraduate student, I received the H.O.P.E. scholarship from the state of Georgia. This scholarship paid tuition and some book costs. As a result, my parents were responsible only for my housing costs (I did not have a vehicle or live off-campus during my first year of college). My parents applied for Parent Plus loans to cover those costs. During college, I also applied for university scholarships (receiving two) and worked part-time to defer costs. I was able to maintain the H.O.P.E. scholarship throughout my entire tenure at Georgia Southern University, which definitely helped me financially (and kept my family and me mostly debt free throughout).

The important relationships are those that I had/have with friends from college. To this day, I am still good friends with the majority of the people that I developed close relationships with while in college. I can say also there were some amazing professors who had an influence on my life and, to this day, have assisted in writing references on my behalf, providing advice, etc. Those relationships were and continue to be definitely important as well.

The University of Georgia is probably one of the first places in my lifetime where I felt inherently "black." The student population and class size immediately highlighted the fact that I was a minority and there is a noticeable divide between students of different ethnicities. I remember distinctly being in a freshman course of over 200 people and there may have been less than 20 black people in the class. Although I did not experience any type of blatant racism, it was one of the first times in my life I was kind of put of notice about being a minority. This may be difficult to understand from someone not coming from a military background, but growing up in that background, everyone is new and different, etc., so being a minority is not highlighted as much (or did not seem to be). I definitely would not tell someone to not choose a university for this reason because ultimately it is your education that is the priority, but I would definitely recommend researching the schools you are interested in and think about your comfort level and possible experience in advance. I believe that comfort directly affects your success in school. At Georgia Southern University, the student population is predominately white; however, there is a comparable number of minority students (and when I say minority I mean all, Hispanic, black, Asian, etc.). I immediately felt more comfortable in classes, seeing professors of different ethnicities and backgrounds, etc., and I did not feel like my gender identity was necessarily an issue at either institution.

Upon entering college, I did not handle any disappointments or failures well because I would feel like I was disappointing my family. I would not talk about struggles or issues because everyone seemed to be counting on me to succeed and do it flawlessly. I definitely had to develop an understanding on how to deal with issues by being open and honest and speaking to others about them as well as learning how to resolve issues. College is also about becoming an adult and learning how to handle issues in a mature way. I was able to do this by being very honest with myself about mistakes, disappointments, and failures and taking realistic measures to deal with any issues (not always expecting my parents to "fix" things for me). I did not have set schedules for studying, etc. I was really focused when I needed to read or complete assignments, write a paper (and I mean actually write, not type), etc. I would set the time to get things completed but no particular strategies.

I would suggest African American students to stay focused! I always tell students at whatever level of education that college has nothing to do with "being smart" or "incredibly bright"; it mostly has to do with focus. If you focus on your goals, then you will succeed and accomplish them. I learned in my freshman year when I was missing classes, sleeping in, and expecting to just read the chapter and do well on an exam that it was not going to work that way because I started receiving grades I had never seen in my life. That propelled me to be better focused on the reason I was in college, which was to ultimately earn and receive a degree.

I was religious but I did not practice my religion (outside of praying) while I was in college. During my last two years, I did start attending church (Christian), tithing, and becoming more active in church. I grew up with extremely traditional views on gender roles. However, in college, my views on femininity changed because I was developing a strongly independent lifestyle and was not focused on being in college to get married, find a mate, etc. Even though my family wanted me to succeed in college, it seems they also wanted me to focus on "finding a husband," which points to a very traditional view of gender roles. What I feel college presented to me was an understanding of financial and professional independence outside of a relationship with a man, which allows for focus on the intrinsic aspects of a relationship instead of the traditional values of a male maintaining the financial and professional stability.

Ultimately, I believe that African American students need a strong support system, which includes family, friends, and developing relationships with professors in school. Even though the number of African Americans who are obtaining postsecondary education is increasing, it is still fairly disproportionate to white students and among gender; that being said, African Americans may be more likely to be the first to attend college in their family, etc. It is important for African Americans to try to align themselves with and develop relationships with their (college-educated) people and other like-minded individuals so that they understand the many options for majors, schools, environments, etc.; that way applying to and attending college will be a more seamless transition.

Algerian Hart

Undergraduate Major: Sociology minor in Black Studies
Highest Degree Obtained: PhD
Parent(s) Occupation: Pre-K and K–12 Educators (retired)
Current Occupation: Graduate Coordinator/Assistant Professor, Department of Kinesiology

I did not apply to my undergraduate institution. Actually, my father filled in the information as a back-up plan without my knowledge. At the time I had come off of my senior season competing in both football and track and field. I was recruited by University of Southern California (USC), University of California Los Angeles (UCLA), Notre Dame University, University of Nevada Las Vegas (UNLV), University of Colorado, University of Florida, University of Michigan, Southern University, University of Utah, University of California Santa Barbara, San Diego State, Cornel University, and Columbia University. However, upon injury during my football season, many of the offers went away. After a successful track-and-field season, scholarship offers to compete for Southern University, Cal State Northridge, and the University of Utah and to walk on at UCLA had promise. Ultimately, I had a conversation with the head coach at Long Beach State University (my father's back-up plan) and earned a track scholarship.

During my time as an undergraduate, I did not transfer, although after my freshman track-and-field season, I was contacted by several coaches and considered transferring schools for the opportunity to play football again. The ultimate deterrent occurred when I was made captain by my teammates and coach. This vote of confidence in my leadership made me accountable to my institution and team. Yet having the beach a quarter mile away from campus was a great encourager to stay.

I graduated from a strong academic high school where attending college was a common conversation. The curriculum, advisors, college fairs, and college prep classes were of great benefit to my transition into college. Throughout high school I never achieved beyond a mid-range 3.0. After my first semester of college, I held a 4.0 GPA.

Confidence was not an issue. My study skills were decent, and I was aware of the campus resources because all freshmen were required to take a summer bridge class that introduced us all to the available resources across campus. In addition, we had great academic support services within athletics. While I had a few academic challenges in some core courses, I was confident about graduating.

I received strong financial aid along with a scholarship. During my time in college, the Pell Grant A and B were funding schools near 100 percent. In addition, supplemental funding was available that included alumni monies and small institutional loans to encourage minority students to complete school. My parents, aunts, uncles, and grandmother were supportive of my undergraduate fiscal needs. In addition, I worked every summer and most of throughout my junior and senior year for the City of Long Beach. The university created partnerships with various entities to assist athletes in finding employment. The partnerships between the university and City Parks and Recreation created jobs that assisted many of my teammates and me to pay bills beyond rent and for incidentals.

Family was always around if and when I needed them, but for the most part, it was my coach and teammates. I had a great roommate and was blessed to have arguably one of the most conscious Black Studies programs in the nation. The faculty in the Black Studies program demanded greatness and created a place of strength, expectation, acknowledgment, and truth. The faculty ranged from Maulana Karenga (department chair) and Omawali Fowles (English professor, Harvard educated) to Paul Williams (first black music history PhD at USC) to Ahmen Rah (seasoned scholar) and a host of others that graduated from premier colleges and universities across the nation. One could make the case that we, as young black men and women, had a highly conscious HBCU faculty accountability structure at a PWI.

Although Long Beach State University was in the heart of Southern California, and there is the perception that it was a progressive state during the 1980s and 1990s, our campus was the recruiting hub for the John Birch Society, Skin Heads, and various White Supremacist groups. Only several miles from the boarders of Orange County, California, many of the described groups flourished within these areas. Our campus life was typically cordial outside of the occasional Aryan Nation or Skin Head flyer. Campus police were somewhat harassing (pulled over for no reason and asked for ID) but not as ornery as the surrounding communities, that is, Signal Hill P.D. (for example, Ron Settles's hanging in the jail cell, circa

1981/1982) and Long Beach P.D. (poor relationship with minority hiring and diverse populations). There was an ever-present tension outside of our classrooms masked by the laid-back Southern Cal vibe, filled with palm trees and rolling green lawns. Our campus was a powder keg that was right next to the epicenter for the civil unrest during the Rodney King trial. Racism was met head-on, and the explosion of the South Central riots was in our campus backyard. As a whole, my campus experience had moments of tension, but elements of cross-cultural inclusion sprouted post King riots.

Primarily, I confided in my teammates and several family members. When it came to academic failures, I went to the Black Studies faculty because there was always an open-door policy for us. Although the athletic department had a student-athlete support services unit, it was not always a comfortable space for minority student athlete social issues/concerns.

As a student-athlete we were pretty much locked into a matriculation model that was connected to eligibility and scholarship. While I did not graduate in four years, I did take advantage of a four-term structure. These terms were fall, winter, spring, and summer sessions. My plan was to take more difficult philosophy, core science, and field science courses during the off-session, that is, winter and summer, to have a singular focus to achieve the best possible outcome. After a poor spring semester of core classes during season, I learned from a senior teammate on how best to take advantage of the system to produce high marks. Mentorship is vital. Having a springboard to bounce questions and concerns off provides a comfort level that nourishes confidence not regularly delivered by faculty across PWIs. Identifying a plan for major or career exploration exposes black students to an arena that many of their peers access. This exploration often leads to internships and other professional development opportunities that can lead to jobs or postgraduate prospects. The key to success is peer group association. Having friends and associates across campus in different majors, holding diverse beliefs and ideas, serving, working, sharing, and willing to challenge your development is critical to student retention and success.

I was active in my Christian faith. I participated in student-athletes for Christ, Double Rock Baptist Church, and occasionally visited my home AME Church. I regularly attended Bible study and shared my faith with others across campus and within the community. I also received constant support and encouragement from the Brothers of Alpha Phi Alpha Fraternity, Inc. and my teammates, many of whom were members of Kappa Alpha Psi Fraternity, Inc. Individuals from each of these organizations were instrumental in my path toward degree completion. In addition, the social support and cultivation by the members of Alpha Kappa Alpha, Delta Sigma Theta, and Sigma Gamma Rho was of great encouragement throughout my undergraduate journey.

My views were very AME centered and male dominant. These views have certainly been developed and matured over the years from travel both abroad and domestic via exposure to diverse beliefs, ideas, and philosophies. However, my core tenets of faith and Christ-centered value have not changed.

I was helped by having a strong consistent faith and identifying with a family unit. For African American students, accessible mentorship is vital. I am talking about mentorship that will pour encouragement and examples of success into them. African American students should seek reliable friends who will challenge your success mission until its completion. It is important for black students that they have an example who has completed the undergraduate journey, so they can have firsthand account of the potential pitfalls and challenges that will arise during their time on campus.

I was track-and-field student-athlete. It was very much a part of my identity throughout my undergraduate experience. It provided obstacles and challenges that translated into academic success. Injuries, conflict, character development, and leadership growth attributed to my success story. Being a captain was monumental to my confidence and value of self. Participating in sports and having a responsibility for others on my team fostered a dominant identity that I rely upon today. This experience sparked relationships and earned respect that exists among a number of my teammates, competitors, and former coaches today. The level of hard work and sacrifice to become a Division 1 student-athlete and compete among your peers is an experience I thank the Lord I had. The obstacles, defeat, triumphs, and challenges all mixed into one have made me a better man and pushed me to pursue academic and athletic balance.

C. Douglas Johnson

Undergraduate Major: Business
Highest Degree Obtained: Doctorate of Philosophy
Parent(s) Occupation: Deceased
Current Occupation: Professor at Georgia Gwinnett College

The main motivation to apply and attend college was to ensure that I had options and an opportunity to travel beyond the confines of the street where I grew up. I wanted options because it was assumed that I would graduate high school (or not) and get a "good job" in one of the local textile mills. I am not suggesting there is anything wrong with working in a textile mill, as I did work there one summer while in college to earn money to pledge a fraternity. That one summer was enough to confirm that I needed a college degree. Another motivation to attend college was I wanted to be in a professional position where I would not have to work in the elements and could wear a coat and tie each day if I chose to do so. I was also motivated to attend college in order to honor my mother's memory and make her proud as she passed away from breast cancer two months prior to my fifth birthday.

My undergraduate institution was chosen because I attended a summer camp there as a rising high school junior and was convinced they had the best program in the state for an aspiring business executive with a focus on accounting and finance. I also met some great friends that summer who planned on going there as it was (is) one of the highest regarded institutions in the state of South Carolina. I attended Clemson University for the four years of my program. I really didn't feel a need to transfer as I had a wonderful experience and was actively engaged in various facets of college life, from Student Government Association (SGA) to gospel choir, from work study job to college ambassador. Further, there wasn't any other college at the time that I thought would be comparable, and I had to finish there within four years to prove those who said I could not and would not wrong.

I had a very smooth transition from high school to college, and I attribute this in large part to being academically prepared and motivated to succeed in college. Further, I was conditionally accepted, so I had to start the summer immediately following high school graduation. I had less than a week to transition, but this turned out to be a great experience and opportunity as I met some great friends that I remain in touch with today some 30 years later. There were also smaller classes and fewer people on campus, so I was able to become very comfortable with navigating the campus and ensuring I was "college material." After my first exam, I was convinced that I would be successful. At the end of the summer, I had a solid grade point average and felt really confident going into the fall semester. My confidence soared from there and only wavered when I started to debate whether or not I was in the correct major. I did have a scholarship (James F. Byrnes Scholarship) that provided more support than your traditional scholarship. We had to meet as a cohort on campus, as well as attend a "Super Weekend" event with scholars from other campus each year in the spring, as well as a summer luncheon where we were introduced to the new scholars. We also had touch points with various members of the foundation throughout the year. This additional support was beneficial as we had our Byrnes's brothers and sisters to encourage us, and all shared the commonality of having lost one or both parents. While they were supportive, the requirements to maintain the scholarship were not that stringent (maintain a 2.0 GPA each semester). This scholarship was awarded based on academic merit, financial need, South Carolina resident, and loss of one or both parents. I also had Pell grants and loans as my family did not have the means of paying for my college career, nor were they all fully supportive and encouraging of me attending college.

Interestingly, some of my family (sister, brothers) were supportive to an extent, but some of my most important relationships were formed while at college. Unfortunately, I did not have many professors who were that supportive or encouraging, but I did form strong relationships with my work study supervisor and the student affairs staff that were advisors/mentors to SGA. I still maintain some of those relationships. I also had the support of my fraternity brothers and advisor, who were an excellent mentor and supporter. There were some friends from high school who attended Clemson with me that I maintained and many new friendships that were formed through my affiliation with SGA and the gospel choir.

The percentage and number of African American students were relatively low, and as a result we were a fairly close-knit group. Even if we were not the best of friends, we still came together at critical times. I do feel that my racial identity did have an impact on my college experience, but in most ways it became a positive. I became a lot more aware of my racial identity while in college. My high school was similar in terms of racial makeup; however, I was able to embrace my cultural heritage and identity without fear of direct discrimination or retaliation. Overall, there was not any outright or institutional racism. I did have one experience that adversely affected me that still makes me question whether I was living in reality and the environment was more hostile than I gave it credit. I had just been elected the SGA vice president and was feeling positive as I was about to enter my senior year on schedule. I was walking across campus and a pickup truck drove by and the driver shouted, "Go home you Nigger." This hit me really hard, but I saw it as an opportunity to attempt to make a difference and know that we had a lot of work to do as a student government. I wasn't sure if that person was a student or a person from the community. Either way, it was an unfortunate incident, but I took it as that individual's ignorance and not an indication of how the vast majority of people affiliated with the campus felt, but it was also a reminder that not everyone saw my personal worth or respected me as a fellow human being.

Overall, I had a very positive experience as an undergraduate. I would say that some of my biggest disappointments were with myself (e.g., not performing as well in a particular class or during a given semester; not getting the girl), and I knew I had not put forth the effort that I should have or that things were beyond my control, so I could not let it stop me from persevering. I looked at prior experiences and the fact that I needed to be a role model for my younger cousins and family to keep me motivated and focused on the goal at hand. I'd had many major disappointments prior to college, so I knew not to take things personally and remain focused on what I wanted to achieve. As an undergraduate, I was extremely involved, which required me to be extremely organized. I would use a calendar and to-do lists on the regular. I was committed to finishing the degree in four years, so I always had a plan and checked it regularly to ensure I was on track to complete the degree, but also knew that I wanted to be involved during my tenure there, and all this helped me remain focused.

One of the things that I wish someone had told me was how important it was to develop relationships not only with your peers but also with your professors. Depending on the person and the school, most professors are open and want you to succeed. At the end of my undergraduate career, I did not have professors whom I could go to for letters of recommendation or career advice. I believe that adversely affected me when I went on the job market. Now, not having a job at graduation was a major disappointment that I didn't mention earlier and I do not feel that was totally my fault. I think I would tell potential students that holistic development is important, but you have to have a solid grade point average, or the involvement will mean very little. My teaching philosophy now is "To Know. To Care. To Act." and I firmly believe that a student needs to understand that it is important for them to learn the course content, have compassion and want to apply it, and then go forth and make a difference. They need to understand it is not all about them, and they are there for a bigger purpose as they need to teach others as they learn and help others climb as they advance. I would also share with them the importance of relationships and building social capital with their human capital.

In college I was spiritual and I still hold that spirituality; it is still important to me. In order to maintain my connection, I was a member of the gospel choir and we were constantly traveling to perform at various churches. When we did not have an engagement, I attended church almost every Sunday as this was a large part of my identity and I knew that without God I could not achieve anything. He had been my source of hope and inspiration all my life, and it continued while I was in college.

I was a very active member of a historically black fraternity and remain active with Kappa Alpha Psi Fraternity today. Upon entry in college, I did not feel as if I would pursue membership in a fraternity as I am a fairly independent, strong-willed person and do not deal with cliques that well; however, given the dynamics experienced in high school and beginning with college, I wanted to see if I could establish relationships with like-minded African American males. Further, while I have biological brothers, we were not similar relative to our academic pursuits/interests, and becoming a Kappa gave me a forum to pursue some of the things I wanted to do in the community and on campus. Initially, I was attracted to Kappa because they stepped with a cane and I wanted to do the same, and they did not actively recruit (I was turned off by recruiting by some of the other fraternities who made me feel as if they wanted me to join to bring popularity to their organization or other ulterior motives that did not seem pure). As I learned more about the organization and their purpose of achievement and the role of community service and training for leadership, I was more convinced this was the right organization for me. I tell my students now that I had a double major and a minor: Kappa and SGA were my majors, and accounting was my minor. With that said, membership enhanced my overall college experience and I do not think it would have been as memorable as it was had it not been for Kappa. At times, I did put Kappa before everything else, and as a result my grade point average was not as high as it may have been, but knowing my personality I would have likely invested the time elsewhere as I knew that I did not want to be an accountant and needed other stimuli to keep me engaged in college. I certainly agree with the research that those who are engaged in other activities are more likely to progress and graduate from college. I was doing it not only for me but also for the reputation of my fraternity.

I do not recall giving much thought to masculinity or femininity while in college, unless jokingly as it relates to stereotypes of certain fraternities or more seriously when certain attributions made about close friends who were female athletes. I think I view it a little differently now as I have additional information on the social construction versus a biological phenomenon. It is far more complex than I thought growing up and while in college. I believe strong will, determination, and resilience are key factors relative to success for African American undergraduates as they are not afforded the benefits of white privilege and may experience discrimination based on stereotypes and lowered expectations. Other than that I think the elements are very similar to non–African American students. I was not an athlete in college by choice. I decided not to pursue an athletic scholarship at a smaller, lesser known college to attend Clemson. It was a difficult decision as I love track and field, but didn't see where I would have a career in that field. I did attend some sporting events from a social perspective mainly. I attended women's basketball on a regular basis as one of my close friends since first grade played on the team. I attended football games on a regular basis after pledging as that was expected—at least through half time.

I have few regrets about college, but I wish I would have accepted the internship that I was offered as that may have helped me decide earlier that accounting was not the right career for me or that I had taken advantage of the services offered by the career services. Also, I wish I had participated in study/educational abroad experiences. I guess those would be things I'd add to my response of advice to give to students.

Joi Reed Fairell

Undergraduate Major: Political Science
Highest Degree Obtained: Juris Doctorate
Parent(s) Occupation: Educator and Truck Driver
Current Occupation: Attorney

When I was growing up, the option of going to college was a constant goal, and my parents did not present me with the option of not applying for college. Not going to college was honestly not something that I even thought about. I always knew I would go to college, but where I would go became a big question. I chose to attend Georgia Southern University because it provided a small college setting but with a large college atmosphere. I also knew this school would provide me with growth because there was a plan that had been implemented and this university had plans to grow, and I wanted to be a part of that growth. Unlike some students, I did not find my transition from high school to college very difficult. I had always been a responsible high school student and had been successful in managing both academics and extracurricular activities. In high school I was a very active student. I participated in several organizations and I was employed throughout my entire high school career. When I started college, I realized that I had learned many of the valuable skills needed to become a successful college student. I discovered that by juggling my job and classwork, I had mastered the same type of time management skills that are greatly needed to be a successful college student, so it was a smooth transition.

In college, I continued with many of the time management techniques that I had utilized in high school. I had a schedule filled with "to do" tasks. Therefore,

I kept a handwritten calendar that helped me manage everything. Even though my calendar was usually packed with activities, I still found time to take part in normal college activities such as attending sporting events and social outings. I was very confident that I would succeed in college and now I am confident as an attorney; failing is not an option that I have ever considered. Sometimes things were difficult, but I never gave up on my dream of graduating and becoming an attorney.

I had a great support system that included my family and friends. I also had great support from my professors and other employees at the university. The best support that I received while in college were the friendships that I developed in college; many of us became lifelong friends. We fed off of each other. We motivated each other; when someone was down, the others would pick them up. Having a great group of friends allowed me to stay focused and prevented me from becoming involved with the wrong crowd.

I did not receive any financial support from my family. It was difficult, but I financed my entire education through student loans. Some might not want to graduate with the amount of student debt as I did, but I viewed it as an investment in myself. While pursuing my undergraduate education, I did not consider transferring. Many students see greener pastures at a larger or popular school, but I believe that if you do very well and make good grades at the school that you attend, then doors will open up for you. After I graduated with my undergraduate degree, I was able to take the Law School Admission Test (LSAT) and get accepted to the law school of my choice. I believe that my undergraduate institution and life experiences helped prepared me well for law school.

I did not directly experience overt racism at my undergraduate institution. People got along fairly well; there were a few incidents that occurred in the city and surrounding areas. However, I was so focused on schoolwork and graduating with a good grade point average that I did not get involved in racial incidents. I also did not experience gender inequality at my undergraduate institution. Of course, I did face disappointment during my undergraduate experience, but I dealt with these by staying focused on my long-term goals. By doing so, I was able to soothe the pain of my disappointments. I have discovered that after a disappointment, there is usually a blessing to follow it. One disappointment I experienced during my undergraduate years involved the desire to become a member of a particular sorority. Since, I was a little girl, I knew I wanted to be a member of Alpha Kappa Alpha. However, at my undergraduate institution, they had been suspended from the campus community for many years. The date they were scheduled to return was a date after my targeted graduation date. I was so disappointed that I would not be able to go through the intake process as an undergraduate. However, this turned out to be a blessing in disguise. I ended up participating in the graduate in-take process after I graduated and this was the best option for me. Looking back I am glad that I did in-take through graduate chapter. There were so many of my friends who participated while they were undergraduates and their priorities changed after becoming a member of the sorority. Their schoolwork became less of a priority, while their work in the sorority became their top priority. My college boyfriend (now husband) had this experience. His grade point average plummeted after joining a fraternity from 3.7 to 2.5. While I did not seek a mentor while in college, there were a few African American professors who encouraged me. I viewed them as role models, and after seeing them and their accomplishments, I knew that I could graduate and achieve great things also.

The best advice that I can offer incoming freshman college students is to stay focused! Students should not get caught up in the hype of college life. Any high-achieving college graduate knows the truth that nerds can be cool too; it is more cool to graduate than to be a dropout. Students should also not succumb to peer pressure. There will always be someone in the crowd who came to college but really does not intend to graduate. Students must remain focused and get their education. In the African American community, I have always heard that education is something that nobody can take away from you, so by all means African Americans should obtain degrees and pursue lifelong education opportunities.

Gregory Gray

Undergraduate Major: BS in Finance/Economic
Highest Degree Obtained: Dual Bachelor of Science and Business
Parent(s) Occupation: Farmers/Textile Workers
Current Occupation: Financial Audit Readiness Manager, Department of Navy

I was motivated to go to college because I had no desire to work on my family's farm. In my hometown, there were limited work opportunities. There were virtually no employment opportunities to make a good and sustainable income within the town. I chose my undergraduate institution because of the stellar reputation for its "School of Business" and I was familiar with the university because I had two other siblings who also attended college there.

My transition from high school to college was very difficult; my high school had very limited advanced classes. Therefore, I was not fully prepared for college work when I started college, I was already behind because my high school had so few resources. As a result, I began my freshman year enrolling in three developmental courses. I was already behind most incoming freshmen, but I used this as a motivation to help me get on the right path and graduate. Although I brought my skills on par with my classmates, it took about five or six years to become very confident in my skills and abilities.

Several factors contribute to a student's success as an undergraduate, but I believe that external sources may be the most important to having success in college. External sources are the financing of a student's undergraduate education: how students pay for their college education. Many students are tethered with thoughts of how to pay for their education, and worrying does not allow them to concentrate fully on their school work. They worry if they will receive a scholarship or grant, or will have to take out loans. I was fortunate; I had a combination of all of the above, and my family paid the other 50 percent of the cost of my undergraduate education. I had a collage of people in my support network. It consisted of family and friends. I also had some faculty and staff members in my support network. I also had a work study job on campus, and those who supervised me at my work study job were helpful by allowing me to study when things were slow at work. They also provided support, so I had a very good encouraging cast of people who helped me along the way.

I believe that some people think African American students, in particular males, do not attend college with the intent of obtaining a degree. I also believe that some professors stereotype us and discount those things that we may truly have interest in. They make erroneous assumptions about us because of the way we speak or carry ourselves. In the classroom setting, I think it is very common for professors to label us by our external appearance. For instance, in an investment class, my professor found it surprising that I had a very good understanding about investment banking and sound investment practices. Also in the classroom, sometimes I found it difficult to engage in class discussion because my professors failed to acknowledge my raised hand as a signal to enter into the discussion. Sometimes, I would just politely interrupt to interject my comments and responses. This took place the entire semester, but I did not let this intimidate me at all. This professor's action motivated me. It forced me to keep up with the class readings and attempt to have a better understanding of the course material before the professor's lectures. I made sure that I did not miss any classes and that I was prepared before every class.

I handled any disappointments and failures as an undergraduate student through my family's tough love and refocusing my attention on my true goal of attending college. On one instance, my grades started to slide downward due to living the college life by having too much fun and not studying enough during my sophomore year. As I previously stated, my parents paid about 50 percent of my tuition. After seeing my grades, my father made me pay my own tuition one semester and take on other financial responsibilities. Having to pay my own tuition for a while opened my eyes and see how truly fortunate I was.

When I first started college, I had no idea about planning. Actually, I had no plan. By my junior year, I discovered that life can go a whole lot smoother if you have a plan. I developed a plan that would ensure I could receive dual Bachelor of Science degrees. I also took on additional employment as a front-desk clerk at a hotel working the night shift. If I did not develop a good plan and stick with it, I knew I was doomed for failure, so I developed a study schedule and took classes around my job.

I would advise students to discover what they want to do early in life and then go do it. I also would advise African American college students to have a plan and understand that a degree alone will not get you much these days. It is really competitive finding employment. Students are not only competing with other college graduates in the United States; they are competing with people in other countries. Students must understand that it takes a combination of having a degree, good grades, and also good social skills to be a success. Students should pick a major of their interest, and if there is a strong workforce or need in that area, then that is a winning combination.

I was involved in a few extracurricular activities as an undergraduate; however, I did not join a fraternity in college. I am not sure these organizations are for everyone. When I was in college, I attended church three to four Sundays a month. I was very active in the Baptist Student Union and their activities. Though I was an athlete in high school, I was not an athlete in college. I did attend all of the home baseball and basketball games. Since my undergraduate school did not have a football team, I watched football games on the campus of HBCU that is located in the city. African American students engaging in these types of activities to help enrich their undergraduate experiences.

In closing, I believe many young black males go to college without any idea of what they want to become or what career path they would like to take. Our social, civic, and religious organizations and institutions should set up mentoring programs and other support programs in place to help black males get prepared for college. For black males, it can be a struggle. I think it is a struggle for us from the initial stage of college. I would like to see black young males being introduced to different careers in high school. This would help them decide if college is the right step for them and it will help them plan their career.

Benjamin Jones

Undergraduate Major: Chemical Engineering
Highest Degree Obtained: Doctorate—Jurist Prudence
Parent(s) Occupation: Father—Farmer/Domestic Worker; Mother—Farmer/Domestic Worker
Current Occupation: Chief Executive Officer, Montgomery Community Action Agency

I am the 15th of 16 children, and my motivation and inspiration for college came from both my parents and my siblings. My parents stressed education but with a sense of excitement as to what it could do for us. They were always talking about how smart we were, and my father gave each of us a nickname (title if you will) in an effort to spark our interest in a particular field of study. I was his lawyer, and he had engineers, professors, and doctors, and he always picked those professions that were extremely hard for us to imagine at that time. My mother would reinforce his statements with her own encouragement by saying to us, "You can be whatever you want to be, you just have to believe in yourself and have a willingness to work hard and achieve it."

I chose Tuskegee University for my undergraduate institution, and again it was tremendously in connection with the path most of my siblings had taken. Tuskegee was so familiar to me because several of my siblings had gone there before me. I had an interest in engineering, and Tuskegee was well known for its engineering school, and although I applied to a couple other schools and was accepted, Tuskegee was my choice from my freshman year in high school. I did not transfer from Tuskegee because I enjoyed my undergraduate experience. I was totally dedicated to my education. I found the faculty and staff of Tuskegee University to be very nurturing. I quickly became engaged in the Tuskegee University's family environment and I had very close friendships that have remained in place through the years. I did not transfer because I found the environment very conducive to learning; I found a tremendous amount of support for my education and I enjoyed my stay.

My transition from high school to college was not difficult, but it was challenging once I was embarking upon it. It wasn't difficult necessarily because I was ready to move forward with my career preparation and at that age I was always eager to move to the next level. The challenge for me was to discover when I arrived at Tuskegee that I was no longer the smartest person in the class, to discover that there were students there who had college prep courses that I had never even heard of while in high school. It was a major challenge for me to have to quickly change my study patterns and habits because this was no longer high school; this was the real deal—it was college. The transition was challenging but not so much so that I couldn't make the necessary adjustments to the college life.

I truly had very good self-esteem leaving my parents' house and having watched my siblings one after the other graduate from high school and then college. Having a close relationship with others who are successful in their endeavors gives one a sense of strength and it also has a way of making you believe in your ability as you watch those closest to you do well. My mother was constantly cheering me on and encouraging me so I immediately felt that success was mine, and I had great confidence in my skills and ability to achieve that success. As an undergraduate student I believe the success of my siblings before mine, the encouragement of my mother, and the tremendous relationships developed early in my arrival were all factors that contributed to my success. At Tuskegee and in chemical engineering (engineering overall), there was a very unique relationship formed among fellow classmates that served as a support system similar to a big brother, big sister mentor relationship. There was always someone there willing to extend to you a helping hand, share old notes, be a study coach or guide, and basically just help your every need. It was a family environment and everyone invested in others and seemingly found a sense of accomplishment in making sure others succeeded.

Along with that there were scholarships, grants, work study, and co-op that assisted financially. My mother was single (with the death of my father), but she was making sure we had what we needed to the best of her ability. A number of my siblings were in college at the same time; therefore, we had to seek ways to help finance our own education as much as possible, and work, work study, and co-op turned out to be the key to making that happen. It turns out that my most important relationships were a blend of family for which I have and had very good relationships with while in my undergraduate program. Family was a key part of my support structure while I was in college, support that I am not sure I could have succeeded without but happy I never had to find out. Then I developed some very strong and lasting friendships as an undergraduate that were important and key to keeping me focused and on track. I developed strong relationships as well with university staff especially in my work study jobs in the business office and in the physical plants warehouse. Those relationships with university staff afforded me the opportunity to enjoy privileges other students did not have access to. I had good student-teacher relationships with my professors, but those relationships were not as strong as my relationships with family, friends, and staff. There were a few professors that I had a very strong relationship with, but relationship with the greater number of professors did not develop until I finished the program and was back on campus recruiting.

At Tuskegee University, I did not experience any racial issues that I can recall. From a gender perspective, often it would appear that the females received better treatment from the male professors and sometimes it was true and other times maybe just an excuse for why the females were making better grades. With Tuskegee University being a historically black college, I did not see any outright racism or at least not toward me as an African American. I did not note any institutional racism either; however, there were plenty of institutional problems, but none of them appeared to me to be racism.

The fortunate thing about my undergraduate experience is the fact that I attended Tuskegee University; I had a tremendous support system from friends who were more like family. The Tuskegee University students were close, attentive to each other's needs, helpful with homework, and always working in small groups. I had two best friends, one male, one female, and we studied together, supported each other in difficult endeavors, and helped each other deal with disappointments and failures. We took the approach that any negative thing that occurred was really opportunity advancing itself as a lesson on how to avoid this path in the future. Then I could always lean on my actual family if there was a need to do that when dealing with issues.

In my undergraduate study, my driving force was the relationship with my two best friends, Scott Jackson and Richie Brown. The relationship we had was one of challenging each other to master the work in every class. While we were all majoring in engineering, it was three totally different areas of the study of engineering. I majored in chemical engineering, Scott majored in mechanical engineering, and Richie majored in electrical engineering; we challenged each other until the end of our undergraduate careers. We had planned study times; we maintained consistent relaxation time to give the mind time to just relax. We also, while taking general courses together, would each take the lead and prepare to act as the teacher in different study sessions. When one was responsible for advancing the lesson, you would always learn the most from being the teacher of a homework study session. We would often invite other groups to join us and always kept learning fun and filled with excitement, joking, laughter, and at the same time very serious.

African American students should focus on making learning fun and keeping focus on the primary reason they are in their undergraduate program, that is, to learn. Don't allow the sudden freedom that has fallen on you to take your focus off of schoolwork; just know that after you've completed your studies, there will be time for other adventures. Try to establish meaningful friendships and relationships with persons who are dedicated to their studies and limit your partying. Make sure your undergraduate experience is fun and exciting but always within reason and never lose focus of your purpose and goal as a student. The undergraduate experience is the most exciting, but yet it is the most important experience for setting your pace and establishing a pattern for future educational endeavors such as master degrees and PhDs.

I grew up in a religious environment, and while in college, I continued my spiritual relationship. I attended church somewhere every Sunday, either near the campus if I were in town, or I went back to my home town and attended church at my home church. I interacted with other religious students and from time to time attended Bible study with campus groups. I was actively engaged in continuing my religious and spiritual quest throughout my undergraduate career.

I was not a part of a historically black fraternity as an undergraduate. However, I was very interested in the fraternity life while in undergraduate but did not join until I had completed my studies. I did not feel that my studies as well as my financial position would allow me to join a historically black fraternity while in the undergraduate program. I joined Alpha Phi Alpha Fraternity, Inc. upon completion of my undergraduate studies.

My views on masculinity and femininity while in college were very much reflective of my rearing back home. I thought certainly men should be strong firm protectors of women. I didn't think men should ever be pretty but handsome and smooth with a manly touch. I thought of course that a woman should be feminine and soft, protected by a man and looking to him for strength and encouragement. I found, however, on campus every possible definition of both; there were plenty of guys who were soft, feminine in their actions and lacking in any type of manly touch. And there were females who were masculine in their actions and less than ladylike in their demeanor. I just tried then, and even to this day, to see life from all perspectives.

I think that African Americans like all Americans are driven when they have been inspired at some point in their young lives. There is no real family structure or perfect scenario that determines who will and will not be successful, but I believe something has to spark an interest within an individual to make them believe enough in themselves that they strive beyond what is before them to achieve greatness and success. So the key in my mind for success is an inspiration that develops into a drive and a motivation from some deep place within. Other elements would include support from wherever it comes: family, friends, and/or both.

I was not actively engaged in any college sport. However, my two best friends and I played tennis on a regular basis for fun and relaxation while I was in my undergraduate program. I did attend football and basketball games on campus very often while in the program. My undergraduate experience was very good, and it was a time in my life when I learned a great deal about myself and what it takes to be successful in one's endeavors. It allowed me to mature and learn how to interact with other people on a wide-scale basis; it challenged me to work and to learn to help others as a means for helping myself. It inspired me and lit a fire inside me that made me want to learn more and earn more and go further and do more in life. It was a great experience.

Shakita B. Jones

Undergraduate Major: Social Work
Highest Degree Obtained: Master of Public Administration
Parent(s) Occupation:Factory Workers
Current Occupation: Administrator for Nonprofit Organization and Social Activist

I always knew that it was my parents' goal for me to attend college, but I can't say that I had any real "motivation." I attended a public school that did not have a true interest in the advancement of black students. My guidance counselor did not discuss college or career goals with me. I was blessed to have a 10th grade English teacher who was able to see the potential in me and helped me to begin thinking about career options and mentored me throughout my high school career. I grew up in a household where both of my parents were blue-collar workers at factories, and the only other exposure I had to college-educated people were some of my parents' friends who were mostly educators. I knew early on that I did not want to work in a factory and I did not want to become a teacher, so I actually went to college searching for a career.

I had a very strong desire to go to the University of Alabama, but due to the cost of attending that particular university, my father said no. I had to attend Troy State University because my father was paying for my education and it was a university that he could afford to pay for with his overtime pay from his factory job. Also, my two older brothers attended Troy State and my father had found that putting them through college there continued to be affordable and they were successful students while attending and graduated from there. Transferring did not cross my mind. I did not transfer to another school because I knew I could not afford to go anywhere else and needed the financial support of my father. I believe I easily adapt to situations, and at that time, I was less rebellious and still trying to figure out life, so I was willing to give it a chance and stay the course at Troy State.

My transition from high school to college was smooth. The classrooms were small and very much like a high school setting in terms of the number of students in my classes. Many of the people from my high school also attended my undergraduate institution. I had journeyed through my transformative years of adolescence with them and now we were in college together, so I saw it as if we were just entering another phase of life together. I did not get homesick because home was only a 45-minute drive away. My parents made sure that my basic needs were met. I did not have to get used to living with a roommate because I grew up with a sister and two older brothers. By the time, I enrolled in college, I had learned to live with others and make compromises. I was grateful for the experience of meeting people from other cultures and varying socioeconomic backgrounds. I have always felt a sense of independence while growing up, being the youngest of four children. I did not feel that I needed anyone to guide me through the college process. My brothers had attended my undergraduate institution so if I had questions I could ask them, and the rest I just figured out on my own. Many people think of the youngest child as the "baby," but in my parents' home, they did not believe in "babying" anyone. My parents encouraged all of us to do things for ourselves with the understanding that we had a family support system when we failed. It was also understood that the family would not serve as a crutch for us. This ideology guided much of my college experiences.

Looking back on my experience, I was not certain that I would be successful. One thing I did know is that I would graduate and anything short of that goal would be a failure. My first couple of years, I spent enormous amounts of time trying to figure out college life. I was trying to balance academic demands with social activities. I was also trying to learn good study skills and habits because I did not find high school to be difficult. However, when I entered college I entered on conditional status and had to take remedial courses in math and English because I did not know some of the basic, fundamental information that I needed for college-level courses. My grades were not impressive in my first semesters in college. My pride and the shame of being a mediocre student kept me from asking for help from the people who were there to assist me through the process. I did not have a strategy in college. I was very unorganized and undisciplined. I did not keep a calendar, and I failed to connect with my advisors, so I actually had to stay in college an extra year for failing to take a course in my major when it was offered. This particular course was offered one time a year. At the time, I did not fully understand what it really took to graduate from college. I was very fortunate that many of my professors saw my potential and chose to provide guidance in navigating the college process. When I finally entered my courses in my career field, social work, I was a slightly better student but still struggled in areas that required analyzing data and writing. Through building my writing and test-taking skills and by taking advantage of programs being offered on campus, I began to see my confidence rise in my academic abilities. It was when I started working in my career and pursuing a graduate degree that I realized that I had not only become a good student but also a good student of life. My father paid my tuition and living expenses; that support definitely contributed to the success of my undergraduate career. My father worked overtime at a paper mill to pay for the cost of my education out of pocket. He did this not only for me, but for all four of his children. My mother also provided money for all of us to attend college as well. They did not get the opportunity to attend college, but they were committed to see all of their children not only attending college but graduating from college.

My most important relationship as an undergraduate student was my best friend, who went to another college. We have been friends since we were five years old and never had been apart from each other until we chose to attend different colleges. While in college, we kept up with each other and our accomplishments. From our college experiences, and as adults, we have developed leadership skills that will help compel us as leaders in our careers. We know each other's strengths and weaknesses. Though we attended different schools and our strengths were on opposite ends of the spectrum, we utilized each other's strengths to assist each other with coursework. I was weak in math and she was an engineering major and daughter of a former mathematics teacher. Needless to say, she helped me get through difficult math assignments and I helped her with courses like sociology and literature.

I grew up in Montgomery, Alabama. My undergraduate institution is located in the South, and there were a growing number of African Americans and other racial and ethnic minorities attending my undergraduate institution during my time there. Self-segregation was prevalent on campus. Though all students attended classes together, campus activities were still very segregated. It was rare to see various racial groups comingling with each other in social settings. There were a few exceptions when people of different races, who held memberships in the same group, would comingle or closely associate with each other.

I really noticed a pattern of self-segregation more as it related to sororities and fraternities. I am a member of Delta Sigma Theta Sorority, Inc., a predominately African American sorority. My sorority found ourselves without a meeting place. The white sororities built large houses on campus and the property was named sorority row, with no black sororities allotted any space or a house to hold our meetings. We advocated for a meeting space and we were given a small, very old house across the street from sorority row. The condition of the house was definitely below the quality of the houses that were provided to the white sororities. It could have been because the white sororities had bigger budgets than our organization, but we were not given any options for relocation in the planning process. I found Greek life to be very helpful during my undergraduate years; being a member of a sorority definitely helped me appreciate service to the community and empowerment of women. Upon entering into this sorority, we had the highest grade point average of all the Panhellenic organizations on campus, and there was self-imposed pressure to maintain this title. To keep our title, we organized designated study sessions. We encouraged and supported each other and we excelled in our coursework. After I became a member of my sorority, I became a part of network of learners and driven women. We shared study tips and developed strategies to be successful in difficult courses.

African American college students should attempt to find a mentor. First-generation college students should form a personal relationship with an academic advisor in particular in their major. I believe it is important to ask for help and seek out on-campus organizations and community programs that will assist them with their personal growth and development. They should seek out diversity in social and school settings. African American students should also begin to network early by volunteering or getting involved with organizations related to their field of interest.

During my college experience, I endured some school-related disappointments, but I managed to get through them with the support of friends. I also had a strong spiritual faith and used prayer as a tool to transform my anger into peace. I was not so much religious but I was very spiritual. I did not regularly attend church during my time in college, but I did attend a Bible study on campus, which was comprised of all black students who mostly participated in the school's gospel choir. Though I was not in the gospel choir, I was still welcomed to attend Bible study. I would also sometimes attend the gospel choir's rehearsal so that I could hear spirit-filled gospel music. In my book, if you put those two things together, it was "church."

I am a feminist and was definitely one in college. I have always been an advocate for women's rights and exercised many of those rights during my formative years. I never looked at a male life partner as someone to take care of me. I always saw my future mate as being my equal partner. I had an expectation that we would build a life together and have equal responsibilities in our relationship as well as advancing our family and careers. I always knew that I did not want to be a stay-at-home mom because of the spirit of advocacy that I have in my being. Since I mostly dated athletes, my thoughts of masculinity were skewed but my thoughts varied. I would sometimes think that a man that cries was weak but I learned, "after college," to appreciate the vulnerability of a man who could be open about sharing his thoughts and passions.

For African American students to be successful, they need financial support and a social support system. We live and interact in a global society. African American students cannot isolate and segregate themselves; they must network with diverse groups and cultures. I believe that it is important for African American students to take advantage of study abroad opportunities to learn outside of the United States.

For the most part, I enjoyed my undergraduate experience, but I have some regrets about my college years. If I could do my undergraduate years over again, I would not allow fear to keep me from enjoying myself and expanding my mind to all of the learning opportunities that were available to me. Reflecting back, I realized that I did not maximize my experience and I missed out. I missed out on the only period in my life that I was truly free of life's responsibilities. This is the time where you can try new things and not be afraid. I let fear of disappointing my parents, fear of venturing into new environments, fear of not measuring up to my peers, and other things keep me from really reaching my full potential during my college years. Do not let fear and the unreasonable expectations of others keep you from pursuing your goals. Others might mean well and believe their negative talk will help you rise to the challenge. I have found this not to be the case. It is your life and you are responsible for your decisions. Move forward by surrounding yourself with positive people and critical thinkers who challenge you to expand your thinking and who aid you in continuing to develop your skills and talents. Make every effort to grow mentally, physically, and spiritually. Lastly, never stop pursuing your dreams and get your degree!

Consuela Ward

Undergraduate Major: English (Creative Writing)
Highest Degree Obtained: Education Doctorate
Parent(s) Occupation: Dad was a minister and police officer, one step-father was a mechanic, one was a migrant worker, mom did some book-keeping but could not hold a job for long
Current Occupation: Speaker, Writer, Educator, and Activist

I was a first-generation college student, and I went to college only to get away from home, not realizing that education would save my life. I did not know the differences in types of degrees or how they could benefit me. I knew I was not wired for the military and getting pregnant like the other girls in my town only seemed to make unhappy situations worse. Mrs. Davis, my black female guidance counselor, planted the seed that college could be real for me and was instrumental (almost pushy although I didn't resist) in helping me by getting me into an upward-bound program, helping me complete my admissions and financial applications, and inundating me with scholarship applications and other opportunities. I applied only to Florida State University and Florida A&M University and was accepted to both. I visited the University of Florida during a debate tournament my senior year and did not like the vibe of the campus. When I visited Florida State University during a summer bridge program the summer before my senior year of high school, I felt at home. I also liked their school colors. I applied to Florida A&M University only to appease Mrs. Davis. At the time, I didn't want to attend an HBCU because I felt awkward around crowds of black people because they made fun of me. White people ignored me, which was fine because at least I was at peace. Mrs. Davis died in October of my freshman year of college, so I felt she was sent to me by God.

I was very glad to be away from my home environment, so I did not let too much to get to me at first. Initially, I lived in a scholarship house with 18 other women, 16 white and two black. This was the first time I lived with white people. Jennifer was our house mother, and she greeted me as I was the first one to arrive. She urged me to room with someone named Lavenia, and I couldn't understand why until she showed up two days later as the only other black girl in the house. I believe she meant well and was sincere in trying to make me comfortable;

nonetheless, it was a loud silence that screamed race is still an issue. Lavenia and I got along, but I could relate only to two other women in the house. I moved out within a year because my GPA fell to a 2.9. Were it not for that, the micro aggressions would have been enough to move out anyway. One particular incident had to do with some girls writing something with backward letters on my bathroom mirror in red lipstick, which I viewed as satanic because of my religious views. They laughed until they saw how distraught I was; then they seemed remorseful. I fought depression because I was trying to balance dealing with my mother, getting accustomed to my environment, making money and decent grades, and basically being in survival mode all day every day. I didn't go home often, but when I did, it was obvious that my new exposure had changed me. It was like I was now seeing in color instead of black and white. I didn't know how to share without making others feel inadequate, and they wanted to be happy for my perceived success but could no longer relate to me. It was like I did not fit in anywhere.

My biggest academic concern was math, so I focused harder and received my first "A" in math ever during my freshman year. If an assignment called for completing questions 1–30 odd, I would do 1–30 all because I found that the repetition made me remember. I even started tutoring some of the football players in my math class, and I always studied this subject with a partner. I was also concerned about my test-taking ability. When I posed "what do I do if I am not a good test taker" to a black female administrator from whom I was seeking advice, she simply said learn. I don't know that I learned that skill in undergrad, but I was able to survive. Although my overall grades hovered only around a 2.9–3.0 average, my academic prowess beyond math and tests was less of my concern because I knew I could write well. My biggest focus was making sure I had enough money for food, water, and shelter and making sure my mental and emotional states of being were intact.

The biggest factor that contributed to my success was that I was goal oriented, persistent, and an effective problem solver. I earned some initial scholarships but because my FASFA identified my family as living in poverty, I was able to maximize my Pell grant. I took out only $7,500 in student loans for undergrad and I worked a lot. Between those three options, my needs were taken care of.

My initial mentors were upperclassmen who were hired by the university to mentor my cohort of freshman in the Summer Enrichment Program (SEP) now expanded to the CARE program at Florida State University. One of those mentors those was Ben Crump, Esq. This program allowed underserved and/or first-generation college students to come to campus the summer before fall of their freshman year to take classes and get a jumpstart on making friends, learning the campus, and getting some much needed guidance on study skills, coping, and navigating new surroundings.

I also made connections with other students through SEP. I also connected with the man I started dating during freshman year who later became my husband and father to my children, the mentorship through black female staff of the Multicultural Student Support Center, and the friends in the gospel choir and the black players guild (an acting troupe). They hired me as a work study student and were instrumental in helping me transition to college and getting me through my freshman year.

Racism was normal in the sun down town where I grew up, so I learned to navigate it. Although I could navigate it, the micro aggressions were hard to identify but impossible to deny even in an institution of higher learning. However, I felt supported when it came to black staff and faculty and a few white liberal faculty, but there was not a buffer when I went off-campus. I remember babysitting a young white boy in the care of his elderly grandmother. She was watching TV and said to me, "Don't you wish we could go back to the 1920's when it was a much simpler time." I responded that the 1920s may not have been a simpler time for me as a black woman in the South. She asked why, and I iterated how black people were treated during that time and place, and she responded, "How do you know, you weren't there." Then she ordered me to go check on the baby. My then boyfriend, however, had a different experience. He used to work for the campus escort service and was habitually stopped by campus police after walking me home from choir rehearsal at night. Perhaps this was because he was black and male.

I viewed disappointments and failures as problems that I had to solve. For instance, my grades were not high enough to get admitted into the School of Communication, so instead, I majored in English and obtained two internships from two different television stations by simply calling them with my interest. If I needed money, I found another job. They usually consisted of babysitting, cleaning, call centers, and/or on-campus clerical jobs. If I needed to talk out my pain, which dealt mostly with my relationship with my mother and was less about school, I would do that with a friend or a staff member of the Multicultural Student Support Center. I did experience one failure that I realized was necessary for my growth. I failed geology during my sophomore year and it challenged my ego and reminded me that I was human. I could always maneuver around failure especially academically until this class. I went through a deep depression for a few days and even felt like I wanted to die. At some point, I realized that I actually did the best I could do in this class. It took about three days for me to get over it, and I got back up and signed up for meteorology and continued to move forward.

Although I advocate for students to plan because it will maximize their experience, I cannot say that is what helped me. I realized my motivation for succeeding was that my alternative would be going home, and that was nonnegotiable. My relationship with my mother was strained and she was homeless part of the time. This means I worked two to three part-time jobs at a time and went to school because I couldn't call home for money. My drive was not in learning; it was in not failing.

African American students should be sure professors know your name by sitting in the front of the classroom and visiting them during office hours whether you are having difficulty or not. Speak to each other in passing even if you do not have a relationship. Get engaged by getting involved in a multicultural organization, a professional organization, and one that excites your passion. Work on campus between 12 and 15 hours per week. Students should not be afraid to ask for help and find a mentor. African American students must prioritize schoolwork and go to class.

I grew up as a Christian fundamentalist and rejected the idea of being in church regularly now that I was away from home. However, because it was imbedded in me to find solace and support in Christianity, I joined the gospel choir and that was my church. I remained active my entire four years of undergraduate school and it was my release. I was a first-generation college student and did not know much about sororities, so what I learned, I learned from watching. I loosely considered joining but was immediately deterred by costs and then rumors of hazing.

I was not aware of issues of masculinity and femininity in undergrad. I became aware of that only when I moved to Georgia at the age of 32. I abode by traditional male/female gender roles created in the church and society at large. I had a boyfriend during college, and we married because that is what you did when you date for five years. Although the relationship was passively toxic, I remained in it because we were defined by others as happy. Where I grew up, if you could find a man who went to college, didn't beat you or curse out, wasn't a crack head or alcoholic, stayed in church, and kept a job, you as a woman had nothing to complain about. I didn't learn about compatibility. My self-esteem was very low, and I thought just because he met these very basic benchmarks, I was lucky because it was better than anything ever modeled for me.

African American students can have a successful undergraduate experience through mentoring, community, participation in student organizations, and leadership opportunities if they are going to fully take advantage of their college experience. As an undergraduate, I spent most of my time in survival mode that I didn't feel free to participate in the full college experience. I made smart and calculated choices. Given my circumstances, I don't regret this. I went to college to get away from home, and I followed my plan of study toward graduation because it was the checklist I was supposed to follow, but I never really considered what graduation meant. What would be my next move and how would I get there? I couldn't find a job and was rejected by the only two graduate programs I applied to; then one day I received a letter from Indiana State University admitting me even though I did not apply. All I had to do was to send in my Graduate Record Exam (GRE) scores and it was a done deal. Turns out, they were heavily recruiting minorities, so I took the opportunity and flew. There again, I was mentored by a black woman and was among the most intellectually respected in my class.

Erica Williams

Undergraduate Major: BS in Business Administration/Accounting
Highest Degree Obtained: Master of Public Administration
Parent(s) Occupation: Rural Letter Carrier
Current Occupation: Federal Financial Management Consultant

Attending college was never optional. Both my parents attended college, as did my older brother. Also, I believe that having a college degree was necessary for me to become a successful accountant. As far as choosing a college, I had my college search narrowed down to two great schools that both offered my intended major. My final decision, however, was based on the fact that one offered freshman housing with single rooms and a bathroom shared with only three other girls, while the other offered freshman housing that had double rooms and a "community bathroom" that was shared with everyone on the hall. I chose the former. I chose to complete my degree at this school. I did not transfer to another institution.

My transition from high school to college went smoothly. As a high school student, I took numerous Advanced Preparation and Honors courses. These courses, I believe, prepared me for the heavy workloads given in college. Also, my high school required seniors to complete a Capstone project, which involved research, job shadowing, and an oral presentation—all of which equipped me for the writing assignments and research projects I had as an undergraduate. I knew that I had the tools necessary to succeed; however, it took some time for me to become confident in those skills. I graduated in the top 25 of my high school class (100 students total), and that was a major feat for me, but when I went to college, I soon realized that there were hundreds of other students who were also at the top of their high school graduating classes. I started to compare myself to them and I had some doubts. Once I learned that some of us are gifted with strengths in areas where others are weak and vice versa, I became more confident in my skills.

Due to financial assistance from my family and external sources such as South Carolina's LIFE scholarship, the Academy of Finance scholarship, and a few other private scholarships, I graduated as an undergraduate student with only $5,500 in student loans. This was definitely a factor that contributed to my success because I was able to focus on my studies and did not have to worry about how my education would be financed. My most important relationships as an undergraduate student were those I formed with my professors. Whether it was by participating in classroom discussions or visiting professors during their office hours, I did everything I could to make sure my professors knew me. I truly believe the initiative I showed contributed to my success in the classroom.

In my experience, I have encountered institutional racism on both ends, as an African American and as a woman. I chose not to attend an HBCU. Therefore, I was definitely a part of the minority at my college. As an African American, I felt a pressure to perform more and to go the extra mile because in the eyes of others, I was just a day away from becoming a statistic (i.e., college dropout, unwed parent, etc.). As a woman, I was expected to exceed and excel in the classroom, without having much sympathy if I sometimes missed the bar. While my male counterparts were given the good ole "he's just being a boy" excuse if they did not respond or perform as expected. Anytime I experienced a setback or failure, I would remember my father telling my brother how important it was for him (my brother) to finish college. My father passed away during my brother's sophomore year of college and my first year of middle school. That memory helped me to get back up and devise a new plan that would allow me to be successful. Whether it was seeking additional tutoring, spending more time in the library, or whatever, I just wanted to make my father proud because I knew that if he were still alive, he would want me to complete college as well.

When dealing with time management, I am a big scheduler. I am always writing down my activities; it helps me remember them. So I kept a planner where I would note each of my assignments and project due dates. I also took advantage of math tutoring and the English tutors at my school's writing center. I saw major grade improvements after I began tutoring. African American students should embrace diversity! There is a lot to be learned from people of other backgrounds and ethnicities. If you get a headstart on developing working relationships with others while in college, you'll be all the more prepared to do so in the "real world."

I do not believe I would have been successful in completing my undergraduate degree if I did not maintain my faith in Jesus Christ and attend church. College opens the door to a lot of experiences, some good and rewarding, others bad and discouraging. I believe that being spiritual in college allowed me to focus on the task at hand, which was to successfully complete my undergraduate degree. I also pledged Delta Sigma Theta Sorority, Inc. as an undergraduate. I believe the opportunities the organization presented contributed to my success. The organization offered resources that improved necessary skills such as communication, leadership, and diversity. The organization also provided me with the chance to create meaningful relationships, both personally and professionally.

My views were that women lived in a world best suited for men. I basically felt that I needed to either adapt or conform to an environment in order to be successful. My views remain the same. However, now I have learned how to best use the knowledge I gained from college within the workforce. I have witnessed a lot of African American undergraduate students who have come from backgrounds in which they have no choice but to succeed. Some of them are first-generation college students; others have parents who have attended college and have set the bar high for their children. These students are tenacious and determined to do their best so that they can make their families proud, set a new standard within their families, and have a successful career. While I was not a college athlete, I attended several basketball and soccer games. I had such a great time cheering on my classmates. I used athletic events as a way to take a much needed break from studying and worrying about exams. It provided a good "work/play" balance that I feel is needed in college.

I had several mentors while in college. One was an upperclassman with the same major as me. She was helpful in telling me which classes to take and which professors to avoid. She also helped encourage me when I didn't think I would make it through a tough semester. Another mentor was an accounting professional. He was instrumental in helping me find internships that would be beneficial for my future career as an accountant.

I believe African American students should find inspiration in the words of others. When I was preparing my statement letter for graduate school, I came across an excerpt from a commencement speech by Steve Jobs. His words were profound and continue to inspire me to follow my dreams daily. I'd like to share it with you. "Your time is limited, so don't waste it living someone else's life. . . . And most important, have the courage to follow your heart and intuition. They somehow already know what you truly want to become. Everything else is secondary."

Ronald Williams

Undergraduate Major: Accounting
Highest Degree Obtained: Education Doctorate
Parent(s) Occupation: Engineer/Pilot and Marketing Executive and Realtor
Current Occupation: Assistant Vice President for Academic Affairs and Assistant Professor

My motivation to attend college was my desire to work in a rewarding career where I could earn enough money to handle my own responsibilities. My undergraduate institution was a small liberal arts college that was founded by the Methodist church, and I chose to attend it because I grew up in a Connectional Methodist church. I have strong ties to the institution that was well established when I was a child. I grew up in Los Angeles, but moved to the South to attend college.

I would describe my transition from high school to college as fairly common. Like many freshmen (especially those who travel thousands of miles away from home), I missed my parents, other family, and friends and at times I was homesick. However, my parents, grandmothers, and others visited campus and gave me the support I needed. Further, I was familiar with many administrators on my campus (as I referenced earlier, I had a strong connection to my undergraduate college), and they provided a welcoming environment on the campus, at church, and in some cases in their homes.

In my family, failure was not an option. I knew I would succeed, and I was confident in my ability to do so. When I needed assistance, I asked for it and I made it a priority to do well in my studies. It would have been an embarrassment and a colossal waste of my parents' money to have failed out of college. I was well prepared, and there would have been no reason for me not to succeed.

Although I received some scholarship support in my freshman year, my parents were committed to paying the majority of my tuition, fees, board, and living expenses. I believe the financial, emotional, academic, spiritual, and social support I received as a college student contributed significantly to my success. My parents were college graduates and I could somewhat rely on their experiences to guide me through some situations; however, some things were vastly different from when they received their degrees. My most salient relationships were with my friends. Attending a small private school lends itself to developing significant and lasting relationships with friends. However, I do value the relationships I established with faculty, administrators, and staff. I attended a historically black college and, fortunately, I did not experience racism on the campus. Unfortunately, I did experience racism as an African American man in a small town in the South. I dealt with racism responsibly and peacefully. Typically, when students experienced incidents of racism, the president of the college addressed issues of racism with the leaders of the city and the county.

Failures are inevitable in life and I have had my share. My faith in God and my spiritual connectedness helped me to navigate failures that I experienced in college. I had great difficulty in statistics; however, I successfully completed those courses with hard work (studying), prayer, and faith. Because I attended a small private school, my degree plan was very static. My classes were offered in a strict rotation, and the course schedule followed a very specific chronological path. If, for any reason, the path was not followed or a student's progress was disrupted, it became very problematic (almost impossible) to complete a degree in four or five years. Therefore, a calendar would not have necessarily helped, but I did schedule study and writing time; I usually completed both tasks early in the evening between dinner and evening (social) activities.

I recommend that students ask for assistance when needed. Typically, the student knows when and/or what he or she needs help with during the semester. Further, students should complete internships during the summers to prepare for a professional career. Faculty members are usually able to assist with the search process. Also, depending on a student's major, a special emphasis should be placed on enhancing writing and speaking skills. Strong writing and speaking skills are most helpful when applying for employment and advancing in one's career.

I was spiritual during my college days, and I usually attended church every Sunday. Also, my college required all students to attend chapel services on Wednesday mornings at 11 am before lunch at noon. I attended chapel and gladly participated in the services when I had an opportunity to do so. I am a member of Alpha Phi Alpha Fraternity, and I joined the fraternity as an 18-year-old undergraduate student. Also, I was a member of several other organizations. I enjoyed, and still enjoy, membership in several organizations I joined in college; however, I do not believe that my participation in said organizations had an impact on my academic achievement. Although I do believe my ability to be chosen for membership in the organizations was a direct result of my academic and social achievements. I believe that support and encouragement coupled with financial resources and advocacy are most salient to students being successful in college.

PART V

Resources and Additional Information

Table 1 Scholarships.

Scholarship	Description	Website/Contact Info	Deadline	Award Amount
AARP Foundation Women's Scholarship	For women 40+ seeking new job skills, training, and educational opportunities to support themselves	http://www. aarp foundationwlc.org/?gclid=COeKnvOUiZ4CFchn5QodR2xQpg	Usually in March	$500–$5,000
Academic Competitiveness Grant	For first-year and second-year college students who graduated from high school	http://www2.ed.gov/about/offices/list/ope/ac-smart.html	Varies	$750–$1,300
Actuarial Diversity Scholarship	For minority students pursuing a degree that may lead to a career in the actuarial profession	http://www.actuarialfoundation.org/research_edu/prize_award.htm#diversity	Usually in May	$1,000–$5,000
Akash Kuruvilla Memorial Scholarship	For students who demonstrate excellence in leadership, diversity, integrity, and academia	https://www.akmscholarship.com/	Usually in June	$1,000
American Copy Editors Society Scholarship	Available to junior, senior, and graduate students who will take full-time copy editing jobs or internships	http://www.copydesk.org/scholarships.htm	Usually in November	$1,000–$2,500
AORN Foundation Scholarship	For students studying to be nurses and perioperative nurses pursuing undergrad and grad degrees	http://www.aorn.org/AORNFoundation/Scholarships/	Usually in June	Up to $20,000
Automotive Hall of Fame Scholarship	For students who indicate a sincere interest in an automotive-related career	http://www.automotivehalloffame.org/	Usually in June	Varies
AWG Minority Scholarship for Women	Encourages young minority women to pursue an education and later a career in the geosciences	http://www.awg.org/eas/minority.html	Usually in June	$6,000

AXA Achievements Scholarship	Provides more than $600K in annual scholarships to 52 students—one from each state	http://www.axa-equitable.com/axa-foundation/AXA-achievement-scholarship.html	Usually in December	$10,000–$25,000
Best Buy Scholarship	For students in grades 9–12 who plan to enter a full-time undergraduate program upon high school graduation	http://www.bestbuy-communityrelations.com/scholarship.htm	Usually in February	$1,000
Burger King Scholars Program	For high school seniors who have part-time jobs and excel academically in school	http://www.haveityourwayfoundation.org/	Usually in January	$1,000
CIA Undergraduate Scholarship Program	Developed to assist minority and disabled students, but open to all who meet the requirements	https://www.cia.gov/careers/student-opportunities/	Usually in October	Up to $18,000
Coca-Cola Scholars Program	Four-year achievement-based scholarships given to 250 high school seniors each year	http://www.coca-colascholars.org/	Usually in October	$10,000–$20,000
Davidson Fellows Scholarship	Recognizes and awards the extraordinary who excel in math, science, and technology	http://www.davidsongifted.org/fellows/	Usually in March	$10,000–$50,000
Davis-Putter Scholarship Fund	Need-based scholarships for college students who are part of the progressive movement in their community	http://www.davisputter.org/	Usually in April	Up to $10,000
Dell Scholars Program	For students who demonstrate a desire and ability to overcome barriers and achieve their goals	http://www.dellscholars.org/	Usually in January	Varies
Discovery Scholarship	Annual scholarship for high school juniors to support continued education and training beyond high school	http://www.discoverfinancial.com/community/scholarship.shtml	Usually in January	$30,000

(*continued*)

Table 1 (*Continued*)

Scholarship	Description	Website/Contact Info	Deadline	Award Amount
Diversity Abroad Scholarships	Study abroad scholarships can make the difference between you going abroad or not	http://www.diversityabroad.com/scholarships	Varies	Varies
Ed Bradley/Ken Kashiwahara Scholarship	Open to full-time students who are pursuing careers in radio and television news	http://www.rtdna.org/pages/education/scholarship-info.php	Usually in May	$2,500
EMPOWER Scholarship Award	Designed to increase diversity in the medical rehabilitation field by awarding students of color	http://www.couragecenter.org/PreviewPages/empower_details.aspx	Usually in May	$1,500
ESA Foundation Computer and Video Game Scholarship Program	For minority and female students majoring in a field related to computer and video game arts	http://www.theesa.com/foundation/scholarship.asp	Usually in May	$3,000
Fulbright Scholar Program	Sends faculty and professionals abroad each year to lecture and conduct research	http://www.cies.org/us_scholars/us_awards/	Usually in August	Varies
Future Engineers Scholarship Program	For students pursuing a career in engineering who show outstanding academic performance	http://www.theesa.com/foundation/scholarship.asp	Usually in May	$3,000
Gates Millennium Scholarship	Funded by the Bill & Melinda Gates Foundation; established to help low-income minority students	http://www.gmsp.org/	Usually in January	Varies
Go on Girl! Book Club Scholarship	Supports authors of the Black African Diaspora who want to write their way to college money	http://www.goongirl.org	Usually in May	$500
Google Anita Borg Scholarship	For women who excel in computing and technology, and are active role models and leaders	http://www.google.com/anitaborg/	Usually in February	$1,000–$10,000

Hallie Q. Brown Scholarship	For African American women who have a minimum C average and can demonstrate financial need	http://www.nacwc.org/programs/scholarships.html	Usually in March	Varies
HBCU Study Abroad Scholarship	Provides travel opportunities for students of color who are traditionally underrepresented in such programs	https://www.iesabroad.org/IES/Scholarships_and_Aid/Diversity_Scholarships/hbcuScholarship.html	Usually in November	$2,000
Jackie Robinson Foundation Scholarship	Minority high school students are invited to apply for scholarships, internships, mentoring, and more	http://www.jackierobinson.org/	Usually in March	$7,500
Jacob K. Javits Fellowship Program	Provides fellowships to students who excel in the arts, humanities, and social sciences	http://www.ed.gov/programs/jacobjavits/index.html	Usually in October	Up to $30,000
Javits-Fraser Teacher Scholarship Fund	To increase diverse students access to talent development opportunities through teacher training	http://www.nagc.org/index.aspx?id=4590	Usually in April	$500
Jeannette Rankin Women's Scholarship Fund	For low-income women who have a vision of how their education will benefit themselves and their community	http://www.rankinfoundation.org/	Usually in March	$2,000
Joe Francis Haircare Scholarship	For cosmetology and barber school students who can demonstrate a financial need	http://www.joefrancis.com/	Usually in June	$1,000
KFC Colonels Scholars Program	For college-bound students who can demonstrate financial need and have a GPA of at least 2.75	http://www.kfcscholars.org/scholarships/	Usually in February	$5,000–$20,000

(continued)

Table 1 (*Continued*)

Scholarship	Description	Website/Contact Info	Deadline	Award Amount
Lincoln Forum Scholarship Essay Contest	A writing contest pertaining to the life and times of Abraham Lincoln and the Civil War era	http://www.thelincolnforum.org/scholarship-essay-contest.php	Usually in July	$250–$1,000
McKesson Pharmacy Scholarship	Designed to assist pharmacy students who plan to continue their education	https://www.scholarshipamerica.org/mckessonpharmacy/	Usually in October	$1,000
National Achievement Scholarship	Established in 1964 to provide recognition for outstanding African American high school students	http://www.nationalmerit.org/nasp.php	Varies	$2,500
National Black Police Association Scholarship	For students pursuing careers in law enforcement, criminal justice, and other related areas	http://www.blackpolice.org/scholarships.html	Usually in June	Varies
National Institute of Grants for Women	Designed to help women and girls find funding for college education, and more	http://www.grantsforwomen.org/	Varies	Varies
National Institute of Health (NIH) Undergraduate Scholarship	For students from disadvantaged backgrounds who are pursuing science and health-related research	https://ugsp.nih.gov/	Usually in March	Up to $20,000
National SMART Grant	Available to full-time students who are majoring in science, math, technology, engineering, and more	http://studentaid.ed.gov/PORTALSWebApp/students/english/SmartGrants.jsp?tab=funding	Varies	$4,000
Ron Brown Scholar Program	Seeks to identify African American high school seniors who will make significant contributions to society	http://www.ronbrown.org/Apply/EligibilityRequirements.aspx	Usually in January	$10,000

Ronald Reagan College Leaders Scholarship	Seeks to recognize outstanding young people who are promoting American values on college campuses	http://www.thephillipsfoundation.org/	Usually in January	$1,000–$7,500
Siemens Competition	Competition for individual or team research projects in science, mathematics, engineering, and technology	http://www.collegeboard.com/siemens/	Usually in October	$1,000
Thurgood Marshall College Fund Scholarship	For first-generation students majoring in business, finance, science, engineering, and more.	http://www.thurgoodmarshallfund.net/	Usually in May	Varies
Tri-Delta Scholarships	For students who excel in chapter and campus involvement, community service, academics, and more	http://www.tridelta.org/	Usually in March	$1,000–$3,000
Tylenol Scholarship	For students pursuing a career in health care who can demonstrate leadership and academic qualities	http://scholarship.tylenol.com/	Usually in May	Up to $10,000
United Negro College Fund Scholarships	Administers 400 different scholarship programs so low-income families can afford college, tuition, and books	http://www.uncf.org/forstudents/scholarship.asp	Varies	$500–$10,000
U.S. Bank Internet Scholarship	For high school seniors planning to enroll or college freshmen, sophomores, and juniors already enrolled	http://www.usbank.com/cgi_w/cfm/studentloans/marketing.cfm	Usually in March	$1,000
USDA/1890 National Scholars Program	For students seeking a bachelor's degree in agriculture, food, or natural resource sciences and related majors	http://www.ascr.usda.gov/1890programs.html	Usually in February	Varies
Vanguard Minority Scholarship Program	Provides merit-based scholarships to minority students studying business, finance, economics, and more	http://sms.scholarshipamerica.org/vanguard/	Usually in November	$10,000

(*continued*)

Table 1 (*Continued*)

Scholarship	Description	Website/Contact Info	Deadline	Award Amount
William B. Ruggles Right to Work Journalism Scholarship	Available to undergraduate and graduate students who are majoring in journalism or a related field	http://www.nilrr.org/scholarships	Usually in December	$2,000
Writer's Digest Annual Short Story Competition	Contest for writers who can compose the best fictional short story, written in 1,500 words or less	http://www.writersdigest.com/short	Usually in December	$100–$3,000
Xerox Technical Minority Scholarship	For academic high-achievers in science, engineering, and information technology	http://www.xeroxstudentcareers.com/why-xerox/scholarship.aspx	Usually in September	$1,000–$10,000

Table 2 Four-Year Accredited Historically Black Colleges and Universities in the United States as of 2013.

School Name	City	State	Year Founded	Type of Institution	Total Enrollment, Fall 2013
Alabama A&M University	Normal	Alabama	1875	Public	5,020
Alabama State University	Montgomery	Alabama	1867	Public	6,075
Albany State University	Albany	Georgia	1903	Public	4,260
Alcorn State University	Lorman	Mississippi	1871	Public	3,848
Allen University	Columbia	South Carolina	1870	Private	651
Arkansas Baptist College	Little Rock	Arkansas	1884	Private	1,027
Benedict College	Columbia	South Carolina	1870	Private	2,512
Bennett College	Greensboro	North Carolina	1873	Private	680
Bethune-Cookman University	Daytona Beach	Florida	1904	Private	3,787
Bluefield State College	Bluefield	West Virginia	1895	Public	1,747
Bowie State University	Bowie	Maryland	1865	Public	5,561
Central State University	Wilberforce	Ohio	1887	Public	2,068
Cheyney University of Pennsylvania	Cheyney	Pennsylvania	1837	Public	1,212
Claflin University	Orangeburg	South Carolina	1869	Private	1,884
Clark Atlanta University	Atlanta	Georgia	1865	Private	3,458
Concordia College	Selma	Alabama	1922	Private	600
Coppin State University	Baltimore	Maryland	1900	Public	3,383
Delaware State University	Dover	Delaware	1891	Public	4,336
Dillard University	New Orleans	Louisiana	1869	Private	1,183
Edward Waters College	Jacksonville	Florida	1866	Private	862
Elizabeth City State University	Elizabeth City	North Carolina	1891	Public	2,421
Fayetteville State University	Fayetteville	North Carolina	1867	Public	6,179
Fisk University	Nashville	Tennessee	1866	Private	646

(continued)

Table 2 *(Continued)*

School Name	City	State	Year Founded	Type of Institution	Total Enrollment, Fall 2013
Florida A&M University	Tallahassee	Florida	1887	Public	10,743
Florida Memorial University	Miami Gardens	Florida	1879	Private	1,560
Fort Valley State University	Fort Valley	Georgia	1895	Public	3,180
Grambling State University	Grambling	Louisiana	1901	Public	5,071
Hampton University	Hampton	Virginia	1868	Private	4,622
Harris-Stowe State University	St. Louis	Missouri	1857	Public	1,298
Howard University	Washington	D.C.	1867	Private	10,297
Huston-Tillotson University	Austin	Texas	1952	Private	973
Jackson State University	Jackson	Mississippi	1877	Public	9,134
Jarvis Christian College	Hawkins	Texas	1912	Private	609
Johnson C. Smith University	Charlotte	North Carolina	1867	Private	1,387
Kentucky State University	Frankfort	Kentucky	1886	Public	2,533
Lane College	Jackson	Tennessee	1882	Private	1,554
Langston University	Langston	Oklahoma	1897	Public	2,533
LeMoyne-Owen College	Memphis	Tennessee	1870	Private	592
Lincoln University	Chester County	Pennsylvania	1854	Public	1,963
Lincoln University of Missouri	Jefferson City	Missouri	1866	Public	3,043
Livingstone College	Salisbury	North Carolina	1879	Private	1,175
Meharry Medical College	Nashville	Tennessee	1876	Private	1,666
Miles College	Fairfield	Alabama	1898	Private	2,203
Mississippi Valley State University	Itta Bena	Mississippi	1950	Public	2,170
Morehouse College	Atlanta	Georgia	1867	Private	2,810
Morehouse School of Medicine	Atlanta	Georgia	1975	Private	372
Morgan State University	Baltimore	Maryland	1867	Public	7,546
Morris College	Sumter	South Carolina	1908	Private	824

Norfolk State University	Norfolk	Virginia	1935	Public	6,728
North Carolina A&T State University	Greensboro	North Carolina	1891	Public	10,561
North Carolina Central University	Durham	North Carolina	1910	Public	8,093
Oakwood University	Huntsville	Alabama	1896	Private	1,903
Paine College	Augusta	Georgia	1882	Private	924
Paul Quinn College	Dallas	Texas	1872	Private	243
Philander Smith College	Little Rock	Arkansas	1877	Private	556
Prairie View A&M University	Prairie View	Texas	1876	Public	8,283
Rust College	Holly Springs	Mississippi	1866	Private	922
Saint Paul's College	Lawrenceville	Virginia	1888	Private	Closed
Savannah State University	Savannah	Georgia	1890	Public	4,772
Selma University	Selma	Alabama	1878	Private	611
Shaw University	Raleigh	North Carolina	1865	Private	2,062
South Carolina State University	Orangeburg	South Carolina	1896	Public	3,463
Southern University at New Orleans	New Orleans	Louisiana	1956	Public	2,292
Southern University and A&M College	Baton Rouge	Louisiana	1881	Public	6,777
Southwestern Christian College	Terrell	Texas	1948	Private	172
Spelman College	Atlanta	Georgia	1881	Private	2,129
St. Augustine's College	Raleigh	North Carolina	1867	Private	1,284
Stillman College	Tuscaloosa	Alabama	1876	Private	863
Talladega College	Talladega	Alabama	1867	Private	932
Tennessee State University	Nashville	Tennessee	1912	Public	8,883
Texas College	Tyler	Texas	1894	Private	971
Texas Southern University	Houston	Texas	1947	Public	8,703
Tougaloo College	Tougaloo	Mississippi	1869	Private	878

(*continued*)

Table 2 (*Continued*)

School Name	City	State	Year Founded	Type of Institution	Total Enrollment, Fall 2013
Tuskegee University	Tuskegee	Alabama	1881	Private	3,118
University of Arkansas at Pine Bluff	Pine Bluff	Arkansas	1873	Public	2,615
University of Maryland Eastern Shore	Princess Anne	Maryland	1886	Public	4,220
University of the District of Columbia	Washington	D.C.	1851	Public	5,371
University of the Virgin Islands	St. Croix and St. Thomas	United States Virgin Islands	1962	Public	2,321
Virginia State University	Petersburg	Virginia	1882	Public	5,763
Virginia Union University	Richmond	Virginia	1865	Private	1,749
Virginia University of Lynchburg	Lynchburg	Virginia	1886	Private	582
Voorhees College	Denmark	South Carolina	1897	Private	536
West Virginia State University	Institute	West Virginia	1891	Public	2,677
Wilberforce University	Wilberforce	Ohio	1856	Private	479
Wiley College	Marshall	Texas	1873	Private	1,392
Winston-Salem State University	Winston-Salem	North Carolina	1892	Public	5,399
Xavier University of Louisiana	New Orleans	Louisiana	1915	Private	3,121

Source: National Center for Education Statistics (2013). *Fall Enrollment, Degrees Conferred, and Expenditures in Degree-Granting Historically Black Colleges and Universities, by Institution*. U.S. Department of Education, Institute of Education Sciences, http://nces.ed.gov/programs/digest/d09/tables/dt09_240.asp.

Table 3 Two-Year Accredited Historically Black Colleges and Universities in the United States as of 2010.

School Name	City	State	Year Founded	Type of Institution	Total Enrollment, Fall 2007
Bishop State Community College	Mobile	Alabama	1927	Public	2,811
Coahoma Community College	Clarksdale	Mississippi	1924	Public	2,216
Clinton Junior College	Rock Hill	South Carolina	1894	Private	93
Denmark Technical College	Denmark	South Carolina	1947	Public	1,571
Gadsden State Community College	Gadsden	Alabama	2003	Public	5,514
H. Councill Trenholm State Technical College	Montgomery	Alabama	1963	Public	1,340
Hinds Community College, Utica Campus	Utica	Mississippi	1903	Public	1,125
J. F. Drake Technical College	North Huntsville	Alabama	1961	Public	694
Lawson State Community College, Birmingham	Birmingham	Alabama	1949	Public	3,320
Saint Philip's College	San Antonio	Texas	1898	Public	9,256
Shelton State Community College, C.A. Fredd Campus	Tuscaloosa	Alabama	1963	Public	5,323
Southern University of Shreveport	Shreveport	Louisiana	1967	Public	2,337

Source: National Center for Education Statistics (2010). *Fall Enrollment, Degrees Conferred, and Expenditures in Degree-Granting Historically Black Colleges and Universities, by Institution: 2006, 2006–07, 2007, and 2007–08*. U.S. Department of Education, Institute of Education Sciences, http://nces.ed.gov/programs/digest/d09/tables/dt09_240.asp.

Table 4 Best U.S. Non-HBCU Schools for Minorities.

School	Address	Web Address	Undergrad Enrollment	Student Body Demographic			
				Black	Latino	White	Other
University of San Francisco	2130 Fulton St San Francisco, CA 94117	usfca.edu	6,392	3%	19%	31%	47%
University of Hawai'i at Mānoa	2500 Campus Rd. Hawaii Hall Honolulu, HI 96882	manoa.hawaii.edu	20,006	1%	9%	19%	71%
Harvard University	Massachusetts Hall, Cambridge, MA	harvard.edu	10,534	6%	9%	48%	37%
Rutgers University	249 University Ave Blumenthal Hall Newark, NJ 01701	rutgers.edu	7,217	18%	23%	25%	34%
San Francisco State University	1600 Holloway Ave San Francisco, CA 94132	sfsu.edu	26,156	5%	24%	23%	48%
Stanford University	Stanford, CA 94305	stanford.edu	7,274	6%	16%	37%	41%
San Jose State University	1 Washington Sq San Jose, CA 95192	sjsu.edu	25,862	3%	24%	22%	51%
California State University	1250 Bellflower Blvd Long Beach, CA 90840	csulb.edu	30,593	4%	37%	21%	38%
University of Houston	212 E Cullen Blvd Houston, TX 77204	uh.edu/students	31,706	11%	30%	29%	30%
New Jersey Institute of Technology	University Heights, Newark, NJ 07102	njit.edu	7,317	8%	19%	31%	42%
Hunter College	695 Park Ave New York, NY 10065	hunter.cuny.edu	16,689	10%	25%	32%	33%
Rensselaer Polytechnic Institute	110 8th St Troy, NY 10065	rpi.edu	5,452	2%	7%	64%	27%
Virginia Commonwealth University	910 W Franklin St, Richmond, VA 23284	vcu.edu	23,356	18%	7%	51%	24%
Southwestern Adventist University	100 W Hillcrest, Keene, TX 76059	swau.edu	791	15%	41%	23%	21%

Pepperdine University	2425 S Pacific Coast HWY Malibu, CA 90263	pepperdine.edu	3,538	7%	15%	42%	36%
Indiana University Purdue Indianapolis	425 University Blvd, Indianapolis, IN 46202	iupui.edu	22,409	11%	5%	72%	12%
Stony Brook University	310 Administration Bldg Stony Brook, NY 11794	stonybrook.edu	15,992	6%	10%	37%	47%
University of Chicago	5801 S EllisAve Chicago, IL 60637	uchicago.edu	5,703	5%	9%	45%	41%
California University of Pennsylvania	250 University Ave California, PA 15419	calu.edu	6,450	9%	3%	78%	10%
Faulkner University	5345 Atlantic Hwy, Montgomery, AL 36109	faulkner.edu	2,617	48%	2%	44%	6%
University of California-Riverside	900 University Ave Riverside, CA 92521	ucr.edu	18,621	5%	36%	14%	45%
Tiffin University	155 Main St Tiffin, OH 44883	tflen.edu	3,764	15%	2%	29%	54%
Seattle University	900 Broadway Ave, Seattle, WA 98122	seattleu.edu	4,608	3%	9%	47%	41%
Florida State University	222 S Copeland, Tallahassee, FL 32306	fsu.edu	32,528	9%	17%	66%	8%
George Washington University	2121 I Street NW Washington, DC 20052	gwu.edu	10,357	7%	7%	60%	26%
University of Louisville	2301 S 3rd St Louisville, KY 40292	louisville.edu	15,954	11%	4%	76%	9%
Iowa State University	3410 Beardshear Hall, Ames, IA 50011	iastate.edu	27,659	3%	4%	77%	16%

Table 5 Notable Alumni of Historically Black Colleges and Universities.*

Name	School	Occupation
Abbott, Robert Sengstacke	Hampton University	Lawyer, Newspaper Publisher, One of the First African American Self-Made Millionaires
Abele, Julian	Cheyney University of Pennsylvania	Architect (designed 250 buildings including Harvard University's Widener Memorial Library, the majority of buildings at Duke University, the Philadelphia Museum of Art, the Philadelphia Free Library, and Gilded Age mansions in Newport and New York)
Abernathy, Ralph David, Sr.	Clark Atlanta University, Alabama State University	Civil Rights Leader
Adams, Eula L.	Morris Brown College	Executive Vice President for First Data Corporation
Adams, John H.	Johnson C. Smith University	Civil Rights Activist
Adams, Victorine Q.	Coppin State University	Baltimore, Maryland, Political Pioneer and Activist
Adams, Willie, Jr.	Meharry Medical College	Mayor of Albany, Georgia
Adams, Yolanda Yvette	Texas Southern University	Grammy Award–Winning Gospel Singer, Radio Personality
Adegbalola, Gaye	Virginia State University	Blues Singer and Civil Rights Activist
Aggrey, James Emman Kwegyir	Livingstone College	Intellectual, Missionary, and Teacher
Alexander, Avery Caesar	Southern University at New Orleans	Civil Rights Activist and Louisiana State Representative
Alexander, Ronald Brent	Tennessee State University	NFL Player with the Arizona Cardinals, Carolina Panthers, Pittsburgh Steelers, and New York Giants
Alexander-Nickens, Myrna	Tougaloo College	Cardiologist
Allen, Allethia Lee	Bennett College	Professor Emeritus, University of Washington
Allen, Deborrah Kaye "Debbie"	Howard University	Choreographer, Dancer, Actress
Allen, Jacqueline A.	Lincoln University	Judge, Court of Common Pleas (5th Judicial District, Trial Division, Philadelphia)
Ambrose, Ashley Avery	Mississippi Valley State University	NFL Player with the Cincinnati Bengals, Indianapolis Colts, New Orleans Saints, and Atlanta Falcons
Anderson, Anthony	Howard University	Actor

Anderson, Bennie T. L.	Tennessee State University	NFL Player with the Baltimore Ravens and Miami Dolphins
Anderson, Ezzrett "Sugarfoot"	Kentucky State University	One of the First African Americans from an HBCU to play Professional Football
Anderson, Ralph	Allen University	Senator in the South Carolina General Assembly
Anderson, Regina M.	Wilberforce University	Playwright, Librarian, Member of the Harlem Renaissance
Anderson, Reuben Vincent	Tougaloo College	First Black Graduate of the University of Mississippi Law School, First Black Judge on the Mississippi Supreme Court, First Black President of the Mississippi Bar Association
Anderson, Rickey Recardo	South Carolina State University	NFL Player with the San Diego Chargers
Anderson, Sunshine	North Carolina Central University	R&B Singer
Anderson, Terry C.	Bethune-Cookman University	NFL Player with the Miami Dolphins, Washington Redskins, and San Francisco 49ers
Ansa, Tina McElroy	Spelman College	Novelist, Filmmaker, Teacher
Antoine, Denis G.	University of the District of Columbia	Grenada's Ambassador to the United States
Armstrong, Chris	Fayetteville State University	Canadian Football League Player
Armstrong, Darrell	Fayetteville State University	Basketball Player with the Global Basketball Association and U.S. Basketball League
Arrington, Marvin S., Sr.	Clark Atlanta University	Politician and Jurist
Arrington, Richard, Jr.	Miles College	First African American Mayor of Birmingham, Alabama
Atkins, Hannah Diggs	St. Augustine's College	First African American Woman Elected to the Oklahoma House of Representatives
Attles, Alvin A. "Al," Jr.	North Carolina A&T State University	One of the First African American NBA Coaches, Second African American Coach to win a NBA Title
Ausbie, Hubert Eugene "Geese"	Philander Smith College	Harlem Globetrotters Player and Coach
Austin, Helen Elsie	Wilberforce University	U.S. Foreign Service Officer
Austin, Joshua Bernard	Tuskegee University	National President of Black Men Incorporated
Azikiwe, Benjamin Nnamdi	Lincoln University	First President of Nigeria

(*continued*)

Table 5 ***(Continued)***

Name	School	Occupation
Badu, Erykah	Grambling State University	R&B Singer
Bailey, Beaufort	Winston-Salem State University	Forsyth County (Winston-Salem) County Commissioner
Baker, Delbert W.	Oakwood University	Administrator, Educator, Author, President of Oakwood University, Member of the White House Board for HBCUs
Baker, Ella Josephine	Shaw University	Leader of the Student Nonviolent Coordinating Committee (SNCC) and Civil Rights Activist
Ballance, Frank W., Jr.	North Carolina Central University	U.S. Congressman
Ballard, Billy Ray	Meharry Medical College	First African American Board-Certified Oral Pathologist, Previous Chair for the AAMC Group on Student Affairs, Former Vice President for Student Affairs and Associate Dean of Students and Admissions, UTMB Galveston Medical School
Ballard, Howard Louis "House"	Alabama A&M University	NFL Pro-Bowler with the Buffalo Bills and Seattle Seahawks
Ballentine, Warren	North Carolina A&T State University	Attorney and Syndicated Radio Talk Show Host
Bama Boyz	Alabama A&M University	Grammy-nominated, Dove Award–Winning Group consisting of Eddie "E-Trez" Smith III, Jesse J. Rankins, and Jonathan D. Wells
Banda, Hastings Kamuzu	Meharry Medical College, Central State University	President of the Republic of Malawi
Bankhead, Lester Oliver	Voorhees College	Pioneering Black Architect
Banks, Gordon	Norfolk State University	Guitarist, Producer, Writer, and Musical Director
Banks, William	Dillard University	Professor of African American Studies at the University of California at Berkeley
Baraka, Nefertari Imani	South Carolina State University	Educator, Author, Radio Host, President of the Riland Educational Corporation
Barbara Mitchell	Paul Quinn College	Lead Singer with Kirk Franklin and God's Property
Barber, Bryan	Clark Atlanta University	Music Video and Motion Picture Director
Barber, Rudolph "Rudy"	Bethune-Cookman University	American Football League Player for the Miami Dolphins

Barlow, Reggie	Alabama State University	NFL Player with the Jacksonville Jaguars and Tampa Bay Buccaneers, Head Coach ASU football
Barnes, Darian Durrell	Hampton University	NFL Player with the New York Giants, Tampa Bay Buccaneers, Dallas Cowboys, Miami Dolphins, New York Jets, Buffalo Bills, Detroit Lions, and New Orleans Saints
Barnes, Ernest “Ernie” Eugene, Jr.	North Carolina Central University	Artist and Professional Football Player
Barnes, Johnnie Darnell	Hampton University	NFL Player with the San Diego Chargers and Pittsburgh Steelers
Barnes, Luther	St. Augustine’s College	Gospel Singer
Barnes, Margaret Elizabeth Sallee	Kentucky State University	Leader in the Republican Party
Barnes, Reggie	Delaware State University	Canadian Football League Player
Barney, Lemuel Joseph “Lem”	Jackson State University	NFL Hall of Fame Cornerback with the Detroit Lions
Barry, Marion S., Jr.	Lemoyne-Owen College, Fisk University	Mayor of Washington, D.C.
Bartley, Lonnie	Fort Valley State University	Head Women’s Basketball Coach at FVSU
Bass, Harry W.	Lincoln University	First African American elected to the Pennsylvania Legislature
Battiste, Harold, Jr.	Dillard University	Jazz Saxophonist, Composer, and Arranger
Baxter, Shelia R.	Virginia State University	U.S. Army Brigadier General, First Female General Officer in the Army Medical Services Corps
Bean, Walter D.	Kentucky State University	First African American Administrator and Recruiter for African American Teachers, Helped Integrate Phi Delta Kappa Fraternity after becoming First African American chartered member, Second African American member of the U.S. American Association of School Personnel Administrators
Beard, Albert “Al”	Norfolk State University	ABA Player with the New Jersey Americans
Beard, Thomas	Winston-Salem State University	Opera Singer

(continued)

Table 5 *(Continued)*

Name	School	Occupation
Beatty, Anthany, Sr.	Kentucky State University	First African American Chief of Police in Lexington, Kentucky
Beatty, Joyce	Central State University	Senior Vice President for Outreach and Engagement at Ohio State University and Member of the Ohio House of Representatives
Beaty, Zelmo	Prairie View A&M University	NBA Player with the St. Louis Hawks and American Basketball Association
Beauchamp, Patrick L.	Kentucky State University	Founder of Beauchamp Distributing Company
Beaumont, James T.	Kentucky State University	First African American councilman in La Grange, Kentucky
Becton, Julius Wesley, Jr.	Prairie View A&M University	Lieutenant General U.S. Army, Federal Emergency Management Agency Director, Educator
Bell, Al	Philander Smith College	Founder of Stax Records and President of Motown Records
Bell, Carl C.	Meharry Medical College	Community Psychiatrist, International Researcher, Academician, Author, President/CEO
Bell, David	Southern University at New Orleans	Chief Judge, Orleans Parish Juvenile Court
Bell, Howie	Benedict College	Comedian
Bell, Marion L.	Bennett College	Educator
Bello, Howie	Benedict College	Comedian
Benjamin, Regina Marcia	Xavier University of Louisiana	U.S. Surgeon General
Bennett, Lerone, Jr.	Morehouse College	Scholar, Author, and Social Historian
Benson, Joanne C.	Bowie State University	Member of the Maryland House of Delegates
Bernard, Annabelle	Xavier University of Louisiana	First Black to Perform as a Principal Player with the Deutsche Opera in Berlin, Germany
Bernard, Michael "Mike"	Kentucky State University	First from KSU to be drafted by the NBA
Berry, Leon Brown "Chu"	West Virginia State University	Jazz Tenor Saxophonist
Berry, Mary Frances	Howard University	Chair of the U.S. Commission on Civil Rights and President of the Organization of American Historians
Betha, Mason "Mase" Durrell	Clark Atlanta University	Rapper

Bethea, Antoine	Howard University	NFL Player for the Indianapolis Colts
Bethea, Elvin Lamont	North Carolina A&T State University	NFL Hall of Fame Player with the Houston Oilers
Bethune, Evelyn	Bethune-Cookman University	CEO of the Mary McLeod Bethune Educational Legacy Foundation, Inc., Granddaughter of Dr. Mary McLeod Bethune
Bethune, Mary McLeod	Barber-Scotia College	Founder of Bethune-Cookman University
Bibby, James "Jim" Blair	Fayetteville State University	MLB Player with the St. Louis Cardinals, Texas Rangers, Cleveland Indians and Pittsburgh Pirates
Biggers, John T.	Hampton University	Harlem Renaissance Muralist and Founder of the Art Department at Texas Southern University
Biggers, Samuel L., Jr.	Dillard University	Chief of Neurosurgery, King/Drew Medical Center, Los Angeles
Bishop, Clyde	Delaware State University	U.S. Ambassador to the Marshall Islands, First African American to earn a doctorate from the University of Delaware
Bishop, Sanford Dixon, Jr.	Morehouse College	U.S. Congressman
Black, Barry C.	Oakwood University	U.S. Navy Chief of Chaplains and Chaplain of the U.S. Senate
Black, Lawrence "Larry" J.	North Carolina Central University	Olympic Gold and Silver Medalist
Blackmon, Edward	Tougaloo College	Member of the Mississippi House of Representatives and Nationally Renowned Attorney
Blake, Elias A., Jr.	Paine College	HBCU Advocate who helped develop the Upward Bound Program and President of Clark College
Blakey, Donald A.	Delaware State University	Member of the Delaware State House of Representatives
Blanton, Jimmy	Tennessee State University	Jazz Musician
Blassingame, John W.	Fort Valley State University	Professor and Chair of African Studies at Yale University
Blaylock, James	Albany State University	Member of the Georgia Department of Veterans Service
Blount, Melvin "Mel" Cornell	Southern University and A&M College	NFL Pro Football Hall of Fame Player with the Pittsburgh Steelers
Blow, Charles M.	Grambling State University	*New York Times* Columnist
Blue, Daniel Terry "Dan," Jr.	North Carolina Central University	First African American Speaker of the House, State of North Carolina
Blunt, Theodore "Ted"	Winston-Salem State University	Wilmington, Delaware City Council President

(*continued*)

Table 5 (*Continued*)

Name	School	Occupation
Blythers, Isaac	Morris Brown College	President of Atlanta Gas Light Company
Board, Dwaine P.	North Carolina A&T State University	NFL Player with the San Francisco 49ers and New Orleans Saints, and Defensive Line Coach
Bogle, Robert W.	Cheyney University of Pennsylvania	President and CEO of the *Philadelphia Tribune*, the oldest black newspaper in circulation
Bohannon, Fred	Mississippi Valley State University	NFL Player with the Cincinnati Bengals and San Francisco 49ers
Bolden, Joyce	Fisk University	First African American Woman to Serve on the Commission for Accreditation of the National Association of Schools of Music
Bolton, Ronald Clifton	Norfolk State University	NFL Player with the New England Patriots and the Cleveland Browns
Bond, Horace Julian	Morehouse College	Civil Rights Leader, Politician, Professor, Author
Bond, Horace Mann	Lincoln University	First President of Fort Valley State University and First African American President of Lincoln University, Father of Julian Bond
Boney, J. Don	Prairie View A&M University	First President of the University of Houston-Downtown
Boone, Herman	North Carolina Central University	High School Football Coach featured in *Remember the Titans*
Boozer, Emerson	University of Maryland Eastern Shore	AFL and NFL Player with the New York Jets
Boseman, Julia	North Carolina Central University	Member of the North Carolina State Senate
Boston, Ralph Harold	Tennessee State University	Olympic Gold Medalist
Boutte, Alvin J., Sr.	Xavier University of Louisiana	Founder and CEO of Indecorp, the largest black-owned financial institution in the United States; Chair and CEO of the Independence Bank and the Drexel National Bank in Chicago, Illinois
Bowman, Leroy	Morris College	One of the original Tuskegee Airmen
Boyd, Dennis Ray “Oil Can”	Jackson State University	Major League Baseball Pitcher
Boyd-Scotland, Joanne	Tougaloo College	President of Denmark Technical College, Denmark, South Carolina
Bradford, Corey Lamon	Jackson State University	NFL Player with the Green Bay Packers, Houston Texans, and Detroit Lions
Bradley, Donald	Winston-Salem State University	President of Newark, NJ City Council

Bradley, Edward Rudolph "Ed," Jr.	Cheyney University of Pennsylvania	Former Anchor of *60 Minutes*
Bradley, Mark Anthony	University of Arkansas at Pine Bluff	NFL Player with the Chicago Bears, Kansas City Chiefs, Tampa Bay Buccaneers, and New Orleans Saints
Bradshaw, Myron C. "Tiny"	Wilberforce University	Jazz and R&B Bandleaders, Singer, Musician
Brady, Saint Elmo	Fisk University	One of the First African Americans to earn a PhD in Chemistry
Branch, Frederick C.	Johnson C. Smith University	First African American Officer in the U.S. Marine Corps
Braxton, Toni Michelle	Bowie State University	Singer, Actress
Brazeal, Aurelia "Rea"	Spelman College	U.S. Ambassador to Ethiopia
Brazile, Robert Lorenzo, Jr.	Jackson State University	Seven-time NFL Pro Bowl outside linebacker with the Houston Oilers
Breland, Floyd	Allen University	Representative in the South Carolina General Assembly
Bridgewater, Pamela E.	Virginia State University	U.S. Ambassador to Ghana
Briggs, Karen	Norfolk State University	Violinist
Briggs, Kerry	Grambling State University	President and CEO of Briggs Field Services
Brise, Ronald A.	Oakwood University	Florida State Representative
Britt, Gwendolyn T.	Bowie State University	Member of the Maryland State Senate
Brock, Louis Clark "Lou"	Southern University and A&M College	MLB Player with the Chicago Cubs and St. Louis Cardinals
Broderick, Shelley	University of the District of Columbia	Dean, David A. Clark School of Law
Bronner, Nathaniel Hawthorne, Sr.	Morehouse College	Founder of Bronner Brothers Beauty Cosmetics
Bronson, Oswald P., Sr.	Bethune-Cookman University	President of Bethune-Cookman University
Brooke, Edward William, III	Howard University	First African American to be elected by popular vote to the U.S. Senate
Brooks, Angie Elizabeth	Shaw University	Only African Female President of the UN General Assembly and Associate Justice to the National Supreme Court of Liberia

(*continued*)

Table 5 (*Continued*)

Name	School	Occupation
Brooks, C. D.	Oakwood University	Evangelist
Brown, Angela M.	Oakwood University	Soprano Opera Singer
Brown, Benjamin	Clark Atlanta University	Civil Rights Activist and Georgia State Representative
Brown, Charles	Prairie View A&M University	Blues Recording Artist and member of Rock & Roll Hall of Fame
Brown, Cora Mae	Fisk University	First African American Woman elected to a U.S. State Senate (in Michigan)
Brown, Corrine	Florida A&M University	U.S. Congresswoman
Brown, Dorothy L.	Bennett College	First African American Woman General Surgeon in the south and to serve on the Tennessee State Legislature
Brown, Ewart Frederick, Jr.	Howard University	Premier of Bermuda
Brown, Hallie Quinn	Wilberforce University	Educator, Writer, Activist
Brown, James Lamont	Virginia State University	NFL Player with the New York Jets, Miami Dolphins, and Cleveland Browns
Brown, Jericho	Dillard University	Author
Brown, Linda B.	Bennett College	Author and Professor of English at Bennett College
Brown, Oscar, Jr.	Lincoln University	Singer, Songwriter, Playwright, Poet, Civil Rights Activist
Brown, Reginald	Edward Waters College	Jacksonville (Florida) City Council Representative
Brown, Roger Lee	University of Maryland Eastern Shore	NFL Player with the Detroit Lions and Los Angeles Rams
Brown, Roosevelt "Rosey," Jr.	Morgan State University	NFL Hall of Fame Player with the New York Giants
Brown, Vincent "The Undertaker"	Mississippi Valley State University	NFL Player with the New England Patriots
Brown, Vivian	Jackson State University	Weather Channel Meteorologist
Brown, W. C.	Allen University	President of Barber-Scotia College
Browne, Roscoe Lee	Lincoln University	Actor
Bruton, Kris Marcus	Benedict College	Basketball Player with the Harlem Globetrotters
Bryant, Wanda G.	North Carolina Central University	Judge, North Carolina Court of Appeals

Bryant-Howroyd, Janice	North Carolina A&T State University	Founder and CEO of ACT-1 Group
Budd, George F.	Delaware State University	President of St. Cloud State University and Kansas State College of Pittsburg (now Pittsburg State University)
Bumbry, Alonzo "Al"	Virginia State University	MLB Player with the Baltimore Orioles
Buren, Courtney Van	University of Arkansas at Pine Bluff	NFL Player with the San Diego Chargers and Detroit Lions
Burke, Selma Hortense	Winston-Salem State University	Artist, developed sculpture of Franklin D. Roosevelt that inspired image on the Dime
Burks, Matthew	Tougaloo College	President of Arkansas Baptist College
Burnham, Margaret A.	Tougaloo College	Professor of Law at Northeastern University
Burris, Roland Wallace	Howard University	U.S. Senator
Burwell, Bryan	Virginia State University	*USA Today* Sports Columnist
Bush, James, III	Bethune-Cookman University	Member of the Florida House of Representatives
Butler, Albert	Alcorn State University	Mississippi State Senator
Butler-McIntyre, Cynthia M.	Dillard University	Twenty-Fourth National President of Delta Sigma Theta, Inc.
Butterfield, George Kenneth, Jr.	North Carolina Central University	Congressman and Former Associate Justice, North Carolina Supreme Court
Butts, Calvin O., III	Morehouse College	Pastor of the Abyssinian Baptist Church in New York City, President of the State University of New York College at Old Westbury, Chairman and Founder of the Abyssinian Development Corporation
Bynum, Kenneth Bernard "Kenny"	South Carolina State University	NFL Player with the San Diego Chargers
Byrd, Howard	Winston-Salem State University	Christian Author
Byrd, Isaac K., Jr.	Tougaloo College	Nationally Renowned Trial Lawyer
Byrd, Thomas J.	Morris Brown College	Actor
Caesar, Shirley	Shaw University	Pastor and Grammy Award–Winning Gospel Singer

(continued)

Table 5 ***(Continued)***

Name	School	Occupation
Cain, Herman	Morehouse College	Founder and CEO of T.H.E. New Voice, Inc., Chairman and CEO of Godfather's Pizza, Newspaper Columnist, Radio Talk Show Host
Calloway, Cabell "Cab," III	Lincoln University	Jazz Singer and Bandleader
Calloway, Donald, Jr.	Alabama A&M University	Member of the Missouri House of Representatives
Campbell, Ralph, Jr.	St. Augustine's College	First African American North Carolina State Auditor
Canady, Hortense Golden	Fisk University	President of Delta Sigma Theta Sorority, Inc. and First African American elected to the Lansing (Michigan) Board of Education
Cannon, Katie G.	Barber-Scotia College	First African American Female ordained as a Minister by the Presbyterian Church
Carmichael, Lee Harold	Southern University and A&M College	NFL Pro-Bowler with the Philadelphia Eagles and Dallas Cowboys
Carmichael, Stokely "Kwame Ture"	Howard University	Civil Rights Activist
Carson, Harold "Harry" Donald	South Carolina State University	NFL Football Hall of Fame Player with the New York Giants, Member of College Football Hall of Fame
Carter, Clarence	Alabama State University	Soul Singer
Carter, James	Hampton University	Olympic Track Athlete
Carter, Lee "Lee G"	Kentucky State University	Rap Artist and Poet
Carter, Ray C.	Tougaloo College	Attorney. Board Member, National Association of Criminal Defense Lawyers (NACDL)
Carter, Walter P.	North Carolina A&T State University	Civil Rights Activist
Carver, Wayman	Clark Atlanta University	Composer (first person to make extensive use of the flute in Jazz)
Carwell, Hattie	Bennett College	Research Scientist and Expert in the Study of Radiation
Casey, Raashaun "DJ Envy"	Hampton University	Disc Jockey
Catto, Octavius Valentine	Cheyney University of Pennsylvania	Influenced the Passage of the Fifteenth Amendment, Founder of the First Black Baseball Team in the United States, Founder of the Equal Rights League

Cauthen, Wayne A.	Central State University	First African American City Manager of Kansas City, Missouri
Chamberlain, Wesley "Wes" Polk	Jackson State University	MLB Player with the Philadelphia Phillies and Boston Red Sox
Champion, Charles	Xavier University of Louisiana	Named among Top 50 Most Influential Pharmacists by American Druggist magazine
Chaney, John	Bethune-Cookman University	Men's Head Basketball Coach at Temple University
Chea, Alvin	Oakwood University	Member of the Gospel Group Take 6
Cheaney, Henry E.	Kentucky State University	Educator and Expert on the history of African Americans in Kentucky
Cheek, James E.	Shaw University	Former President of Shaw University, President Emeritus of Howard University, 1983 Recipient of the Presidential Medal of Freedom
Cheesborough, Chandra Danette	Tennessee State University	Olympic Gold Medalist
Cherry, Travis	St. Augustine's College	Grammy-Nominated Music Producer
Chestnutt, Charles Waddell	Fayetteville State University	Author, Essayist, and Political Activist
Childs, Ted	Virginia State University	Vice President of Workforce Diversity for IBM
Chilembwe, John	Virginia University of Lynchburg	Missionary and Political Leader of Malawi, Africa
Chisholm, Samuel	Virginia State University	CEO and President of Chisholm-Mingo Group
Christian, Spencer	Hampton University	Weatherman for Good Morning America
Christy, Earl	University of Maryland Eastern Shore	NFL Player with the New York Jets
Claitt, Rickey	Bethune-Cookman University	NFL Player with the Washington Redskins
Clark, Charles Lee "Boobie"	Bethune-Cookman University	NFL Player with the Cincinnati Bengals and Houston Oilers
Clark, Dave Earl	Jackson State University	MLB Player with the Cleveland Indians and Pittsburgh Pirates
Clark, Kenneth Bancroft	Howard University	Conducted Groundbreaking Child Psychology Studies with Wife Mamie Phipps Clark
Clark, Mamie Phipps	Howard University	Conducted Groundbreaking Child Psychology Studies with Husband Kenneth Bancroft Clark

(continued)

Table 5 (*Continued*)

Name	School	Occupation
Clarke, Anna Mac	Kentucky State University	Member of Women's Army Corps during World War II, First African American Officer of an all-white company
Clay, William	Benedict College	U.S. Congressman
Clayton, Eva M.	Johnson C. Smith University	First African American Elected to the North Carolina House of Representatives since 1898
Clayton, Xernona	Tennessee State University	Creator of the Trumpet Awards and Executive Vice President with Turner Broadcasting/CNN
Cleage, Pearl	Spelman College, Clark Atlanta University	Novelist, Playwright, Poet, Essayist, and Journalist
Cleaver, Emanuel, II	Prairie View A&M University	U.S. Congressman
Clemon, U. W.	Miles College	One of the First Two Blacks elected to the Alabama Senate after Reconstruction and Alabama's First Black Federal Judge
Clemons, Clarence	University of Maryland Eastern Shore	Saxophonist with Bruce Springsteen & The E Street Band
Cleveland, E. E.	Oakwood University	Evangelist, Author, Civil Rights Activist
Clifford, John Robert "J. R."	Storer College	West Virginia's first African American Attorney
Clifton, Gregory	Johnson C. Smith University	NFL Player with the Washington Redskins and the Carolina Panthers
Clinkscales, Keith	Florida A&M University	Senior Vice President for Content Development and Enterprises at ESPN
Clyburn, James E.	South Carolina State University	U.S. Congressman
Clyburn, William	Allen University	Representative in the South Carolina General Assembly
Coachman, Alice Marie	Tuskegee University, Albany State University	First Black Woman to win an Olympic Gold Medal
Cochran, Donnie L.	Savannah State University	U.S. Navy Captain who completed two tours with the U.S. Navy Flight Demonstration Squadron, the Blue Angels
Coffin, Alfred O.	Fisk University	First African American to earn a Doctorate in Zoology

Coggs, Tandy Washington, Sr.	Arkansas Baptist College	Educator and President of Arkansas Baptist College
Colbert, Tom	Kentucky State University	First African American Oklahoma Supreme Court Justice
Cole, James	Talladega College	Senior Executive Vice President of MBNA Bank
Cole, Johnnetta B.	Fisk University	First African American Female President of Spelman College, President of Bennett College, Director of the Smithsonian Institution's National Museum of African Art
Cole, Rebecca J.	Cheyney University of Pennsylvania	Second African American Female Physician in the United States, First Woman to Graduate from the Medical College of Pennsylvania
Coleman, Alonzo	Hampton University	NFL Player with the Dallas Cowboys
Coleman, Bessie	Langston University	First Female African American Pilot
Coleman, James H.	Virginia State University	First African American to serve on the New Jersey Supreme Court
Coleman, Maida	Lincoln University of Missouri	Senate Minority Leader in Missouri
Coleman, Phonte	North Carolina Central University	Member of Little Brother and The Foreign Exchange (Hip-Hop Groups)
Coleman, Ronald "OG Ron C"	Prairie View A&M University	DJ/Record Executive, Co-founder of Swishahouse Records, creator of the FAction Series
Coleman, Ronald S.	Cheyney University of Pennsylvania	Lieutenant General and Deputy Commandant for Manpower and Reserve Affairs for the U.S. Marine Corps
Coleman, Ronnie Dean "Big Ron"	Grambling State University	Eight-Time Mr. Olympia
Coleman, Vince Maurice	Florida A&M University	MLB Player with the St. Louis Cardinals
Coles, Togo	Alabama State University	Tennis Player
Collins, Marva N.	Clark Atlanta University	Educator, Founder and Director, Westside Preparatory School in Garfield Park, Chicago
Collins, Nicholas	Bethune-Cookman University	NFL Player with the Green Bay Packers
Combs, Shawn "P-Diddy"	Howard University	Hip-Hop Music Executive, Actor, Entrepreneur

(continued)

Table 5 (*Continued*)

Name	School	Occupation
Cone, James Hal	Philander Smith College	Leader in Systematic Theology and Liberation Theology
Conley, Elizabeth	Huston-Tillotson University	Texas Philanthropist and Equal Rights Activist
Conyers, Monica Ann	Bennett College, University of the District of Columbia	Detroit City Council Member
Cook, Damion Lamar	Bethune-Cookman University	NFL Player with the Baltimore Ravens
Cooper, Anna J.	St. Augustine's College	Writer, Educator, One of the First African American Women to Receive a PhD
Cooper, Cecil Celester "Coop"	Prairie View A&M University	MLB Player and Manager
Cooper, Curtis V.	Savannah State University	Notable Savannah-area Civil Rights leader
Cooper, Edward S.	Meharry Medical College	President of the American Heart Association
Coopwood, Reginald	Oakwood University, Meharry Medical College	CEO of the Metropolitan Hospital Authority
Copeland, Alvin J.	Fort Valley State University	State Championship Athletic Director and Girls High School Basketball Coach at Northeast Health Science Magnet High School in Macon, Georgia
Corcoran, Caitlin	Virginia State University	Music Editor, *Ebony* Magazine
Counts, Dorothy	Johnson C. Smith University	First Black student admitted to the Harry Harding High School
Covington, Grover	Johnson C. Smith University	Seven-Time All-Star Canadian Football League Defensive End for the Hamilton Tiger-Cats
Cox, William E.	Alabama A&M University	President and Co-founder of Cox, Matthews and Associates (CMA), Inc., Fairfax, Virginia
Craft-Kerney, Alice	Southern University at New Orleans	Founder and Executive Director, Lower 9th Ward Health Clinic
Crawford, Bennie Ross "Hank," Jr.	Tennessee State University	Jazz Musician
Crawford, Ruth B.	Paine College	Director of Shiloh Community Center and Designer of the Paine College Flag

Crockett, Victoria	Tougaloo College	Computational Chemist
Crooms, Michael "Mr. Collipark"	Alabama A&M University	Hip-Hop Producer and President of Collipark Records
Crutchfield, Danielle	Hampton University	Deputy Assistant to the President and White House Director of Scheduling
Culmer, John Edwin	Bethune-Cookman University	Minister and Civil Rights leader
Culp, Daniel W.	Johnson C. Smith University	Medical Doctor and Essayist
Cummings, Elijah Eugene	Howard University	U.S. Congressman
Cunnigen, Donald	Tougaloo College	Sociologist
Cunningham, Louis	Lane College	Physician
Curry, George E.	Knoxville College	Editor-in-Chief of the National Newspaper Publishers Association News Service (NNPA) and www.BlackPressUSA.com.
Curry, Walter Morrell, Jr.	Albany State University	NFL Player with the Jacksonville Jaguars
Cuthrell, Kimberly Morton	Bennett College	Author
Dandridge, Robert L. "Bob"	Norfolk State University	NBA Player with the Milwaukee Bucks and the Washington Bullets
Daniel, James	Alabama State University	Tight Ends Coach for the Pittsburgh Steelers
Daniels, David	Allen University	Bishop of 14th Episcopal District of the African Methodist Episcopal Church
Daniels, Gregory	Albany State University	First African American Vice President of Nissan North America
Dannelly, Charlie S.	Johnson C. Smith University	North Carolina General Assemblyman
Darby, Chartric "Chuck" Terrell	South Carolina State University	NFL Player with the Tampa Bay Buccaneers, Seattle Seahawks, and Detroit Lions
Das EFX	Virginia State University	Rap Group
Davenport, William "Willie" D.	Southern University and A&M College	Olympic Gold Medalist
David, Marvin	Southern University and A&M College	NFL and CFL Player
Davis, "Ossie" Raiford Chatman	Howard University	Actor, Director, and Social Activist
Davis, Amanda	Clark Atlanta University	Anchor of Fox 5 News, Atlanta, Georgia

(*continued*)

Table 5 (*Continued*)

Name	School	Occupation
Davis, Cassandra "Cassi"	Spelman College	Actress
Davis, Clifton Duncan	Oakwood University	Actor, Pastor, Songwriter
Davis, Danny K.	University of Arkansas at Pine Bluff	U.S. Congressman
Davis, Karey A.	Alabama State University	Music Producer and Musician
Davis, Kimberly B.	Spelman College	President, JP Morgan Chase Foundation
Davis, Lamar	Dillard University	Deputy Chief of Staff in the Office of Arkansas Governor Mike Beebe
Davis, Lee	North Carolina Central University	American Basketball Association All-Star
Davis, Leroy	South Carolina State University	President of South Carolina State University
Davis, Marianna White	South Carolina State University	Teacher, Author, and Black Historian
Davis, Miles Henry	Arkansas Baptist College, University of Arkansas at Pine Bluff, Lincoln University	Prominent Dentist and Father of Jazz Legend Miles Davis
Davis, Ruth A.	Spelman College	Director General of the U.S. Foreign Service
Davis, Willie D.	Grambling State University	NFL Hall of Fame Player with the Cleveland Browns and Green Bay Packers
Dawson, Andre Nolan	Florida A&M University	MLB Player with the Montreal Expos, Chicago Cubs, Boston Red Sox, and Florida Marlins
Dawson, Phire	Spelman College	Model on the *Price Is Right*
Dawson, William Levi	Fisk University	U.S. Congressman
Delany, Bessie	St. Augustine's College	African American who published her best-selling memoir, *Having Our Say*, at the age of 102 with Sadie Delany
Delany, Sadie	St. Augustine's College	African American who published her best-selling memoir, *Having Our Say*, at the age of 104 with Bessie Delany
Deloatch, Curtis Lee	North Carolina A&T State University	NFL Player with the New York Giants, New Orleans Saints, and Carolina Panthers

DeMesme, Ruby Butler	St. Augustine's College	Assistant Secretary of the Air Force for Manpower, Installations and Environment
Dent, Richard Lamar	Tennessee State University	NFL Player with the Chicago Bears
Desselle-Reid, Natalie	Grambling State University	Actress
DeVaughn, Raheem	Coppin State University	R&B and Neo-Soul artist
Dewitty, Thelma	Wiley College	First African American to teach in the Seattle, Washington, Public Schools
Diallo, Dazon Dixon	Spelman College	Founder/CEO SisterLove, Inc.
Diggs, Charles Coles, Jr.	Fisk University	First African American elected to the U.S. Congress from Michigan, First Chairman of the Congressional Black Caucus
Dinkins, David Norman	Howard University	First African American Mayor of New York City
Dixon, Hewritt	Florida A&M University	NFL All-Star and Pro-Bowler with the Denver Broncos and Oakland Raiders
Dixon, Ivan	North Carolina Central University	Actress
Dixon, Richard Clay	Central State University	City Commissioner and Mayor of Dayton, Ohio
Dixon, Waliyy	Benedict College	Professional Streetball Player
Dobbs, Mattiwilda	Spelman College	Opera Singer
Doctor, Henry, Jr.	South Carolina State University	Lieutenant General in the U.S. Army
Donaldson, Lou	North Carolina A&T State University	Jazz Musician
DoQui, Robert	Langston University	Actor
Dorrough, Dorwin Demarcus "Dorrough"	Prairie View A&M University	Rapper
Dortch, Thomas "Tommy" W.	Fort Valley State University	Former President of 100 Black Men of America, Inc.
Douglas, Aaron	Fisk University	Painter and major figure in the Harlem Renaissance
Douglas, Hugh Lamont	Central State University	New York Jet and Philadelphia Eagle Defensive Lineman
Douglas, Marques Lamont	Howard University	NFL Player for the Miami Dolphins
Douglas, Walter	North Carolina Central University	CEO, Avis Ford

(*continued*)

Table 5 (*Continued*)

Name	School	Occupation
Dowdy, Lewis	Allen University	President of North Carolina A&T State University
Dowers, Donte	Alcorn State University	NFL Player with the Baltimore Ravens
Downing, Will	Virginia Union University	R&B Singer
Dowse, Denise	Norfolk State University	Actress
Drake, Karen	Dillard University	Perinatologist, Iowa Methodist Medical Center, Des Moines, Iowa
Drakeford, Rashad	Hampton University	Trip Coordinator for the U.S. Secretary of Energy
Driver, Donald Jerome	Alcorn State University	NFL Pro-Bowler with the Green Bay Packers
Drummond, Isaiah	Virginia State University	World War I Veteran
Du Bois, W. E. B.	Fisk University	Educator, Writer
Dudley, Edward R.	Johnson C. Smith University	First African American Ambassador of the United States (to Liberia)
Dudley, Joe Louis, Sr.	North Carolina A&T State University	Founder of Dudley Products Inc.
Duncan, Allyson Kay	Hampton University	U.S. Circuit Court Judge
Duncan, Jim	University of Maryland Eastern Shore	NFL Player with the Baltimore Colts
Duncan, Leslie “Speedy”	Jackson State University	Four-Time NFL Pro-Bowl cornerback with the San Diego Chargers and Washington Redskins
Duncan, Michael Clark	Alcorn State University	Actor
DuPois, Starletta	University of Maryland Eastern Shore	Actress
Durant, Justin	Hampton University	NFL Football Player with the Jacksonville Jaguars
Dymally, Mervyrn M.	Lincoln University of Missouri	California Senator, Congressman, and Lieutenant Governor
Earls, Julian	Norfolk State University	Scientist and Deputy Director for Operations, NASA
Easley, Michael Francis “Mike”	North Carolina Central University	North Carolina Governor
Eaton, Cleveland Josephus “Cleve,” II	Tennessee State University	Jazz Musician
Eckford, Wendel	Prairie View A&M University	Ralph Bunche Distinguished Professor of History, Los Angeles City College, First African American to earn PhD in History at the Claremont Graduate University, California

Eckstein, Billy	Saint Paul's College	Singer and Bandleader
Edelman, Marian Wright	Spelman College	President and Founder of the Children's Defense Fund
Edmonds, Albert J.	Morris Brown College	Lt. Gen. of the U.S. Air Force
Edwards, Alfred L.	Livingstone College	Deputy Assistant Secretary of Agriculture by President John F. Kennedy
Edwards, Glen	Florida A&M University	NFL Player with the Pittsburgh Steelers and San Diego Chargers
Elam, Cleveland	Tennessee State University	NFL Player with the San Francisco 49ers and Detroit Lions
Elders, (Minnie) Joycelyn	Philander Smith College	Surgeon General of the United States
Elders, Christopher	Morehouse College	Rhode Scholar
Ellis, Aunjanue L.	Tougaloo College	Actor
Ellis, James "Jim"	Cheyney University of Pennsylvania	Inspiration for the Lead Character in the Movie *Pride*
Ellis, Ted	Dillard University	Artist and Educator
Ellis, Terry	Prairie View A&M University	Member of Female R&B group En Vogue
Ellison, Ralph Waldo	Tuskegee University	Author and Scholar
Elmore, Rick	North Carolina Central University	Judge, North Carolina Court of Appeals
Elzy, Ruby	Rust College	Opera Singer who created the role of Serena in *Porgy and Bess*
Ender, Clara Adams	North Carolina A&T State University	U.S. Army Brigadier General, Georgetown University Professor
Eneas, Cleveland W., Sr.	Meharry Medical College	Senator, Government of the Bahamas
English, Albert Jay (A. J.)	Virginia Union University	NBA Player with the Washington Bullets
Epps, Raymond Edwards, Jr.	Norfolk State University	NBA Player with the Golden State Warriors
Erwin, Richard Cannon	Johnson C. Smith University	First Black Federal Judge in North Carolina
Espy, Alphonso Michael "Mike"	Howard University	First African American U.S. Secretary of Agriculture
ETU Evans	South Carolina State University	Shoe and Accessory Designer
Evans, Donald Lee	Winston-Salem State University	NFL Player with the Los Angeles Rams, Philadelphia Eagles, Pittsburgh Steelers, and New York Jets
Evans, Hugh	North Carolina A&T State University	NBA Referee
Evers, Medgar Wiley	Alcorn State University	Civil Rights Activist

(*continued*)

Table 5 (*Continued*)

Name	School	Occupation
Falconer, Etta Zuber	Fisk University, Clark Atlanta University	One of the First African American Woman to earn a PhD in Mathematics, Chair of the Mathematics Department at Spelman College
Farmer, James Leonard, Jr.	Wiley College	Civil Rights Activist
Farris, Vera King	Tuskegee University	President of Richard Stockton College of New Jersey
Fauntroy, Michael K.	Hampton University	Professor and Political commentator
Feacher, Richard	Mississippi Valley State University	NFL Player with the Cleveland Browns and New England Patriots
Felder, Damon	Alcorn State University	NFL Player with the Miami Dolphins
Fenty, Adrian Malik	Howard University	Mayor of Washington, D.C.
Ferguson, Kevin "Kimbo Slice"	Bethune-Cookman University	Street Fighter and Martial Arts Fighter
Fields, Evelyn J.	Norfolk State University	First African American and Woman Director of the Office of the National Oceanic and Atmospheric Administration (NOAA) Corps Operations and the NOAA Commissioned Corps
Fields, Sandy	Claflin University	Player with the World Basketball Association
Finley, Stephanie	Grambling State University	Nominated as U.S. Attorney for Louisiana's Western District by President Barack Obama
Finney, Gus	Paul Quinn College	Coach of the Harlem Globetrotters and Member of the Michigan Sports Hall of Fame
Fishburne, Lillian E.	Lincoln University	First African American Woman Promoted to Admiral in the U.S. Navy
Fisher, Ada Lois Sipuel	Langston University	Fought for Integration of Southern Law Schools
Flack, Roberta	Howard University	Singer, Songwriter, and Musician (Enrolled at Howard at the age of 15)
Flake, Floyd Harold	Wilberforce University	U.S. Congressman, President of Wilberforce University
Flipper, Henry O.	Clark Atlanta University	First African American Graduate of West Point
Floyd, Virginia Davis	Spelman College	Vice President of PROMETRA International and Executive Director of PROMETRA USA

Fobbs, Brandon	Hampton University	Actor
Folarin, Olubowale Victor "Wale"	Bowie State University	Rapper
Folarin, Oluwabusayo Tope	Morehouse College	Rhode Scholar
Ford, Alphonso	Mississippi Valley State University	Euroleague Basketball Player
Ford, Harold Eugene, Sr.	Tennessee State University	U.S. Congressman
Ford, John N.	Tennessee State University	Member of the Tennessee State Senate
Ford, Johnny L.	Knoxville College	Mayor of Tuskegee, Alabama
Ford, Leonard "Len" Guy, Jr.	Morgan State University	NFL Hall of Fame Player with the Cleveland Browns and Green Bay Packers
Fordham, Walter Wraggs	Oakwood University	Author, President of Several SDA Regional Conferences
Foster, Belinda	Bennett College	First African American District Attorney in North Carolina
Foster, Frank	Wilberforce University	Musician
Foster, Justin C.	Oakwood University	Medical Doctor in Greensboro, North Carolina
Foster, Marcus Albert	Cheyney University of Pennsylvania	First Black Superintendent of the Oakland Unified School District in Oakland, California
Fox, John Robert	Wilberforce University	Recipient of the Medal of Honor
Foxx, Martha Louise Morrow	Hampton University	Blind Educator
Foy, Kevin C.	North Carolina Central University	Mayor of Chapel Hill, North Carolina
Franklin, John Hope	Fisk University	U.S. Historian and President of Phi Beta Kappa
Franklin, Shirley Clarke	Howard University	Mayor of Atlanta, Georgia
Frazer, Victor O.	Fisk University, Howard University	U.S. Congressman
Frazier, Leslie Antonio	Alcorn State University	NFL Player with the Chicago Bears, Defensive Coordinator with the Minnesota Vikings, Special Assistant Coach with the Indianapolis Colts
Frazier-Page, Lisa	Dillard University	Staff Writer, the *Washington Post*

(*continued*)

Table 5 (*Continued*)

Name	School	Occupation
Freeman, Marvin "Starvin' Marvin"	Jackson State University	MLB Pitcher with the Philadelphia Phillies and Colorado Rockies
French, Bob	Grambling State University	Jazz Artist
Frye, Henry E.	North Carolina A&T State University	First African American Justice and Chief Justice of the North Carolina Supreme Court, First African American member of the North Carolina General Assembly in the 20th century
Fuller, Randy	Tennessee State University	NFL Player with the Denver Broncos, Pittsburgh Steelers, Atlanta Falcons, and Seattle Seahawks
Futrell, Mary Hatwood	Virginia State University	President of the National Education Association
Gadsden, Oronde Benjamin	Winston-Salem State University	NFL and Arena Football League Player
Gadson, Sandra L.	Meharry Medical College	President of the National Medical Association
Gailliard, Amos M., Jr.	South Carolina State University	Brigadier General in the New York Guard
Gaines, Lloyd L.	Lincoln University of Missouri	Primary plaintiff in *Missouri ex rel. Gaines v. Canada*, 305 U.S. 337 (1938)
Gaither, Alonzo Smith "Jake"	Knoxville College	Legendary Florida A&M University football coach who won more than 85 percent of his games over a 24-year period, from 1945 to 1969
Gale, Michael "Mike" Eugene	Elizabeth City State University	NBA Player with the New York Nets, San Antonio Spurs, Portland Trail Blazers, and Golden State Warriors
Galimore, Willie "The Wisp"	Florida A&M University	NFL Player with the Chicago Bears, Father of Ron Galimore, who was the First Black U.S. Olympic Gymnast
Gant, Kenneth Dwayne	Albany State University	NFL Player with the Dallas Cowboys and the Tampa Bay Buccaneers
Garner, James A.	Winston-Salem State University	Mayor of Hempstead, New York, First African American Mayor on Long Island, and President of U.S. Conference of Mayors
Gary, Willie E.	North Carolina Central University, Shaw University	Attorney, Motivational Speaker, and Cable Television Executive

Gaskin, Walter E.	Savannah State University	Major General in the U.S. Marine Corps, Vice Director of Joint Staff, Senior Ranking Active-Duty African American Marine and First African American to Command a Marine Corps Division
Gavin, James R., III	Livingstone College	Clinical Professor of Medicine and Senior Health Advisor on Health Affairs, Emory University School of Medicine, and Adjunct Professor of Medicine, Morehouse School of Medicine, Atlanta, Georgia
Gay, Blenda Glen	Fayetteville State University	NFL Player with the San Diego Chargers and Philadelphia Eagles
Gayles, Joseph N., Jr.	Dillard University	President of Talladega College, Morehouse School of Medicine Vice President for Development
Gentry, Howard, Jr.	Tennessee State University	Vice Mayor of the Metropolitan Government of Nashville, Tennessee and Davidson County, President of the Metropolitan Council, CEO of the Nashville Chamber Public Benefit Foundation
Gibson, Althea	Florida A&M University	First Black Woman on the World Tennis Tour, Grand Slam Title Winner in 1956
Gilbert, Elias	Winston-Salem State University	Track and Field World Record Holder
Gilbert, John Wesley	Paine College	First African American Archaeologist
Gilchrest, Wayne Thomas	Delaware State University	U.S. Congressman
Giles, Jimmy	Alcorn State University	NFL Player with the Tampa Bay Buccaneers
Gilford, Henry	Alabama A&M University	President and CEO of the Gilford Corporation
Gilliam, Joseph, Jr.	Tennessee State University	NFL Player with the Pittsburgh Steelers
Gilmore, Vanessa Diane	Hampton University	U.S. District Court Judge
Giovanni, Yolanda Cornelia "Nikki"	Fisk University	Grammy Award–Winning Poet, Activist, Professor
Gipson, Mack, Jr.	Paine College	NASA Consultant, First African American to obtain a PhD in Geology
Glenn, Clement E.	Prairie View A&M University	2010 Democratic Candidate for Texas Governor

(continued)

Table 5 (*Continued*)

Name	School	Occupation
Gloste, Hugh M.	Lemoyne-Owen College	President of Morehouse College
Glover, Nathaniel, Jr.	Edward Waters College	Sheriff of Jacksonville, Florida, Interim President of Edward Waters College
Golphin, Robert X.	St. Augustine's College	Actor
Gooden, Beverly	Hampton University	Best-Selling Author
Graham, Trevor	St. Augustine's College	Athletics Coach
Grant, C. LeFoy	Clark Atlanta University	Television Editor and Producer, Founder of HBCU Unit Network
Grant, Travis	Kentucky State University	NBA Player with the Los Angeles Lakers and Indiana Pacers
Grattan, C. Hartley	Clark Atlanta University	Economist and Historian
Graves, Earl Gilbert, Sr.	Morgan State University	Publisher of *Black Enterprise* Magazine
Graves, Mildred Netter	Alcorn State University	Olympic Gold Medalist
Graves, William H.	Lane College	Senior Bishop and CEO of the Christian Methodist Episcopal Church
Gray, Fred	Alabama State University	Attorney for Rosa Parks during the Montgomery Bus Boycott and the First African American President of the Alabama State Bar
Gray, Quinn F., Sr.	Florida A&M University	NFL Player with the Jacksonville Jaguars and the Kansas City Chiefs
Grays, Mattelia Bennett	Dillard University	18th International President of Alpha Kappa Alpha, Inc.
Green, Louis Edward	Alcorn State University	NFL Player with the Denver Broncos
Green, Ronald G.	Texas Southern University	City Controller of Houston, Texas
Green-Ridley, Gloria	University of the District of Columbia	First African American Recipient of the James Davenport Memorial Award
Greenwood, L. C. Henderson	University of Arkansas at Pine Bluff	NFL Player with the Pittsburgh Steelers
Gregory, Louis George	Fisk University, Howard University	Hand of the Cause in the Bahá'í Faith
Gregory, Roger L.	Virginia State University	Judge, U.S. Court of Appeals for the Fourth Circuit
Grigsby, Eugene J., Jr.	Johnson C. Smith University	Artist and Art Educator

Grimke, Archibald Henry	Lincoln University	Lawyer, Journalist, Diplomat, and Community Leader
Grimsley, Chet F.	Johnson C. Smith University	First White CIAA and All-American at JCSU and at an HBCU, and Author
Grissom, Marquis Deon	Florida A&M University	MLB Player with the Montreal Expos, Atlanta Braves, Cleveland Indians, Milwaukee Brewers, Los Angeles Dodgers, and San Francisco Giants
Gunn, Moses	Tennessee State University	Actor
Guy-Sheftall, Beverly	Spelman College	Author, Feminist Scholar, Founder of Women's Research and Resource Center at Spelman College
Hairston, Carl Blake	University of Maryland Eastern Shore	Coach with the United Football League, NFL Player with the Green Bay Packers, Kansas City Chiefs, and St. Louis Rams
Hairston, Lorraine	Winston-Salem State University	Mayor of Evanston, Illinois
Hale, William H.	Langston University	Past President of Langston University and Alpha Phi Alpha Fraternity, Inc.
Haley, Alex	Alcorn State University	Author
Haley, Brick	Alabama A&M University	Defensive Line Coach of the Chicago Bears and Louisiana State University Tigers
Haley, Oretha Castle	Southern University at New Orleans	Civil Rights Activist
Hall, Aaron	Virginia State University	R&B Singer
Hall, Alex	St. Augustine's College	NFL Player with the Cleveland Browns, Philadelphia Eagles, New York Giants, and Arizona Cardinals
Hall, Damion	Virginia State University	R&B Singer
Hall, Larry D.	Johnson C. Smith University	Member of North Carolina House of Representatives
Hamilton, George, Sr.	North Carolina Central University	President of Dow Automotive
Hamm, Barbara	Bennett College	First African American Woman to serve as a Television News Director in the United States

(*continued*)

Table 5 (*Continued*)

Name	School	Occupation
Hammonds, Evelynn M.	Spelman College	Professor of the History of Science and African American Studies and Senior Vice Provost for Faculty Development and Diversity at Harvard University
Hardy, Rob	Florida A&M University	Movie Producer
Hare, Julia	Langston University	Psychologist, Wife of Nathan Hare
Hare, Kefla	Alabama State University	Actor, Educator, Motivational Speaker
Hare, Nathan	Langston University	Founding publisher of *The Black Scholar: A Journal of Black Studies and Research*, Author, Wrote First Proposal for the First Black Students' Department
Harper, Fredrick Douglass	Edward Waters College	Author and Scholar
Harper, Nick	Fort Valley State University	NFL Player with the Tennessee Titans
Harper, Thelma	Tennessee State University	Member of the Tennessee State Senate
Harpool, Marsha	Kentucky State University	First African American Mayor of Blountstown, Florida
Harris, Herman	Morris College	Participated in the Freedom Rides during the 1960s
Harris, James Larnell "Shack"	Grambling State University	Senior Personnel Executive for the Detroit Lions, NFL Player with the Buffalo Bills, Los Angeles Rams, and San Diego Chargers
Harris, Marcelite J.	Spelman College	First African American Female to obtain the rank of General in the U.S. Air Force
Harris, Patricia Roberts	Howard University	First African American and only Woman to Serve in Three Cabinet-Level Positions, First Black Female Ambassador, First Female to serve in the United Nations, First Female Dean of a Law School
Harris, William H.	Paine College	President of Paine College, Texas Southern University, and Alabama State University
Harris, Willie	Virginia State University	Lt. Col., Chief of Command Information U.S. Army Reserve
Harris-Hooker, Sandra A.	Dillard University	Associate Dean of Research at Morehouse School of Medicine

Harrison, Charles "Tex"	North Carolina Central University	Coach and Member of the Harlem Globetrotters
Hart, Tommy Lee	Morris Brown College	NFL Player with the San Francisco 49ers, Chicago Bears and New Orleans Saints
Harvey, William R.	Talladega College	President of Hampton University
Hastings, Alcee Lamar	Fisk University	U.S. Congressman
Hatchette, Matthew "Rook"	Langston University	NFL Player with the Minnesota Vikings, New York Jets, Oakland Raiders, Jacksonville Jaguars
Hathaway, Donny Edward	Howard University	Soul Singer and Musician
Hawkins, Erskine Ramsey	Alabama State University	Jazz Musician
Hayes, Burnalle "Bun"	Johnson C. Smith University	Star Pitcher in the Negro Leagues
Hayes, Robert Lee "Bullet Bob"	Florida A&M University	Olympic Gold Medalist
Hayes, Roland	Fisk University	Tenor and First African American Male Concert Artist to receive international acclaim
Hayes, William Quintin	Winston-Salem State University	NFL Player with the Tennessee Titans
Haygood, Lawrence F., Sr.	Stillman College	First Black to attend the Union Theological Seminary in Richmond, Virginia; Founder of Southern Community College in Tuskegee, Alabama
Haynes, Marques	Langston University	Basketball Player with the Harlem Globetrotters and Member of the Basketball Hall of Fame
Haysbert, Raymond V., Sr.	Wilberforce University	Business Executive and Civil Rights Leader
Hefner, James A.	Clark Atlanta University, North Carolina A&T State University	Economist, President of Tennessee State University and Jackson State University
Helterbrand, Jayjay	Kentucky State University	Filipino Player of the Barangay Ginebra Kings in the Philippine Basketball Association
Helton, Audwin	North Carolina Central University	President and CEO of Spatial Data Integrations, Inc.
Hemphill, Julius	Lincoln University of Missouri	Jazz Musician

(*continued*)

Table 5 (*Continued*)

Name	School	Occupation
Henderson, "Big" James	Albany State University	Title Holder in the International Power-Lifting Federation, Offensive Lineman for the 1985 SIAC Conference Championship Football Team
Henderson, Francis C.	Dillard University	Professor of Medicine and Special Assistant to the Director of the Jackson Heart Study—Jackson, Mississippi
Henderson, James Fletcher Hamilton, Jr.	Clark Atlanta University	Pianist, Band Leader, and Composer
Henderson, Thomas "Hollywood"	Langston University	NFL Player with the Dallas Cowboys
Henley, Vernard	Virginia State University	Chairman and CEO of Consolidated Bank and Trust Company
Henry, James T., Sr.	Central State University	First Black Mayor and City Commissioner of Xenia, Ohio
Henry, Philip B. IV	Delaware State University	CEO of Mahogany Communications LLC
Henson, Taraji Penda	North Carolina A&T State University	Actress
Herenton, Willie Wilbert	Lemoyne-Owen College	Mayor of Memphis, Tennessee
Herman, Alexis Margaret	Xavier University of Louisiana	First African American U.S. Secretary of Labor, Director of the White House Office of Public Liaison
Hicks, Maurice	North Carolina A&T State University	NFL Player with the Chicago Bears, San Francisco 49ers, and Minnesota Vikings
Hill, Cleo	Winston-Salem State University	First from a CIAA School Drafted in the First Round of the National Basketball Association
Hill, Hallerin Hilton	Oakwood University	Radio Talk Show Host
Hill, Henry A.	Johnson C. Smith University	First African American President of the American Chemical Society
Hill, Rodrick	Kentucky State University	NFL Player with the Dallas Cowboys, Buffalo Bills, Detroit Lions, and Los Angeles Raiders
Hill, Sammie Lee	Stillman College	NFL Player with the Detroit Lions

Hill, Winston	Texas Southern University	NFL Pro-Bowler with the New York Jets and Los Angeles Rams
Hines, Lovett	Grambling State University	Jazz Artist
Hines, Paul	Norfolk State University	High School Football Coach who coached with Herman Boone, who was portrayed by Denzel Washington in *Remember the Titans*
Holbert, Clarence	Eritrea	Designed the Currency for Eritrea (Africa)
Holland, Ebony	Oakwood University	Member of the Gospel Group Virtue
Holloway, Ernest L.	Langston University	President of Langston University
Holmes, Corey	Mississippi Valley State University	CFL Player, Mayor of Metcalfe, Mississippi
Holmes, Earl	Florida A&M University	NFL Player with the Pittsburgh Steelers, Cleveland Browns, and Detroit Lions
Holmes, James	Albany State University	First African American Director of the U.S. Census Bureau
Holzendorf, Betty	Edward Waters College	Florida State Senator
Honeysucker, Robert E.	Tougaloo College	Opera Singer
Honeywood, Varnette	Spelman College	Artist
Hooks, Benjamin Lawson	Lemoyne-Owen College	Executive Director of the NAACP
Horsey, Michael J.	Cheyney University of Pennsylvania	Member of the Pennsylvania House of Representatives
Houston, Kenneth Ray	Prairie View A&M University	Member Pro Football Hall of Fame (Houston Oilers and Washington Redskins)
Howard, Alexander	Huston-Tillotson University	African American Feminist Studies Theoretician
Howard, Daniel	Claflin University	Winner of New York Emmy Award for Excellence in Teen Programming for *Bullets in the Hood*, also featured in the Sundance Film Festival
Howard, George, Jr.	Lincoln University of Missouri	First African American Federal Judge in Arkansas
Howard, Perry Wilbon, Jr.	Rust College, Fisk University	Assistant U.S. Attorney General
Howard, Theodore Roosevelt Mason	Oakwood University	Civil Rights Leader, Surgeon, Entrepreneur, Mentor to Medgar Evers and Fannie Lou Hamer
Howell, Maria	Winston-Salem State University	Actress and Singer

(continued)

Table 5 (*Continued*)

Name	School	Occupation
Hrabowski, Freeman A., III	Hampton University	President of the University of Maryland, Baltimore County
Hubbard, Trenidad Aviel	Southern University and A&M College	MLB Player with the Colorado Rookies and several other teams
Huff, Michelle	Bennett College	Founder of Huff Entertainment
Hughes, James Mercer Langston	Lincoln University	Author
Hughes, Nate	Alcorn State University	NFL Player with the Jacksonville Jaguars
Hugine, Andrew, Jr.	South Carolina State University	President of South Carolina State University and Alabama A&M University
Humphrey, Claude B.	Tennessee State University	NFL Player with the Atlanta Falcons and Philadelphia Eagles
Humphries, Frederick S.	Florida A&M University	President of Florida A&M University
Hundley, Lynn "Mandisa"	Fisk University	Grammy and Dove Award–nominated Christian contemporary singer/songwriter, Finalist on *American Idol*
Hunt, Cletidus Marquell	Kentucky State University	NFL Player with the Green Bay Packers, and in the Arena Football League
Hunter, Julius	Harris-Stowe State University	St. Louis, Missouri News Anchorman
Hunter, Lindsey Benson, Jr.	Jackson State University	NBA Player with the Chicago Bulls, Detroit Pistons, and the Los Angeles Lakers
Hunter, William C.	Hampton University	Dean of the Tippie College of Business at Iowa University
Huntley, Richard Earl	Winston-Salem State University	NFL Player with the Atlanta Falcons, Pittsburgh Steelers, Carolina Panthers, and Detroit Lions
Hurley, Walter "Doc"	Virginia State University	Founder of the Walter Hurley Foundation
Hurston, Zora Neale	Morgan State University and Howard University	Folklorist, Anthropologist, Author
Hyde, Deborah	Tougaloo College	One of four African American Female Neurosurgeons in the United States
Hytche, William P.	Langston University	President of University of Maryland Eastern Shore
Iglehart, Floyd	Wiley College	NFL Player with the Los Angeles Rams

Imes, Elmer Samuel	Fisk University	Second African American to earn a PhD in Physics and Scientist who made major contributions to modern physics
Ireland, Roderick L.	Lincoln University	First African American Associate Justice of the Massachusetts Supreme Judicial Court
Irons, Roy L.	Tougaloo College	Vice President, National Dental Association
Irving, Barrington, Jr.	Florida Memorial University	First and Youngest African American Pilot
Jackson, Cynthia	University of the District of Columbia	New Jersey Judge
Jackson, Edna P.	Savannah State University	Member of the National League of Cities Board of Directors and Mayor of Savannah, Georgia
Jackson, Grady O'Neal	Knoxville College	NFL Player with the Oakland Raiders, New Orleans Saints, Green Bay Packers, Jacksonville Jaguars, Atlanta Falcons, and Detroit Lions
Jackson, Harold Leon	Jackson State University	NFL Wide Receiver with the Los Angeles Rams and New England Patriots, NFL Wide Receiver Coach
Jackson, Jamaal	Delaware State University	National Football League Player with the Philadelphia Eagles
Jackson, Jesse Louis, Jr.	North Carolina A&T State University	U.S. Congressman, Son of Jesse L. Jackson Sr.
Jackson, Jesse Louis, Sr.	North Carolina A&T State University	Civil Rights Activist, Founder and CEO of the Rainbow PUSH Coalition
Jackson, Jonathan Luther	North Carolina A&T State University	Civil Rights Activist, Businessman, Professor, National Spokesman for the Rainbow PUSH Coalition, Son of Jesse L. Jackson Sr.
Jackson, LaTanya Richardson	Spelman College	Stage, Film, and Television Actress
Jackson, Lewis	Alabama State University	NBA Player, Educator, and ASU Basketball Coach
Jackson, Maynard Holbrook, Jr.	Morehouse College, North Carolina Central University	First African American Mayor of Atlanta, Georgia
Jackson, Randall Darius "Randy"	Southern University and A&M College	American Idol Judge, Musician
Jackson, Samuel L.	Morehouse College	Actor
Jackson, Tarvaris Fox	Alabama State University	Quarterback for the Minnesota Vikings

(continued)

Table 5 ***(Continued)***

Name	School	Occupation
Jacobs, Mary	Bennett College	Member of the Durham City Council and Durham Board of Commissioners
James, Daniel "Chappie," Jr.	Tuskegee University	First African American Four Star General
James, Jerome Keith	Florida A&M University	NBA Player with the Sacramento Kings, Seattle SuperSonics, New York Knicks, and Chicago Bulls
James, Kay Coles	Hampton University	Director of the U.S. Office of Personnel Management, President and Founder of the Gloucester Institute
James, Robert	Fisk University	NFL Player with the Buffalo Bills
Jamison, Judith Anna	Fisk University	Artistic Director for the Alvin Ailey American Dance Theater
Janzon, Mattiwilda Dobbs	Spelman College	First African American to perform opera at the La Scala Opera House in Milan, Italy
Jarmon, Gene C.	North Carolina Central University	General Counsel, Texas Department of Insurance
Jarrett, Ted	Fisk University	Songwriter, Musician
Jarrett, Vernon	Knoxville College	First African American Columnist for the *Chicago Tribune* and President of the National Association of Black Journalists (NABJ)
Jarvis, Leon Raeminton "Ray"	Norfolk State University	NFL Player with the Atlanta Falcons, Buffalo Bills, Detroit Lions, and the New England Patriots
Jefferson, Joseph H.	Claflin University	Member of the South Carolina House of Representatives
Jefferson, Mildred	Texas College	First Black Woman to Graduate from Harvard University Medical School
Jenkins, Terrence "Terrence J"	North Carolina A&T State University	Radio and TV Personality; BET's Host of 106 & Park
Jeter, Charles	Fisk University	Substance Abuse Counselor and Father of MLB Player Derek Jeter
Jiles, Everett C.	Selma University	International Poet and Actor
Johns, Vernon N.	Virginia University of Lynchburg	Civil Rights Leader and President of Virginia University of Lynchburg
Johnson, Adrienne-Joi	Spelman College	Actress

Johnson, Avery	Southern University and A&M College	2006 NBA Coach of the Year, NBA Coach of Dallas Mavericks and New Jersey Nets, NBA Player with the Seattle SuperSonics, Denver Nuggets, San Antonio Spurs, Houston Rockets, Golden State Warriors, and Dallas Mavericks
Johnson, Clinton "Trey," III	Jackson State University	NBA Player with the New Orleans Hornets
Johnson, Conrad O.	Wiley College	Music Educator and Inductee into the Texas Bandmasters Hall of Fame
Johnson, Edward A.	Shaw University	First African American Member of the New York State Legislature
Johnson, Ella Mae Cheeks	Fisk University	At the age 105 years, she traveled to Washington, D.C., to attend the Inauguration of President Barack Obama
Johnson, Eunice Walker	Talladega College	Executive of Johnson Publishing Company
Johnson, Ezra	Morris Brown College	NFL Player with the Green Bay Packers, Indianapolis Colts, and Houston Oilers
Johnson, Harry E.	Xavier University of Louisiana, Texas Southern University	Attorney, Professor at Texas Southern University, President of Alpha Phi Alpha Fraternity, Inc., and President of the Washington, D.C., Martin Luther King Jr. National Memorial Project Foundation, Inc.
Johnson, Harvey, Jr.	Tennessee State University	Mayor of Jackson, Mississippi
Johnson, Henry C. "Hank"	Clark Atlanta University	U.S. Congressman
Johnson, Jack B.	Benedict College	County Executive for Prince George's County, Maryland
Johnson, James Weldon	Clark Atlanta University	Writer of the Negro National Anthem
Johnson, Jon	Southern University at New Orleans	New Orleans City Councilman
Johnson, Joseph D.	Winston-Salem State University	Attorney
Johnson, Larry	Elizabeth City State University	NFL Linebacker, Defensive Line Coach at Penn State University, and Six-Time Maryland High School "Coach of the Year"
Johnson, Lee	Norfolk State University	NBA Player with the Detroit Pistons
Johnson, Lee, Jr.	Shaw University	President and CEO of Mechanics & Farmers Bank

(*continued*)

Table 5 (*Continued*)

Name	School	Occupation
Johnson, Lonnie George	Tuskegee University	Inventor of the Super Soaker and NASA Aerospace Engineer
Johnson, Marcus	Howard University	Record Company CEO
Johnson, Norma Holloway	University of the District of Columbia	U.S. Federal Judge
Johnson, Okoro Harold	Tougaloo College	Actor, Director, and Playwright
Johnson, Otis Samuel	Clark Atlanta University	Mayor of Savannah, Georgia
Johnson, Robert Edward "Bon"	Morehouse College	Former Executive Editor and Associate Publisher, *JET Magazine*
Johnson, Robert Walker	Meharry Medical College	Tennis Instructor for Althea Gibson and Arthur Ashe, Physician, and Educator
Johnson, Yvonne J.	Bennett College	First Black Mayor of Greensboro, North Carolina
Johnston, Gladys Styles	Cheyney University of Pennsylvania	Chancellor of the University of Nebraska at Kearney
Jolly, Samuel D., Jr.	Fort Valley State University	President of Morris Brown College
Jones, Bobby	Tennessee State University	Television Evangelist
Jones, Caldwell "Pops"	Albany State University	Basketball Player with the American Basketball Association and National Basketball Association
Jones, Charles "Gadget"	Albany State University	NBA Player with the Philadelphia 76ers, Chicago Bulls, Washington Bullets, Detroit Pistons, and Houston Rockets
Jones, Charles Price	Arkansas Baptist College	Founder of the Church of Christ (Holiness) U.S.A.
Jones, Cleon Joseph	Alabama A&M University	MLB Player with the New York Mets and Chicago White Sox
Jones, David D. "Deacon"	Mississippi Valley State University	NFL Hall of Fame Player with the Los Angeles Rams, San Diego Chargers, and Washington Redskins
Jones, Ed Lee "Too Tall"	Tennessee State University	NFL Player with the Dallas Cowboys
Jones, Edith Irby	Knoxville College	First Female President of the National Medical Association
Jones, Jamal Aman	North Carolina A&T State University	NFL Player with the St. Louis Rams, Green Bay Packers, and New Orleans Saints
Jones, Leroy	Norfolk State University	NFL Player with the San Diego Chargers

Jones, Lewis Wade	Fisk University	Sociologist and Julius Rosenwald Foundation Fellow at Columbia University
Jones, Major James Brooks	Albany State University	NBA Player with the Houston Rockets and Detroit Pistons
Jones, Michael D.	Dillard University	Attorney and Partner, Kirkland & Ellis
Jones, Paul William Lawrence	Kentucky State University	Educator, Historian, and Athlete
Jones, Samuel "Sam"	North Carolina A&T State University	NBA Hall of Famer with the Boston Celtics
Jones, Tayari	Spelman College	Author
Jones, Tyrone	Southern University and A&M College	Canadian Football League All-Star and MVP
Jones, Warren A.	Dillard University	Distinguished Professor of Health Policy; Executive Director for the Mississippi Institute for Geographic Minority Health, University of Mississippi Medical Center; First African American elected President of the American Academy of Family Physicians
Jones, Wilbert "Wil"	Albany State University	Basketball Player with the American Basketball Association and National Basketball Association
Jones, Willa Saunders	Arkansas Baptist College	Playwright
Jordan, Barbara Charline	Texas Southern University	U.S. Congresswoman
Jordan, David	Mississippi Valley State University	Member of the Mississippi State Senate
Jordan, Vernon Eulion, Jr.	Howard University	Head of UNCF and the Urban League
Joyner, Marjorie Stewart	Bethune-Cookman University	Inventor of the Permanent Wave Machine
Joyner, Thomas "Tom"	Tuskegee University	Radio Talk Show Host, Founder of REACH Media, Inc., Founder of the Tom Joyner Foundation, Founder of BlackAmericaWeb.com
Jude, China	Alabama State University	First Black Female Athletic Director, Cheyney University of Pennsylvania
Just, Ernest Everett	South Carolina State University	Biologist, First Recipient of the NAACP's Spingarn Medal, One of the Founders of Omega Psi Phi Fraternity
Kelly, Bernadine Weaver	Southern University at New Orleans	First African American New Orleans Police Department Officer to be promoted to Captain

(*continued*)

Table 5 ***(Continued)***

Name	School	Occupation
Kelly, Leroy	Morgan State University	NFL Hall of Famer with the Cleveland Browns
Kelly, Sharon Pratt	Howard University	Mayor of Washington, D.C.
Kendall, Joseph "Tarzan"	Kentucky State University	All-American College Football Player and Member of the College Football Hall of Fame
Kennedy, Yvonne	Alabama State University	President of Bishop State Community College
Kent, George E.	Savannah State University	Professor, Scholar, First African American Professor of English at the University of Chicago
Keymah, T'keyah Crystal	Florida A&M University	Actress, Writer, Director, Producer, Singer, and Comedienne
Kibble, Joel "Joey"	Oakwood University	Member of the Gospel Group Take 6
Kibble, Mark	Oakwood University	Member of the Gospel Group Take 6
Kilcrease, Orlando	Alcorn State University	Appointed by President Barack Obama as the Chairman of the Mississippi Farm Service Agency State Committee
Kilpatrick, Kwame Malik	Florida A&M University	Mayor of Detroit, Michigan
Kilson, Martin L.	Lincoln University	First African American to be granted Tenure at Harvard University
Kimoni, Shombay	South Carolina State University	Author, Entrepreneur, and Artist
King, Alberta Williams	Hampton University, Spelman College	Mother of Dr. Martin Luther King Jr.
King, Bernice Albertine	Spelman College	President of the Southern Christian Leadership Conference and Daughter of Dr. Martin Luther King Jr.
King, Martin Luther, Jr.	Morehouse College	Civil Rights Activist, Writer, Winner of the Nobel Peace Prize
King, Melvin H.	Claflin University	Professor at the Massachusetts Institute of Technology, Activist, and Writer
King, Reatha Clark	Clark Atlanta University	Former President and Executive Director of General Mills Foundation Scientist, Philanthropist, and Educator
Kinney, George	Wiley College	NFL Player with the Houston Oilers
Kirkland, Thaddeus	Cheyney University of Pennsylvania	Member of the Pennsylvania House of Representatives
Kiser, Roosevelt	Florida A&M University	NFL Player with the Jacksonville Jaguars

Knight, Genevieve Madeline	Fort Valley State University	1987 Recipient of the Outstanding Faculty Award for Mathematics and Mentoring of Minority Youth from the White House Initiative on Historically Black Colleges and Universities
Knowles, Matthew	Fisk University	Music Industry Executive, Father of Beyoncé and Solange Knowles
Ladner, Joyce Ann	Tougaloo College	First Female President of Howard University
Laffall, LaSalle D., Jr.	Florida A&M University and Howard School of Medicine	First Black President of the American Cancer Society
Lake, Oliver	Lincoln University of Missouri	Jazz Musician
Land, Dan	Albany State University	NFL Player with the Tampa Bay Buccaneers and the Los Angeles/Oakland Raiders
Langhorne, Reginald "Reggie" Devan	Elizabeth City State University	NFL Player with the Cleveland Browns and Indianapolis Colts
Lanier, Willie Edward	Morgan State University	NFL Hall of Fame Player with the Kansas City Chiefs
Lassiter, Darryl	Alabama State University	Producer and Director
Lassiter, Ike	St. Augustine's College	First American Professional Football Player from St. Augustine's College
Lavender, Catherine Hardy	Fort Valley State University	Olympic Gold Medalist
Law, Westley Wallace	Savannah State University	Civil Rights Leader and Preservationist
Lawlah, Gloria Gary	Hampton University	Secretary of Aging for the State of Maryland
Lawrence, Henry	Florida A&M University	NFL Pro-Bowler with the Oakland Raiders
Lee, Joseph E.	Cheyney University of Pennsylvania	One of the First Blacks to practice Law in Florida, Member of the Florida State Congress
Lee, Shelton Jackson "Spike"	Morehouse College	Filmmaker
Lee-Weldon, Nikki	Spelman College	Educator
Leigh, Ronald M., Sr.	Elizabeth City State University	NFL defensive end for the New England Patriots

(*continued*)

Table 5 (*Continued*)

Name	School	Occupation
Leland, George Thomas "Mickey"	Texas Southern University	Antipoverty Activist, U.S. Congressman, and Chairman of the Congressional Black Caucus
Lemelle, Ivan L. R.	Xavier University of Louisiana	U.S. Federal Judge, U.S. District Court in New Orleans
Leon, Kenny	Clark Atlanta University	Actor and Former Artistic Director of Atlanta's Alliance Theatre
Lester, Julius	Fisk University	Author and Professor
Letton, James C.	Kentucky State University	Chemist and Inventor
Lewis, Amanda	Howard University	Television Personality
Lewis, David Levering	Fisk University	Two-Time Pulitzer Prize Winner
Lewis, Emmanuel	Clark Atlanta University	Actor
Lewis, Frederick "Fred" Deshaun	Southern University and A&M College	MLB Player with the San Francisco Giants and Toronto Blue Jays
Lewis, Garry	Alcorn State University	NFL Player with the Oakland Raiders
Lewis, George R.	Hampton University	President and CEO, Phillip Morris Capital Corporation; Listed among the Top 50 Black Executives by *Ebony* Magazine
Lewis, John Robert	Fisk University	U.S. Congressman
Lewis, Leo	Lincoln University of Missouri	Member of the Canadian Football League Hall of Fame
Lewis, Martha S.	Clark Atlanta University, University of Arkansas at Pine Bluff	Government Official in New York City and State
Lewis, Maxine R.	Delaware State University	Publicist, ABC Television Network
Lewis, Michael "Mike" Henry	Wiley College	NFL Player with the Atlanta Falcons and Green Bay Packers
Lewis, Reginald F.	Virginia State University	CEO of TLC/Beatrice
Lewis, William H.	Virginia State University	U.S. Assistant Attorney General
Lightner, Clarence Everett	North Carolina Central University	First African American Mayor of Raleigh, North Carolina
Lincoln, C. Eric	Lemoyne-Owen College	Author and Duke University Professor
Linder, Rozlyn	Clark Atlanta University	Educator and Author
Linsey, Nathaniel L.	Paine College	Senior Bishop of the Christian Methodist Episcopal Church

Little, Lawrence "Larry" Chatmon	Bethune-Cookman University	NFL Hall of Fame Player with the San Diego Chargers and Miami Dolphins
Littlejohn, Sherrie Brown	Xavier University of Louisiana	Vice President and Chief Information Officer for SBC Messaging in Ramon, California
Lloyd, Earl Francis	West Virginia State University	First African American to play in the NBA
Lloyd, Gregory "Greg" Lenard	Fort Valley State University	NFL Pro-Bowl Player with the Pittsburgh Steelers
Lomax, L. J. "Stan"	Fort Valley State University	Georgia Sports Hall of Famer
Lomax, Michael	Morehouse College	President and Chief Executive Officer of the United Negro College Fund, College President, Educator
London, Robert, II	Delaware State University	National Football League Sports Agent
Long, Eddie Lee	North Carolina Central University	Senior Pastor, New Birth Missionary Baptist Church, Lithonia, Georgia
Love, Arthur	South Carolina State University	NFL Player with the New England Patriots
Love, Robert (Bob) Earl "Butterbean"	Southern University and A&M College	NBA All-Star with the Chicago Bulls
Loveday, Shari	Oakwood University	Playwright from Christian Fellowship Halla
Lowery, Joseph Echols	Paine College	President of the Southern Christian Leadership Conference
Lucas, Jeanne Hopkins	North Carolina Central University	First African American elected to the North Carolina Senate
Lucas, Quincy A.	Delaware State University	Advocate against Domestic Violence, Speaker at the 2008 Democratic National Convention
Luetkemeyer, Blaine	Lincoln University of Missouri	U.S. Congressman
Lunceford, James Melvin "Jimmie"	Fisk University	Jazz Alto Saxophonist and Bandleader
Lundy, Harold, Sr.	Dillard University	President of Grambling State University
Lundy, Larry	Dillard University	President of Lundy Enterprises, LLC (a *Black Enterprise* Top 100 Company)

(continued)

Table 5 (*Continued*)

Name	School	Occupation
Lynn, Lonnie Rashied "Common," Jr.	Florida A&M University	Hip-Hop Artist, Actor
Lyons, Henry J.	Bethune-Cookman University	President of the National Baptist Convention, USA, Inc.
Lysonge, E. M.	Fisk University	Senior Director of the Churchill Downs Racetrack (Home of the Kentucky Derby)
Mack, Milton Jerome	Alcorn State University	NFL Player with the New Orleans Saints, Tampa Bay Buccaneers, and Detroit Lions
Mahorn, Derrick (Rick) Allen	Hampton University	NBA Player Detroit Pistons, WNBA Detroit Shock Head Coach
Malachi, Mike	Coppin State University	Hip-Hop Artist
Mallett, Martell	University of Arkansas at Pine Bluff	NFL Player with the Cleveland Browns
Mallory, Arenia C.	Bethune-Cookman University	Founder of Saints Academy
Malone, Vernon	Shaw University	Member of the North Carolina General Assembly
Manigault, Earl "The Goat"	Johnson C. Smith University	Rucker Park Legend
Manigault-Stallworth, Omarosa	Central State University	Actress
Manley, Audrey F.	Spelman College, Meharry Medical College	Deputy Surgeon General of the United States, President of Spelman College
Mann, Marion	Tuskegee University	Dean of the College of Medicine at Howard University and U.S. Army Brigadier General
Manning, Edward (Ed) R.	Jackson State University	NBA Player, Coach, and Scout
Marsalis, Branford	Southern University	Saxophonist, Composer, and Bandleader
Marsalis, Ellis M., Jr.	Dillard University	Jazz Pianist and Music Educator; Father of Jazz artists Branford Marsalis, Wynton, and Delfeayo; Retired Director of Jazz Studies, University of New Orleans
Marsh, Henry L.	Virginia Union University, Howard University	First African American Mayor of Richmond, Virginia
Marshall, Thurgood	Lincoln University, Howard University	First African American Supreme Court Justice

Marshall, Walter	Winston-Salem State University	Forsyth County (Winston-Salem, North Carolina) County Commissioner
Martin, Chris "DJ Premier"	Prairie View A&M University	Member of Gang Starr
Martin, Heather	Oakwood University	Member of the Gospel Group Virtue
Mason, Anthony George Douglas	Tennessee State University	NBA All-Star Player with the New Jersey Nets, Denver Nuggets, New York Knicks, Charlotte Hornets, Milwaukee Bucks and Miami Heat
Mason, Frank J.	Dillard University	Owner, FranGlo (McDonald's Franchise Owner)
Mason, Judi-Ann	Grambling State University	Writer
Massey, Walter E.	Morehouse College	Bank of America Chairman
Masten, Charles C.	Albany State University	Inspector General, U.S. Department of Labor
Mathis, Rashean Jamil.	Bethune-Cookman University	NFL Player with the Jacksonville Jaguars
Mathis, Robert Nathan	Alabama A&M University	NFL Pro-Bowler with the Indianapolis Colts
Matthews, Vincent "Vince" Edward	Johnson C. Smith University	Olympic Gold Medalist
Maupin, John E.	Meharry Medical College	President of Morehouse School of Medicine
Mayfield, Jody	Clark Atlanta University	Composer, Jazz Musician
Maynor, Dorothy	Hampton University	Concert Singer
Mays, Charles "Charlie," Sr.	University of Maryland Eastern Shore	Olympic Long Jumper and New Jersey State Assemblyman
McAuliffe, Christa	Bowie State University	Astronaut
McBay, Henry Cecil	Wiley College	Chemist and College Professor
McBay, Shirley Mathis	Paine College, Clark Atlanta University	First African American Dean at Massachusetts Institute of Technology
McBryar, William	St. Augustine's College	Medal of Honor Recipient
McCain, James T.	Morris College	Civil Rights Activist and Local President of the Congress of Racial Equality (CORE)
McCain, Lillie	Tougaloo College	Psychologist

(*continued*)

Table 5 (*Continued*)

Name	School	Occupation
McCall, Nathan	Norfolk State University	Reporter for the Virginian Pilot-Ledger Star, the Atlanta Journal-Constitution, and *the Washington Post*; Author
McCants, Darnerien	Delaware State University	National Football League Wide Receiver with the Baltimore Ravens
McCloud-Bethune, Mary	Barbara Scotia College	HBCU Founder
McConnell, Ira Wayne	Grambling State University	Managing Partner with McConnell Jones Lanier & Murphy, LLP
McCorvey, Woody	Alabama State University	Assistant Head Football Coach for The Mississippi State University Bulldogs
McCottry, Catherine McKee	Johnson C. Smith University	First African American Female Physician, First African American Female Practitioner in Obstetrics and Gynecology
McCray, Talia	Bennett College	Research Scientist
McCree, Wade Hampton, Jr.	Fisk University	Second African American U.S. Solicitor General, and First African American Justice of the U.S. Court of Appeals for the Sixth Circuit
McCullin, James L.	Kentucky State University	Tuskegee Airman
McDemmond, Marie V.	Xavier University of Louisiana	First Female President at Norfolk State University
McDonald, Charles J.	North Carolina A&T State University	Chair, Dermatology Department, Brown University Medical School
McDuffie, Mildred Weathers	Allen University	Summary Court Judge for Richland County, South Carolina
McGee, Bill	Virginia State University	Jazz Singer
McGee, James H. "Jim"	Wilberforce University	First African American Mayor of Dayton, Ohio
McGee, Sherri A.	Spelman College	Author
McGee-Anderson, Kathleen	Spelman College	Television Producer and Playwright
McGirt, Eddie C.	Johnson C. Smith University	CIAA Football Coach, Member of the CIAA Hall of Fame
McGuire, Edith Marie	Tennessee State University	Olympic Gold and Silver Medalist
McIntosh, Edward	Hampton University	Scholar and Educator

McIver, Everett	Elizabeth City State University	NFL Player with the New York Jets, Miami Dolphins and Dallas Cowboys
McKay, Claude	Tuskegee University	Jamaican Writer and Poet, Harlem Renaissance
McKee, Tywain	Coppin State University	Basketball Player in Australia for the Wollongong Hawks
McKenna, George, III	Xavier University of Louisiana	Superintendent of the Inglewood Unified School District in Los Angeles, California, Principal Who Inspired the Movie "The George McKenna Story"
McKenzie, Vashti Murphy	Howard University	First Woman Bishop of the African Methodist Zion Church
McKinney, Jon	Norfolk State University	NBA Player with the Boston Celtics
McKnight, Brian	Oakwood University	R&B Singer and Musician
McKnight, Claude	Oakwood University	Member of the Gospel Group Take 6
McNair, Ronald Ervin	North Carolina A&T State University	First African American Astronaut, died in the Space Shuttle Challenger explosion in 1986
McNair, Steve LaTreal	Alcorn State University	NFL Pro-Bowl Player with the Houston Oilers, Tennessee Titans and Baltimore Ravens
McNeal, Glenda Goodly	Dillard University	Senior Vice President, American Express Company
McNealey, Ernest	Alabama State University	President of Stillman College
McPhee, Sidney A.	Prairie View A&M University	President of Middle Tennessee State University
McPherson, James Alan	Morris Brown College	Pulitzer Prize–Winning Author
McRae, Harold "Hal" Abraham	Florida A&M University	MLB Player and Manager
McSwain, Lawrence	North Carolina A&T State University	District Court Judge
Means, Carey	Lincoln University of Missouri	Voice of Frylock on *Aqua Teen Hunger Force*
Meek, Carrie P.	Florida A&M University	First African American Female elected to the Florida State Senate, U.S. Congresswoman
Meek, Kendrick Brett	Florida A&M University	U.S. Congressman
Meek, Leslie Dixon	Fisk University	Administrative Law Judge and Wife of Congressman Kendrick Meek
Mfume, Kweisi	Morgan State University	President/CEO of the NAACP

(*continued*)

Table 5 ***(Continued)***

Name	School	Occupation
Michaux, Henry M. "Mickey," Jr.	North Carolina Central University	Member of the North Carolina House of Representatives
Mickens, Ronald Elbert	Fisk University	Physicist and Author
Middleton, John	Allen University	President of Morris Brown College
Midnight Star	Kentucky State University	R&B Group
Milburn, Rodney "Rod," Jr.	Southern University and A&M College	Olympic Gold Medalist
Miles, Leo	Virginia State University	First African American Official to officiate a Super Bowl
Miles, Sir Edward, III	Clark Atlanta University	Philanthropist and Designed DTG, Inc. Facility, Son of Royal Court
Millen, Herbert E.	Lincoln University	First African American Judge in Pennsylvania
Miller, Cleophus "Cleo"	University of Arkansas at Pine Bluff	NFL Player with the Kansas City Chiefs and Cleveland Browns
Miller, Jerome	Savannah State University	Toyota Motor Sales Vice President for Diversity and Inclusion—Toyota Motor Sales, U.S.A., Inc.
Miller, Rosalind	Xavier University of Louisiana	Director of the J. B. Henderson Family Investment Center in New Iberia, Louisiana
Miller, Tangi	Alabama State University	Actress
Miller, Yvonne B.	Norfolk State University	Virginia State Senator
Milner, Eddie	Central State University	MLB Player with the Cincinnati Reds and San Francisco Giants
Miranda, Africa	Alabama State University	Singer
Mishoe, Luna Isaac	Allen University	President of Delaware State University
Mitchell, Parren James	Morgan State University	U.S. Congressman
Mix, Bryant	Alcorn State University	NFL Player with the Houston Oilers
Mobley, Barbara J.	Savannah State University	First African American Woman elected to DeKalb County Georgia State Court Bench, Member of the Georgia House of Representatives
Monroe, Earl "The Pearl"	Winston-Salem State University	NBA Player with the Baltimore Bullets and New York Knicks
Monroe, Lee	Shaw University	President of Voorhees College

Monroe, Randy	Cheyney University of Pennsylvania	Head Coach of the University of Maryland, Baltimore County Men's Basketball Team
Moody, Anne	Tougaloo College	Author and Civil Rights Activist
Moore, Earl	Oakwood University	Pastor and Civil Rights Activist
Moore, Jerry	Morris College	Participated in the Freedom Rides during the 1960s
Moore, Lee Terry	Alcorn State University	NFL Player with the Oakland Raiders
Moore, Peter Wedderick	Shaw University	First President of Elizabeth City State University
Moore, Ron	West Virginia State University	NBA Player with the New York Knicks
Moore, Steve E.	Tennessee State University	NFL Player with the New England Patriots
Moore, Undine Smith	Fisk University	First Fisk University Graduate to receive a Scholarship to Juilliard, Pulitzer Prize Nominee
Moore, Zeke	Lincoln University of Missouri	NFL Player for the Houston Oilers, Jacksonville Jaguars, Tennessee Titans, and the Buffalo Bills
Morgan, Kimberly Nicole	Alcorn State University	Miss Mississippi 2007
Morris, Garrett	Dillard University	Comedian and Actor
Morris, Thomas	Norfolk State University	Corresponding Write for *America's Most Wanted*
Morrison, Toni	Howard University	Nobel Prize and Pulitzer–Winning Author
Morton, Azie Taylor	Huston-Tillotson University	U.S. Treasurer
Morton, Leo	Tuskegee University	Chancellor, University of Missouri at Kansas City
Moses, Edwin Corley	Morehouse College	Olympic Gold Medalist
Motley, Constance Blake	Fisk University	Civil Rights Activist, Lawyer, Judge, State Senator, and President of Manhattan, New York City
Moton, LeVelle	North Carolina Central University	Basketball Coach at NCCU
Moton, Robert Russa	Hampton University	Principal of Tuskegee Institute
Moultrie, Mae Francis	Morris College	Participated in the Freedom Rides during the 1960s
Murphy, Margaret "Peggy"	Coppin State University	First Black Woman to Chair the Baltimore City Delegation

(*continued*)

Table 5 (*Continued*)

Name	School	Occupation
Murphy, Philip J.	South Carolina State University	NFL Player with the Los Angeles Rams and Principal for P. J. Murphy Co. Investment Banking Services
Murphy, Rob	Central State University	Basketball Assistant Coach at Syracuse University
Murray, Albert L.	Tuskegee University	Literary and Jazz Critic, Novelist and Biographer
Murray, Angela Burt	Hampton University	Editor in Chief of *Essence* Magazine
Murray, Conrad	Meharry Medical College	Cardiologist and personal physician of Michael Jackson
Murray, Ronald "Flip"	Shaw University	NBA Player with the Chicago Bulls
Myers, Lou Leabengula	West Virginia State University	Actor and Theatrical Director
Nagin, Clarence Ray, Jr.	Tuskegee University	Mayor of New Orleans, Louisiana
Nance, Milligan Maceo, Jr.	South Carolina State University	President of South Carolina State University
Narcisse, Donald "Don"	Texas Southern University	Canadian Football League Player
Nash, Bob J.	University of Arkansas at Pine Bluff	White House Director of Personnel for President Bill Clinton
Nash, Diane Judith	Fisk University	Founding Member of the Student Nonviolent Coordinating Committee (SNCC)
Neal, Fred "Curly"	Johnson C. Smith University	Basketball Player with the Harlem Globetrotters
Neal, Lloyd	Tennessee State University	NBA Player with the Portland Trail Blazers
Neal, Toni	Oakwood University	Traffic Anchor, WSB-TV Atlanta, Georgia
Nelson, Gertrude DeWitt	Tuskegee University	American Red Cross Nurse, College Administrator from Louisiana
Nelson, Lorenzo Raymond Sylvanus	Meharry Medical College	Regimental Surgeon
Newsome, Timmy A.	Winston-Salem State University	NFL Player with the Dallas Cowboys
Newton, Ernest E., II	Winston-Salem State University	Deputy President Pro Tempore of the Connecticut Senate and Chairman of Public Safety
Newton, Nathaniel "Nate"	Florida A&M University	NFL Player with the Dallas Cowboys, Carolina Panthers
Nhleko, Phuthuma Freedom	Clark Atlanta University	CEO of the MTN Group
Nichols, Waddell	Allen University	President of Allen University

Nielsen, Aldon Lynn	University of the District of Columbia	Poet
Nix, Robert N. C., Sr.	Lincoln University	Pennsylvania's First African American U.S. Congressman
Nkrumah, Osagyefo Kwame	Lincoln University	First President of Ghana, First Prime Minister of Ghana
Noel, Rachel Bassette	Fisk University	First African American to serve on the Denver Public Schools Board of Education, and First African American Woman elected to Public Office in Colorado
Norful, W. R. "Smokie," Jr.	University of Arkansas at Pine Bluff	Pastor, Gospel Singer and Pianist
Norman, Jessye	Howard University	Opera Singer
Norman, Maidie	Bennett College	Actress
Norman, Pettis Burch	Johnson C. Smith University	NFL Player with the Dallas Cowboys and San Diego Chargers
Norris, Audie James	Jackson State University	NBA Player with the Portland Blazers
Norwood, Bryan T.	Hampton University	Chief of the Bridgeport Police Department
Nunn, Eleanor	Shaw University	Civil Rights Activist, Founder of the Student Nonviolent Coordinating Committee (SNCC), Educator
O'Leary, Hazel R.	Fisk University	U.S. Secretary of Energy
Oakley, Charles	Virginia Union University	NBA Player Chicago Bulls, New York Knicks, Toronto Raptors, Washington Wizards, and Houston Rockets
O'Leary, Hazel Reid	Fisk University	First African American and First Female to serve as U.S. Secretary of Energy
Oliver, David	Howard University	Olympic Bronze Medalist
Oliver, Kimberly	Hampton University	2006 National Teacher of the Year
Oliver, Pamela "Pam" Donielle	Florida A&M University	NFL and NBA Sportscaster
O'Neal, Alexander	Alcorn State University	R&B Singer and Musician
O'Neil, Buck	Edward Waters College	Negro League Baseball Player
Ortique, Revius Oliver, Jr.	Dillard University	First African American to serve on the Louisiana State Supreme Court
Osbey, Brenda Marie	Dillard University	Poet

(*continued*)

Table 5 (*Continued*)

Name	School	Occupation
Owens, Robert P.	University of the District of Columbia	Federal Immigration Judge
Packer, William	Florida A&M University	Movie Producer
Paige, Roderick Raynor "Rod"	Jackson State University	U.S. Secretary of Education
Palmer, Douglas Harold	Hampton University	Mayor of Trenton, New Jersey
Parker, CeCi	Alabama State University	Actress
Parker, Henry E.	Hampton University	Former State Treasurer of Connecticut
Parker-Smith, Bettye	Tougaloo College	First Female President of Dillard University
Parks, Rosa Louise McCauley	Alabama State University	Civil Rights Activist
Parmon, Earline W.	Winston-Salem State University	Member of North Carolina State Legislature
Parrish, Daniel	Florida A&M University	NFL Player with the Jacksonville Jaguars and New York Giants
Parrish, Lemar R.	Lincoln University of Missouri	NFL Pro-Bowler with the Cincinnati Bengals, Washington Redskins, and Buffalo Bills
Patterson, Frederick Douglass.	Prairie View A&M University	Founder of United Negro College Fund
Patterson, Kay	Allen University	Senator in the South Carolina General Assembly
Patterson, Obie	Johnson C. Smith University	Member of the Maryland House of Delegates
Patterson, Samuel J.	Cheyney University of Pennsylvania	CEO of Shepard Patterson Systems and Information Consulting Firm
Payton, Benjamin Franklin	South Carolina State University	President of Tuskegee University and Benedict College
Payton, Edward "Eddie"	Jackson State University	NFL Kick Returner and Jackson State Golf Coach
Payton, Walter	Jackson State University	NFL Hall of Fame Running Back with the Chicago Bears
Pena, Dorian Alan	Coppin State University	Philippine Basketball Association Player, San Miguel Beermen
Pendleton, Louis Christopher	Meharry Medical College	Dentist and Civil Rights Leader in Shreveport, Louisiana
Penniman, Richard Wayne "Little Richard"	Oakwood University	Rock-and-Roll Pioneer
Pennington, Richard	University of the District of Columbia	Atlanta, Georgia Chief of Police
Perkins, James, Jr.	Alabama A&M University	First Black Mayor of Selma, Alabama

Perry, Matthew James, Jr.	South Carolina State University	U.S. Federal Judge
Peterkin, Freddie Lee	Florida Memorial University	Soul and Gospel Singer
Peterson, Greg	North Carolina Central University	NFL Player with the Tampa Bay Buccaneers and Jacksonville Jaguars
Pettigrew, Antonio	St. Augustine's College	Track Star
Philips, Jack	Alcorn State University	NFL Player with the Kansas City Chiefs
Phillips, Charles E.	Hampton University	President of Oracle Corporation
Phillips, Melvin "Mel"	North Carolina A&T State University	NFL Player and Miami Dolphins Coach
Phillips, Seandell K.	Dillard University	First Chief Financial Officer of Alpha Phi Alpha Fraternity, Inc.
Phills, Bobby Ray, II	Southern University and A&M College	NBA Player with Cleveland Cavaliers and Charlotte Hornets
Phipps, Wintley Augustus	Oakwood University	Pastor, Founder, and President of U.S. Dream Academy
Pigford, Eva (Eva Marcille)	Clark Atlanta University	Model and Actress
Pinanko, Frank Atta Osam	Livingstone College	African Missionary
Pinckney, Clemente	Allen University	Senator in the South Carolina General Assembly
Pittman, Marcus "The Novelist"	Kentucky State University	Christian Rap Artist
Pitts, Elijah Eugene	Philander Smith College	NFL Player with the Green Bay Packers, Los Angeles Rams and New Orleans Saints
Pitts, Lucius	Paine College	First African American President of Paine College
Poindexter, Hildrus Augustus	Lincoln University	Bacteriologist, Head of the Howard University Medical College
Pollard, Emily F.	Meharry Medical College	Plastic Surgeon
Pollard, William L.	Shaw University	President of Medgar Evers College
Ponder, Henry	Langston University	President of Fisk University, Talladega College, Benedict College, NAFEO, and Alpha Phi Alpha Fraternity, Inc.
Poole, Tyrone	Fort Valley State University	NFL Player with Carolina Panthers, Indianapolis Colts, Denver Broncos, New England Patriots, Oakland Raiders, and Tennessee Titans
Pope, David	Norfolk State University	NBA Player with the Utah Jazz, Kansas City Kings, and the Seattle SuperSonics

(*continued*)

Table 5 (*Continued*)

Name	School	Occupation
Pope, M. T.	Shaw University	Physician
Porcher, Robert	South Carolina State University	NFL Player with the Detroit Lions
Poston, Ersa Hines	Kentucky State University	First African American to head the U.S. Civil Service Commission, First Black to hold a Presidential Cabinet Position
Powell, Alma Vivian	Fisk University	Audiologist, Wife of Collin Powell
Pratt, Joan M.	Hampton University	Comptroller City of Baltimore
Pratt, Tanya Walton	Spelman College	U.S. District Court Judge nominated by Barack Obama
Preston, Charles A., Jr.	Lincoln University	First African American U.S. Postal Inspector
Price, George B.	South Carolina State University	Brigadier General in the U.S. Army
Price, Leontyne	Central State University, Wilberforce University	Opera Singer
Price, Marcus	Alabama A&M University	President of the Dynamix Corporation
Printers, Casey J.	Florida A&M University	Football Player with the Canadian Football League
Prosser, Inez Beverly	Prairie View A&M University	First African American Woman to receive a Doctoral Degree in Psychology
Prothrow-Stith, Deborah	Spelman College	First Woman to head the Department of Public Health in Massachusetts, Associate Dean for Faculty Development and Director at the Harvard University School of Public Health
Pugh, Jethro, Jr.	Elizabeth City State University	NFL Player with the Dallas Cowboys
Pullen, Don	Johnson C. Smith University	Jazz Pianist and Organist
Pulliam, Keshia Knight	Spelman College	Actress
Puryear, Samuel G.	Tennessee State University	Michigan State University Head Golf Coach
Putnam, Glendora M.	Bennett College	First African American Woman to serve as President of YWCA
Randolph, A. Philip	Bethune-Cookman University	Civil Rights Activist
Randolph, Bernard P.	Xavier University of Louisiana	USAF General, Third African American Four-Star General in the U.S. Armed Forces

Randolph, Leonard, Jr.	Meharry Medical College	Acting Deputy Assistant Secretary of Defense, Health Plan Administration
Randolph, Zilner Trenton	Johnson C. Smith University	Jazz Trumpeter and Music Educator
Rankin, E. Anthony	Meharry Medical College	Chief of Orthopedic Surgery at Providence Hospital and Founder of Rankin Orthopedics and Sports Medicine, Second Vice President of the Board of Directors of the American Academy of Orthopedic Surgeons (AAOS).
Rashad, Phylicia	Howard University	Actress
Ray, Tanika	Spelman College	Actress and Television Personality
Ready, Stephanie	Coppin State University	First Female Head Coach in Professional Men's Basketball
Reagon, Bernice Johnson	Albany State University	Singer, Composer, Scholar, Social Activist, Professor Emeritus of History at American University, Curator Emeritus at the Smithsonian Institution's National Museum of American History in Washington, D.C., Cosby Chair Professor of Fine Arts at Spelman College in Atlanta Georgia
Reaves, Kenneth "Ken" Milton	Norfolk State University	NFL Player with the Atlanta Falcons, New Orleans Saints, and the St. Louis Cardinals
Reavis, Rafael Pangilinan "Rafi"	Coppin State University	Philippine Basketball Association Player with the Derby Ace Llamados
Redman, (Walter) Dewey	Prairie View A&M University	Jazz Saxophonist
Redman, Isaac	Bowie State University	NFL Player with the Pittsburgh Steelers
Reed, Joe L.	Alabama State University	Civil Rights Pioneer
Reed, Mohammed Kasim	Howard University	Mayor of Atlanta, Georgia, Member of the Georgia State Senate
Reed, Pearlier S.	University of Arkansas at Pine Bluff	Assistant Secretary for Administration, U.S. Department of Agriculture
Reed, Robi	Hampton University	Casting Director
Reed, Willis	Grambling State University	NBA MVP and All-Star with the New York Knicks

(continued)

Table 5 (*Continued*)

Name	School	Occupation
Reese, Booker	Bethune-Cookman University	NFL Player with the Tampa Bay Buccaneers and Los Angeles Rams
Reid, Jacque	Clark Atlanta University	Television and Radio Personality, News Anchor of The BET Nightly News
Reid, Timothy L. "Tim"	Norfolk State University	CEO Filmmaker, Director, Actor
Revels, Hiram Rhodes	Rust College	First African American to Serve in Congress and in the U.S. Senate, First President of Alcorn State University
Rhoden, William C.	Morgan State University	*New York Times* Sports Columnist, Author
Rhodes, Eugene Washington	Lincoln University	Editor and Publisher of the *Philadelphia Tribune*, the Oldest Black-Owned Newspaper in the United States
Rice, Angelena Ray	Miles College	Mother of U.S. Secretary of State Condoleezza Rice
Rice, Jerry Lee	Mississippi Valley State University	NFL Hall of Fame Wide Receiver
Rice, John Wesley	Johnson C. Smith University	Dean of Students at Stillman College and Father of Condoleezza Rice
Richardson, Earl S.	University of Maryland Eastern Shore	President of Morgan State University
Richardson, LaTanya	Spelman College	Actress
Richie, Lionel Brockman	Tuskegee University	Singer, Songwriter
Riddle, Kenneth L.	Hampton University	Recording Artist
Riley, Kenneth Jerome	Florida A&M University	NFL Player with the Cincinnati Bengals
Riley, Warren J.	Southern University at New Orleans	Superintendent, New Orleans Police Department
Ritter, Sylvester "Junkyard Dog"	Fayetteville State University	NFL Player and Professional Wrestler
Roberts, Kay George	Fisk University	Founder and Music Director of the Lowell-based New England Orchestra
Robertson, Isiah "Butch"	Southern University and A&M College	NFL Pro-Bowler with the Los Angeles Rams and Buffalo Bills
Robinson, Amelia Boynton "Queen Mother Amelia"	Tuskegee University	Civil and Human Rights Activist, First Woman from Alabama to run for U.S. Congress

Robinson, Bishop L.	Coppin State University	First African American Police Commissioner of Baltimore City, Maryland
Robinson, Charles, Jr.	Fort Valley State University	First African American Certified by the American College of Healthcare Administrators
Robinson, Eddie	Alabama State University	NFL Player for the Houston Oilers, Jacksonville Jaguars, and the Buffalo Bills
Robinson, Faye	Bennett College	Opera Singer
Robinson, James H.	Lincoln University	Founder of Crossroads Africa, the model for the U.S. Peace Corps
Robinson, Jo Ann Gibson	Clark Atlanta University	Civil Rights Activist
Robinson, Prezell R.	St. Augustine's College	President of Saint Augustine's College
Robinson, Randall	Virginia Union University	African American Lawyer, Author, Activist, Founder of Trans-Africa
Robinson, Shaun	Spelman College	Co-anchor of *Access Hollywood*, Host of *TV One Access*
Robinson, Will	West Virginia State University	First African American to Coach Division I Basketball, First African American NFL Scout
Roche, Joyce M.	Dillard University	President and CEO of Girls, Inc., Former President and Chief Operating Officer of Carson, Inc., First Female Chairperson of the Dillard University Board of Trustees
Rod Z	Bethune-Cookman University	Actor and Comedian
Rodgers, Barbara	Knoxville College	Anchor for KPIX TV in San Francisco
Rodgers-Cromartie, Dominique	Tennessee State University	NFL Player with the Arizona Cardinals
Roe, James Edward	Norfolk State University	NFL Player with the Baltimore Ravens and Arena Football League Player
Rogers, Oscar Allen	Tougaloo College	President of Claflin University
Rolle, Esther	Spelman College	Actress
Roman, Charles V.	Meharry Medical College	President of the National Medical Association
Rose, Donovan	Hampton University	NFL Player with the Kansas City Chiefs and Miami Dolphins, Player with the Canadian Football League

(*continued*)

Table 5 (*Continued*)

Name	School	Occupation
Rose, Anika Noni	Florida A&M University	Tony Award–Winning Actress
Roseboro, John Junior	Central State University	MLB Player with the Brooklyn/Los Angeles Dodgers, Minnesota Twins, and Washington Senators
Ross, Monte	Winston-Salem State University	Head Basketball Coach University of Delaware
Ross, Quinton T., Jr.	Alabama State University	Member of Alabama Senate
Rosser, James M.	Langston University	President of California State University at Los Angeles
Rouson, Leon	North Carolina Central University	National Black Teacher of the Year
Rowan, Carl Thomas	Tennessee State University	Author, Journalist, and Columnist for the *Washington Post* and *Chicago Sun-Times*
Rowe, Audrey	University of the District of Columbia	Vice President for Lockheed Martin
Royal, Roderick V.	Tuskegee University	President of the Birmingham City Council, Acting Mayor of Birmingham, Alabama
Rudolph, Wilma Glodean	Tennessee State University	Olympic Gold Medalist
Ruffin, John	Dillard University	First Associate Director for Research on Minority Health and Health Disparities at the National Institutes of Health
Russell, George Allen	Wilberforce University	Jazz Composer and Theorist
Russell, H. C., Jr.	Kentucky State University	Third African American Commissioned Officer in the Coast Guard, Executive with Coca Cola
Russell, Herman J.	Tuskegee University	President and CEO of H. J. Russell Construction Co., the largest minority-owned construction company in the nation
Rustin, Bayard	Cheyney University of Pennsylvania	Civil Rights Activist
Sample, Johnny B., Jr.	University of Maryland Eastern Shore	NFL Player with the Baltimore Colts, Pittsburgh Steelers, and Washington Redskins
Satcher, David	Morehouse College	U.S. Surgeon General
Saunders, Marlene	Delaware State University	2008 Delaware Social Worker of the Year
Sawyer, Eugene	Alabama State University	Mayor of Chicago, Illinois

Scott, Franklyn	Claflin University	President of the National Dental Association, President of the Philadelphia Tennis Club, which is the oldest African American–owned tennis club in the United States
Scott, Marvin	Johnson C. Smith University	Republican Candidate for the U.S. Senate
Scott, Shirley	Cheyney University of Pennsylvania	Jazz Pianist
Scott, Stephanie	Spelman College	Associate Beauty Editor for *Essence* Magazine
Scott, Winnie A.	Kentucky State University	Educator
Scott-Heron, Gil	Lincoln University	Poet, Musician, Author, Spoken Word Performer
Segars, Joseph Monroe	Cheyney University of Pennsylvania	U.S. Ambassador
Sellers, Cleveland L., Jr.	Voorhees College	President of Voorhees College
Seymour, Teddy	Central State University	First African American to sail around the world solo
Shabazz, Betty	Medgar Evans College	Civil Rights Activist, Wife of Malcolm X
Shackelford, Lottie H.	Philander Smith College	First Female Mayor of Little Rock, Arkansas, Longest-Serving Vice Chair of the Democratic National Committee
Shanks, Simon	Tennessee State University	NFL Player with the Arizona Cardinals
Shannon, John W.	Central State University	U.S. Undersecretary of the Army
Sharpe, Shannon	Savannah State University	NFL Player with the Denver Broncos and Baltimore Ravens, and NFL Commentator
Shaw, Alexander Preston	Rust College	Methodist Bishop and Preacher
Shaw, Charles Alexander	Harris-Stowe State University	Federal Judge for the U.S. District Court for the Eastern District of Missouri
Shaw, Richard G.	South Carolina State University	First African American to serve as Insurance Commissioner in West Virginia
Sheares, Bradley T.	Fisk University	CEO of Reliant Pharmaceuticals, Inc. and President of the U.S. Human Health Division of Merck & Co., Inc.
Sheats, Jimmy	Albany State University	Developed the Formula for Manufacturing Multicolored Carpet
Shell, Arthur "Art"	University of Maryland Eastern Shore	Hall of Fame NFL Player and Head Coach of the Oakland Raiders

(*continued*)

Table 5 (*Continued*)

Name	School	Occupation
Shell, Donnie	South Carolina State University	NFL Player with the Pittsburgh Steelers
Shelton, Ralph	North Carolina A&T State University	Founder of Southeast Fuels
Shepard, James E.	Shaw University	Founder and President of North Carolina Central University
Sherrod, Jessie L.	Tougaloo College	Physician
Sherrod, Martha Lynn	Fisk University	District Court Judge and First African American to win an at-large election in North Alabama since Reconstruction
Shirley, Aaron	Tougaloo College, Meharry Medical College	Founder of Jackson Medical Mall and Recipient of MacArthur Award
Short, Purvis	Jackson State University	NBA Player with the Golden State Warriors
Shuttlesworth, Fred Lee	Alabama State University	Clergy, Civil Rights Leader
Sias, Mary Evans	Tougaloo College	Second Female President of Kentucky State University
Sibert, Sam Lewis	Kentucky State University	NBA Player with the Kansas City Omaha Kings (Cincinnati Royals)
Simmons, Jake, Jr.	Tuskegee University	Oil Broker and Civil Rights Advocate
Simmons, Jerry Bernard	Bethune-Cookman University	NFL Player with the Pittsburgh Steelers, New Orleans Saints, Atlanta Falcons, Chicago Bears, and Denver Broncos
Simmons, Ruth J.	Dillard University	First African American President of an Ivy League University (18th President of Brown University, Providence, Rhode Island) and the First African American President of a "Seven Sisters" School (9th President of Smith College)
Simmons, Tyree Cinque "DJ Drama"	Clark Atlanta University	Hip-Hop Producer
Simon, Levy Lee	Cheyney University of Pennsylvania	Award-Winning Playwright
Simpson, Frank	Kentucky State University	Educator, High School Principal
Simpson, Ralph	Alabama State University	First African American to earn a PhD (in music) from Michigan State University and former Dean of the School of Music at Tennessee State University

Skerritt, Richard	University of the Virgin Islands	University of the Virgin Island's First Rhodes Scholar, Businessman, and Manager of the West Indies Cricket Team
Slade, Leonard	Elizabeth City State University	Professor and chairman of the Department of African and Afro-American Studies, University of New York, and Author
Slater, Jackie Ray	Jackson State University	NFL Hall of Fame Offensive Tackle with the Los Angeles/ St. Louis Rams
Slaughter, Chad	Alcorn State University	NFL Player with the Baltimore Ravens, Dallas Cowboys, New York Jets, and Jacksonville Jaguars
Slaughter-Harvey, Constance	Tougaloo College	Attorney and First African American Female Graduate of the University of Mississippi Law School
Sleet, Gregory M.	Hampton University	U.S. District Court Judge
Sleet, Moneta, Jr.	Kentucky State University	Photographer for *Ebony*, Won a Pulitzer Prize for the picture of Coretta Scott King at the funeral of Dr. Martin Luther King Jr.
Sloan, Albert J.	Albany State University	President of Miles College
Small, George M.	North Carolina A&T State University	NFL Player and Florida A&M Associate Head Coach
Small, Lola Kelly	Claflin University	Research Scientist for Proctor and Gamble Company
Small, Torrance Ramon	Alcorn State University	NFL Player with the New Orleans Saints, St. Louis Rams, Indianapolis Colts, Philadelphia Eagles, and New England Patriots
Smalls, Evelyn	North Carolina Central University	President and CEO of the United Bank of Philadelphia
Smiley, Rickey	Alabama State University	Comedian and Actor
Smith, Brenda V.	Spelman College	Law Professor at American University, Appointed by Nancy Pelosi to the National Prison Rape Elimination Commission
Smith, Calvin Bernard "Bernie"	Southern University and A&M College	MLB Player with the Milwaukee Brewers
Smith, Edgar E.	Tougaloo College	Biochemist and Molecular Biologist, Professor Emeritus, University of Massachusetts School of Medicine
Smith, Effie Waller	Kentucky State University	Educator and Poet

(*continued*)

Table 5 (*Continued*)

Name	School	Occupation
Smith, Elmore	Kentucky State University	NBA Player with the Buffalo Braves, Los Angeles Lakers, Milwaukee Bucks, and Cleveland Cavaliers
Smith, James "Bonecrusher"	Shaw University	First Heavyweight Boxing Champion with a College Degree
Smith, Jesse	Alcorn State University	American Gladiator
Smith, Jimmy Lee	Jackson State University	NFL Player with the Dallas Cowboys and Jacksonville Jaguars
Smith, Larry	Alcorn State University	NBA Player with the Golden State Warriors, Houston Rockets, and San Antonio Spurs; Assistant Coach of the Houston Rockets; Assistant Coach of the Los Angeles Sparks (WNBA)
Smith, Louise	Winston-Salem State University	Helped establish the First Kindergarten Program in North Carolina
Smith, Meta	Spelman College	Television Personality, DJ, and Author
Smith, Sandra	Bennett College	Activist
Smith, Stephen Anthony	Winston-Salem State University	*The Philadelphia Inquirer* Sports Columnist and ESPN Sports Show Host
Smoots, Jason	North Carolina Central University	Professional Track Athlete
Smyre, Calvin	Fort Valley State University	Youngest Member Elected to the Georgia House of Representatives, Executive Vice President of $34 Billion Financial Corporation (Synovus Foundation)
Speed, James	North Carolina Central University	President and CEO of the North Carolina Mutual Life Insurance Company
Spellman, Mitchell W.	Dillard University	Founding Dean of the Charles R. Drew University of Medicine and Science; Professor of Surgery Emeritus of Harvard University Medical School; Director, Academic Alliances and International Exchange Programs at Harvard Medical International
Spencer, Anne	Virginia University of Lynchburg	Harlem Renaissance Poet
Spencer, Danielle	Tuskegee University	Television Actress
Spencer, Richard Lewis	Johnson C. Smith University	Grammy Award–Winning Composer and Performer

Spiller, Charlie	Alcorn State University	NFL Player with the Tampa Bay Buccaneers
Spinks, John Robert "Jack"	Alcorn State University	NFL Player with the Pittsburgh Steelers, Chicago Cardinals, Green Bay Packers, and New York Giants; The Stadium for the Alcorn State Braves is named in his honor
Spurlock, Jeanne	Meharry Medical College	Psychiatrist
Stallworth, Johnny Lee	Alabama A&M University	NFL Pro-Bowler with the Pittsburg Steelers and Founder of Madison Research Corporation (MRC)
Stanley, Clifford L.	South Carolina State University	U.S. Secretary of Defense for Personnel and Readiness
Stephens, Clarence F.	Johnson C. Smith University	Ninth African American to receive a PhD in Mathematics
Stevenson, Rodrick A.	Dillard University	Director of the Organ Transplant Department at Meharry Medical College
Steward, Carl E.	Dillard University	Judge of the U.S. Fifth Circuit Court of Appeals
Steward, Theophilus Gould	Wilberforce University	U.S. Chaplain and Buffalo Soldier
Stewart, Carl E.	Dillard University	Judge, U.S. Court of Appeals for the Fifth Circuit
Stewart, Doug	South Carolina State University	Talk Radio Host of *2 Live Stews* with this Brother Ryan Stewart in Atlanta, Georgia
Stewart, Larry	Coppin State University	NBA Player with the Washington Bullets and Seattle SuperSonics
Stewart, Tonea	Jackson State University	Actress and University Professor
Stiaes, Charmaine Marchand	Southern University at New Orleans	Louisiana State Representative
Still, William Grant	Wilberforce University	First African American to conduct a Major American Orchestra
Stockton, Dmitri	North Carolina A&T State University	President and CEO of GE Capital, Global Banking
Strahan, Michael Anthony	Texas Southern University	NFL Pro-Bowl Player with the New York Giants and Football Analyst on *Fox NFL Sunday*
Street, John Franklin	Oakwood University	Mayor of Philadelphia, Pennsylvania
Strickland, Haywood L.	Stillman College	President of Wiley College
Stroger, Todd H.	Xavier University of Louisiana	President of the Cook County, Illinois Board
Studdard, (Christopher) Ruben	Alabama A&M University	American Idol Winner

(*continued*)

Table 5 (*Continued*)

Name	School	Occupation
Stukes, Charlie	University of Maryland Eastern Shore	NFL Player with the Baltimore Colts
Suber, Dianne Boardley	Hampton University	President of Saint Augustine's College
Sullivan, Leon Howard	West Virginia State University	Baptist Minister and Civil Rights Leader
Sullivan, Louis Wade	Morehouse College	Secretary of Health and Human Services, Founded the Morehouse School of Medicine
Sullivan-Huffman, Sharmell	Spelman College	Miss Black America
Sutton, William W.	Dillard University	President of Mississippi Valley State University
Sweatt, Heman Marion	Wiley College	Plaintiff in *Sweatt v. Painter*, 339 U.S. 629 (1950)
Sweeney, Donald	Mississippi Valley State University	Arena Football League Player
Sweet, Dennis C.	Tougaloo College	Nationally Renowned Trial Lawyer
Sweet, Ossian	Wilberforce University	African American Doctor who was acquitted in the "Sweet Trials"
Swinton, Sylvia	Allen University	President of Allen University
Sykes, Wanda	Hampton University	Comedian, Actress
Talley, Andre Leon	North Carolina Central University	Editor-at-Large for *Vogue* magazine
Tarrant, Shawn Z.	Norfolk State University	Member of the Maryland House of Delegates
Tate, Horace E.	Clark Atlanta University	George State Senator and Education
Taylor, Billy	Virginia State University	Jazz Musician
Taylor, Cordell Jerome	Hampton University	NFL Player with the Jacksonville Jaguars and Seattle Seahawks
Taylor, Harley F.	Delaware State University	Housing Developer and Creator of oldest African American Housing Development in Dover, Delaware
Taylor, John Gregory	Delaware State University	NFL Wide Receiver with the San Francisco 49ers
Taylor, Jonathan "Steel Arm" Boyce	Johnson C. Smith University	Star Pitcher in the Negro Leagues
Taylor, Otis	Prairie View A&M University	NFL Player with the Kansas City Chiefs
Tharpe, Larry James	Tennessee State University	NFL Player with the Detroit Lions, Arizona Cardinals, New England Patriots, and Pittsburgh Steelers

The A&T Four	North Carolina A&T State University	Ezell A. Blair Jr., David Richmond, Joseph McNeil, and Franklin McCain, who started the major Sit-In Movement of the 1960s that began at a Greensboro, NC Woolworths
The Commodores	Tuskegee University	R&B Group
Theopolis, Theodore, II	Hampton University	Associate Judge of the Court of Appeals, New York
Thierry, John	Alcorn State University	NFL Player with the Chicago Bears, Cleveland Browns, and Atlanta Falcons
Thigpen, Yancey Dirk	Winston-Salem State University	NFL All-Pro Player with the San Diego Chargers, Pittsburgh Steelers, and Tennessee Oilers/Titans
Thomas, Amos Leon, Jr.	Tennessee State University	Singer
Thomas, Carla	Tennessee State University	Singer
Thomas, Dwayne	Dillard University	CEO, Medical Center of Louisiana, New Orleans
Thomas, Iris Little	Spelman College	Actress
Thomas, Jason	Central State University	September 11 Hero
Thomas, Lee	Wiley College	NFL Player with the San Diego Chargers and Cincinnati Bengals
Thomas, Michael A.	Grambling State University	Jazz Artist
Thomas, Phelan	Albany State University	First African American Cosmetic Dentist certified as a Diplomat of the American Board of Aesthetic Dentistry by the American Society for Dental Aesthetics
Thompson, Bennie G.	Tougaloo College, Jackson State University	U.S. Congressman
Thompson, Bonsu	Delaware State University	Editor with *XXL* Magazine
Thompson, Brian	University of the District of Columbia	Banknote Designer
Thompson, James	Allen University	President Talladega College
Thompson, Jeffrey	University of the District of Columbia	President and CEO of Thompson, Cobb, Bazilio, and Associates
Thompson, John W.	Florida A&M University	Former Vice-President at IBM and the Former CEO of Symantec Corporation

(*continued*)

Table 5 (*Continued*)

Name	School	Occupation
Thompson, Thelma	University of the District of Columbia	President of the University of Maryland Eastern Shore
Thompson, William Allen "Billy"	University of Maryland Eastern Shore	NFL Pro-Bowl Player with the Denver Broncos
Thorton, Carlos	Alcorn State University	NFL Player with the San Francisco 49ers
Thurman, Sue Bailey	Spelman College	Founder and First chairperson of the National Council of Negro Women's National Library
Thurmond, Michael	Paine College	Attorney and First African American elected as Georgia Labor Commissioner
Tillman, Cedric Cornell	Alcorn State University	NFL Player with the Denver Broncos and Jacksonville Jaguars
Tisdale, Danica	Spelman College	First African American Miss Georgia
Tlou, Sheila	Dillard University	Member of Parliament in Botswana, Africa
Tolbert, Campbell Aurelius "Skeets"	Johnson C. Smith University	Jazz Clarinetist
Tolson, Melvin B.	Lincoln University	Poet, Educator, Columnist, Politician, Inspiration for Lead Character in the Movie *The Great Debaters*
Tompkins, Jessie	Alabama State University	Athlete, Head Coach for the East Montgomery Track Club, First African America Student to challenge the State of Alabama's White-Only Race-Based scholarships
Torry, Joe	Lincoln University of Missouri	Actor and Comedian
Totten, Willie "Satellite"	Mississippi Valley State University	Head Coach of the Delta Devils Football Team
Townes, Sandra L.	Johnson C. Smith University	District Judge for the U.S. District Court for the Eastern District of New York
Towns, Edolphus "Ed"	North Carolina A&T State University	U.S. Congressman
Trawick, Herb	Kentucky State University	First African American in the Canadian Football League
Traynham, Robert	Cheyney University of Pennsylvania	Television Personality
Troy, Kali Bianca "Kittie"	University of the District of Columbia	Voice-Over Actress

Troy, Micah "Pastor Troy"	Paine College	Hip-Hop Musician
Tucker, Cleopatra G.	Miles College	Member of the New Jersey General Assembly
Tucker, Norma Jean	Langston University	President of Merritt College
Tucker, Walter R., Jr.	Meharry Medical College	Mayor of Compton, California
Turk, Godwin Lee	Southern University and A&M College	NFL Player with the New York Jets and Denver Broncos
Turnbull, Walter	Tougaloo College	Founder of the Boys Choir of Harlem
Turner, Abraham J.	South Carolina State University	Major General in the U.S. Army
Turner, David G.	Delaware State University	Bank of America Executive, Fortune Magazine list of "50 most powerful Black executives in America"
Twiggs, Leo Franklin	Claflin University	First African American to receive a Doctorate of Arts from the University of Georgia
Twyman, Luska	Kentucky State University	First Black Mayor of a Kentucky City (Glasgow, Kentucky)
Tyus, Wyomia	Tennessee State University	Olympic Gold Medalist
Tyus-Shaw, Tina	Tennessee State University	Reporter
Usry, James Leroy	Lincoln University	First African American Mayor of Atlantic City, New Jersey
Vance, Jim	Cheyney University of Pennsylvania	Member of the Association of Black Journalists Hall of Fame
Veal, Frank R.	Allen University	President of Allen University
Viaer, Anthony E.	Huston-Tillotson University	Philanthropist
Waddell, RaSheeda A.	Hampton University	Miss Black North Carolina 2009
Wade-Gayles, Gloria	Lemoyne-Owen College	Author and Spelman College Professor
Wagner, Barry	Alabama A&M University	Arena Football League Player
Walker, Alice Malsenior	Spelman College	Pulitzer Prize–Winning Author
Walker, Joseph Edison	Alcorn State University	President of University Life Insurance Company in Memphis, Tennessee
Walker, LeRoy T.	Benedict College	First Black President of the U.S. Olympic Committee
Walker, Lucius	Shaw University	Baptist Minister, Opposed U.S. Embargo against Cuba
Walker, Nathaniel L.	Alabama A&M University	Alabama District Court Judge

(continued)

Table 5 ***(Continued)***

Name	School	Occupation
Wallace, Ben Carney "Big Ben"	Virginia Union University	NBA Player with the Washington Bullets/Wizards, Orlando Magic, Detroit Pistons, Chicago Bulls, and Cleveland Cavaliers
Walters, Ronald G. "Ron"	Fisk University, Howard University	Political Scholar
Walton, Johnnie	Elizabeth City State University	NFL Quarterback with the Philadelphia Eagles
Ward, Anita	Rust College	R&B Singer
Ward, Horace T.	Morehouse College, Clark Atlanta University	First African American to challenge the racially discriminatory practices at the University of Georgia; Member of the Georgia State Senate, U.S. District Court Judge
Ward, Jerry, Jr.	Tougaloo College	Author University Professor
Ward, William "Kip"	Morgan State University	First Commanding Officer of the U.S. Africa Command
Warfield, Nima	Morehouse College	Rhode Scholar
Warren, Dave	Cheyney University of Pennsylvania	Radio Talk Show Host
Warren, Mervyn	Oakwood University	Member of the Gospel Group Take 6
Warren, Reuben	Meharry Medical College	Associate Director for Minority Health, Centers for Disease Control and Prevention
Warren, Terrence Lamonte	Hampton University	NFL Player with the Seattle Seahawks and San Francisco 49ers
Washington, Booker Taliaferro	Hampton University	College President, Educator, Writer
Washington, Craig Anthony	Prairie View A&M University	U.S. Congressman
Washington, Lisa	Clark Atlanta University	News Anchor of WHNT TV, Huntsville, Alabama
Washington, Walter	Tougaloo College	General President of Alpha Phi Alpha Fraternity, Inc. and President of Alcorn State University
Washington, Walter Edward	Howard University	First Home-Rule Mayor of Washington, D.C., President of the Board of Commissioners of Washington, D.C.
Washington-Williams, Essie Mae	South Carolina State University	African American Daughter of former U.S. Congressman Strom Thurmond
Waters, Andre	Cheyney University of Pennsylvania	NFL Player with the Philadelphia Eagles and Arizona Cardinals

Watkins, Craig	Prairie View A&M University	First African American District Attorney in Texas
Watts, Rolonda	Spelman College	Journalist, Actor, Writer, Talk Show Host
Wayans, Keenan Ivory	Tuskegee University	Actor, Filmmaker, Director
Webb, Eric C.	Lincoln University	Author, Poet, and Editor-in-Chief of *Souls of People*
Webber, Clemmie Embly	South Carolina State University	Author and Educator
Webster, Ben	Wilberforce University	Jazz Musician
Webster, Dave A., Jr.	Prairie View A&M University	American Football League All-Pro Football Player (Dallas Texans/ Kansas City Chiefs), One of the First Blacks to play professional football in the American Football League
Weeks, Rickie Darnell	Southern University and A&M College	MLB Player with the Milwaukee Brewers
Weems, Eric	Bethune-Cookman University	NFL Player with the Atlanta Falcons
Welburn, Craig T.	Cheyney University of Pennsylvania	Owner of the Largest African American Franchise of McDonalds Restaurant
Welcome, Verda Freeman	Coppin State University	First Black Woman to be elected to a State Senate (Maryland)
Wells, Ida B.	Fisk University	Newspaper Editor, Feminist, and Anti-lynching Crusader
Wesley, Charles Harris	Fisk University	President of Wilberforce University, President of Central State College, and Third African American to earn a PhD from Harvard University
Wesley, Dante Julius	University of Arkansas at Pine Bluff	NFL Player with the Detroit Lions and Carolina Panthers
Wesley, Fred	Alabama State University	Jazz and Funk Trombonist
Wesley, Greg Lashon	University of Arkansas at Pine Bluff	NFL Player with the Kansas City Chiefs
Wesley, Richard	Howard University	Playwright, Screenwriter, and Professor at New York University
Westerfield, Louis	Southern University at New Orleans	Lawyer, Law Professor, First African American Dean of the University of Mississippi School of Law
Whalum, Kirk	Texas Southern University	Jazz Musician
Wharton, A. C., Jr.	Tennessee State University	Mayor of Memphis, Tennessee; First African American Mayor of Shelby County (Tennessee)

(*continued*)

Table 5 (*Continued*)

Name	School	Occupation
Wheatley, Jake, Jr.	North Carolina A&T State University	Member of the Pennsylvania House of Representatives
Wheaton, James Lorenzo	Wiley College	Actor, Director, and Educator
Whisenton, Joffre T.	Tougaloo College	President of Southern University
White, Dwayne Allen "The Road Grader"	Alcorn State University	NFL Player with the New York Jets and St. Louis Rams
White, Jesse Clark	Alabama State University	First African American Secretary of State of Illinois
White, Tracy Donnel	Howard University	NFL Player with the Seattle Seahawks, Jacksonville Jaguars, Green Bay Packers, Philadelphia Eagles, and New England Patriots
White, Walter Francis	Clark Atlanta University	NAACP Leader
Whitfield, Fredricka	Howard University	Anchor of CNN Newsroom
Whitfield, Lynn	Howard University	Actress
Whitley, Kym Elizabeth	Fisk University	Comedian and Actress
Whitley, Kym Elizabeth	Fisk University	Actress and Comedienne
Wilbekin, Emil	Hampton University	Entertainment Journalist
Wilcoxon, D. Etta	Alabama A&M University	Publisher of the *Renaissance Observe*
Wilder, L. Douglas	Virginia Union University, Howard University	First Black Governor in the United States (Virginia)
Wiley, Ralph	Knoxville College	Author, Speaker, and Sports columnist for the *Oakland Tribune*, *Sports Illustrated*, and ESPN
Wilkerson, Doug	North Carolina Central University	NFL Player with the San Diego Chargers
Wilkerson, Pinkie C.	Grambling State University	Louisiana House of Representatives
Wilks, Bobby C.	Harris-Stowe State University	First African American Coast Guard Aviator and the First African American Coast Guard Captain
Williams, Aeneas Demetrius	Southern University and A&M College	NFL Pro-Bowler with the Arizona Cardinals and St. Louis Rams
Williams, Alvin	Tennessee State University	Cable Executive, Producer, Songwriter
Williams, Avon N., Jr.	Johnson C. Smith University	Tennessee State Senator

Williams, Camilla Ella	Virginia State University	First African American to receive a contract from a major American Opera Company
Williams, Cecil	Huston-Tillotson University	Community Leader and Minister
Williams, Doug	Alabama State University	Comedian and Actor
Williams, Douglas Lee “Doug”	Grambling State University	NFL MVP Quarterback with the Washington Redskins
Williams, Erik George	Central State University	NFL Player with the Dallas Cowboys and Baltimore Ravens
Williams, George	St. Augustine’s College	Track and Field Coach
Williams, Hosea L.	Morris Brown College, Clark Atlanta University	Civil Rights Activist
Williams, James “Big Cat”	Cheyney University of Pennsylvania	NFL Pro-Bowler with the Chicago Bears
Williams, Jesse J.	Wiley College	Chemical Engineer and Theologian
Williams, Kenneth “Kenny”	Elizabeth City State University	NBA Player with the Indiana Pacers
Williams, Lee	Bethune-Cookman University	NFL Player with the San Diego Chargers and Houston Oilers
Williams, Madaline A.	Clark Atlanta University	First African American Woman elected to the New Jersey Legislature
Williams, Peyton, Jr.	Fort Valley State University	Highest Ranking African American in the U.S. Department of Education for Twenty-Five Years
Williams, Robert F.	Johnson C. Smith University	Civil Rights Leader, Author, and President of Monroe, North Carolina NAACP Chapter
Williams, Robert L.	Philander Smith College	Noted Figure in the History of African American Psychology
Williams, Samuel Arthur “Samm-Art”	Morgan State University	Tony Award–Nominated Playwright and Actor
Williams-Omilami, Elizabeth	Hampton University	Chief Executive Officer, Hosea Feed the Hungry and Homeless
Willis, Hulon	Virginia State University	First African American Alumnus from the College of William & Mary
Wilson, Bobby	Clark Atlanta University	Singer
Wilson, Cassandra	Jackson State University	Jazz Singer and Musician

(*continued*)

Table 5 (*Continued*)

Name	School	Occupation
Wilson, Harrison B.	Kentucky State University	Second President of Norfolk State University
Wilson, Nancy	Central State University	Jazz Singer
Wilson, Theodore Shaw "Teddy"	Tuskegee University	Jazz Pianist
Wilson, William Julius	Wilberforce University	Sociologist and Harvard University Professor
Winbush, Angela	Howard University	R&B and Soul Singer and Songwriter
Winfield, W. Montague	Virginia State University	U.S. Army Major General
Winfrey, Oprah Gail	Tennessee State University	Television Talk Show Host, Media Mogul, Philanthropist
Wingate, James G.	Allen University	President of LeMoyne-Owen College
Winn, Marcus	Alabama State University	Linebacker for the Winnipeg Blue Bombers of the Canadian Football League
Winston, Kelton	Wiley College	NFL Player with the Los Angeles Rams
Witherspoon, Brian	Stillman College	NFL Player with the Jacksonville Jaguars and Detroit Lions
Womble, Larry W.	Winston-Salem State University	Member of North Carolina State Legislature
Wood, Brenda Blackmon	Oakwood University	News Anchor, WXIA-TV Atlanta, Georgia
Woods, Kevin Jamal	Bethune-Cookman University	Actor
Woodson, Robert L.	Cheyney University of Pennsylvania	Founder and President of the National Left for Neighborhood Enterprise (NCNE)
Woodson, S. Howard	Cheyney University of Pennsylvania	First African American to serve as Speaker for the New Jersey General Assembly since Reconstruction
Woodyard, Mark Anthony	Bethune-Cookman University	MLB Player with the Detroit Lions
Woolfolk, Odessa	Talladega College	President Emerita of the Birmingham Civil Rights Institute
Wooten, Roy Wilfred "Future Man"	Norfolk State University	Percussionist and Member of the Jazz Quartet Béla Fleck and the Flecktones
Work, John W, Jr.	Fisk University	Composer, Musicologist
Work, John W., III	Fisk University	Composer, Musicologist
Work, John W., Sr.	Fisk University	Composer, Musicologist

Wrensford, Granville	University of the Virgin Islands	Chair of Albany State University's Department of Natural Sciences
Wright, Charles H.	Meharry Medical College	Founder of the Charles H. Wright Museum of African American History
Wright, Henry M.	Oakwood University	Evangelist
Wright, James E.	Savannah State University	Flight Instructor for the Tuskegee Airmen
Wright, Larry Rayfield	Fort Valley State University	NFL Hall of Fame Player with the Dallas Cowboys
Wright, Louis Tompkins	Clark Atlanta University	First African American Surgeon to Head the Department of Surgery at Harlem Hospital in New York City
Wright, Melvin R.	University of the District of Columbia	Associate Judge, Superior Court of the District of Columbia
Wright, Milton S. J.	Wilberforce University	Economist
Wright, Richard R.	Clark Atlanta University	First African American Paymaster in the U.S. Army and First President of Savannah State University
Wyatt, Alvin B.	Bethune-Cookman University	NFL Player with the Oakland Raiders, Buffalo Bills, and Houston Oilers
Wynn, Cordell	Fort Valley State University	President of Stillman College
Yancy, Dorothy Cowser	Clark Atlanta University	President of Johnson C. Smith University
Yates, Ella Gaines	Spelman College	First African American Director of the Atlanta-Fulton Public Library System
Yates, Josephine Silone	Cheyney University of Pennsylvania	Writer, Teacher, and Civil Rights Advocate
Yearwood, Lennox, Jr.	University of the District of Columbia, Howard University	President of the Hip-Hop Caucus
Yerby, Frank Garvin	Paine College	First African American Author to write a Best Seller, First African American to have a book purchased for screen adaption
Young, Alfred "Al"	South Carolina State University	NFL Player with the Pittsburgh Steelers
Young, Andrew Jackson	Howard University	Former Mayor of Atlanta, Georgia; UN Ambassador; Civil Rights Activist
Young, Jerome Tony "New Jack"	Clark Atlanta University	Professional Wrestler

(continued)

Table 5 (*Continued*)

Name	School	Occupation
Young, Roynell	Alcorn State University	NFL Player with Philadelphia Eagles
Young, Whitney M., Jr.	Kentucky State University	Civil Rights Leader, Director of the National Urban League, Educator and Executive
Young, Yetta	Fisk University	First to Produce the All–African American Celebrity Cast of the Obie Award–Winning Play *The Vagina Monologues*
Youngblood, Johnny Ray	Dillard University	Pastor, Saint Paul Community Baptist Church in Brooklyn, New York
Younger, Paul Lawrence "Tank"	Grambling State University	First Black Football Player drafted into the NFL from an HBCU
Zulu, Chaka	Clark Atlanta University	Hip-Hop Producer, Manager

*Note that some alumni graduated from more than one HBCU.

Table 6 Twenty-Five Best Community Colleges.

Community College	Address	Web Address	Tuition		Undergrad Enrollment	Student Body Demographic			
			In State	Out of State		Black	Latino	White	Other
Walla Walla Community College	500 Tausick Way, Walla Walla, WA 99362	www.wwcc.edu/CMS/	$5,376.00	$6,675.00	5,109	6%	15%	64%	15%
Santa Barbara City	721 Cliff Dr Santa Barbara, CA 93109	www.sbcc.edu/	$3,054.00	$8,516.00	19,331	3%	31%	42%	24%
Lake Area Technical Institute	1201 Arrow Ave Watertown, SD 57201	www.lakeareatech.edu	$6,180.00	Not found	1,559	0%	1%	90%	9%
East San Gabriel Valley Regional Occupational Program & Technical Center	1501 W Del Norte St West Covina, CA 91790	www.esgvrop.org	$6,615.00	Not found	983	6%	72%	11%	11%
New Mexico Military Institute	101 W College Blvd Roswell, NM 88201	www.nmmi.edu	$6,036.00	$11,147.00	470	20%	23%	33%	24%
North Central Kansas Technical College	3033 US Hwy 24 Beloit, KS 67420	www.ncktc.edu	$6,548.00	Not found	844	2%	3%	92%	3%
Valencia College	190 South Orange Ave Orlando, FL 32801	www.valenciacollege.edu	$3,740.00	$10,649.00	42,180	17%	32%	33%	18%
Snow College	150 College Ave Ephraim, UT 84627	www.snow.edu	$5,888.00	$13,842.00	4,605	1%	4%	85%	10%

(continued)

Table 6 (*Continued*)

Community College	Address	Web Address	Tuition		Undergrad Enrollment	Student Body Demographic			
			In State	Out of State		Black	Latino	White	Other
Saint Paul College	235 Marchall Ave St Paul, MN 55102	www.saintpaul.edu	$6,678.00	Not found	6,740	30%	8%	39%	23%
Mayland Community College	100 Mayland Dr Spruce Pine, NC 28777	www.mayland.edu	$3,812.00	$9,747.00	985	3%	2%	92%	3%
Northwest Iowa Community College	603 W Park St Sheldon, IA 51201	www.nwicc.edu	$6,710.00	$7,100.00	1,628	0%	4%	89%	7%
Southeast Community College Lincoln	301 South 68th St Place Lincoln, NE 68510	www.southeast.edu	$4,339.00	$4,946.00	9,751	6%	5%	82%	7%
Victor Valley College	18422 Bear Valley Rd Victorville, CA 92395	www.vcc.edu	$2,860.00	$7,492.00	11,504	12%	47%	33%	8%
Georgia Military College	201 E Greene St Milledgeville, GA 31061	www.gmc.edu	$6,282.00	Not found	Not found				
DeAnza College	21250 Stevens Creek Blvd Cupertino, CA 9501	www.deanza.edu	$3,252.00	$9,732.00	23,630	3%	15%	23%	59%
Marion Military Institute	1101 Washington St Marion, AL 36756	www.marionmilitary.edu	$9,978.00	$15,978.00	418	23%	10%	58%	9%
Kingsborough Community College	2001 Oriental Blvd Brooklyn, NY 11235	www.kbcc.cuny.edu	$6,154.00	$8,854.00	18,634	30%	21%	31%	18%

Western Wyoming Community College	2500 College Dr Rock Springs, WY 82902	www.wwcc.wy .edu	$3,400.00	$7,384.00	3,620	2%	11%	84%	3%
North Iowa Area Community College	500 College Dr Mason City, IA 50401	www.niacc.edu	$5,645.00	$7,606.00	3,207	3%	5%	87%	5%
Northeast Alabama Community College	138 Hwy 35 Rainsville, AL 35986	www.nacc.edu	$6,230.00	$9,620.00	2,834	2%	6%	88%	4%
Colorado Mountain College	802 Grand Ave Glenwood Springs, CO 81601	www. coloradomtn.edu	$3,804.00	$8,988.00	5,893	1%	16%	68%	15%
Mitchell Technical Institute	1800 E Spruce St Mitchell, SD 57301	www.mitchell tech.edu	$5,922.00	Not found	1,203	0%	0%	94%	6%
Alexandria Technical & Community College	1601 Jefferson St Alexandria, MN 56308	www.alextech .edu	$6,597.00	Not found	2,845	1%	2%	89%	8%
West Kentucky Community & Technical College	4810 Alben Barkley Dr Paducah, KY 42002	www.west kentucky.kctcs .edu	$4,624.00	$13,456.00	7,104	8%	2%	80%	10%

Index

About the Authors

F. Erik Brooks is a professor and chair of the Department of African American Studies at Western Illinois University. He holds a doctorate in public policy and administration from the L. Douglas Wilder School of Government and Public Affairs at Virginia Commonwealth University.

Glenn L. Starks is a senior acquisition division chief for the U.S. Department of Defense. He holds a doctorate in public policy and administration from the L. Douglas Wilder School of Government and Public Affairs at Virginia Commonwealth University.